SANDRA BETZINA

ALL NEW
FABRIC SAVVY

HOW TO CHOOSE & USE FABRICS

A QUICK REFERENCE GUIDE

The Taunton Press

The Taunton Press, Inc.
63 South Main Street, PO Box 5506
Newtown, CT 06470-5506
email: tp@taunton.com

Editor: Carolyn Mandarano
Technical Editor: Bernie Bacon
Copy Editor: Betty Christiansen
Indexer: Barbara Mortenson
Jacket/Cover design: Stacy Wakefield Forte
Interior design: Carol Petro, Stacy Wakefield Forte
Layout: Stacy Wakefield Forte
Illustrators: Bob La Pointe, Heather Lambert
Photographers: Jack Deutch: pp. 4, 6, 14, 18, 20, 22, 24, 28, 44, 48, 60, 62, 64, 68, 72, 74, 78, 88, 100, 108, 110, 114, 116, 120, 126, 132, 134, 136, 138, 142, 144, 148, 152, 154, 156, 158, 166, 174, 186, 188, 190, 192, 194, 196, 198, 204, 208, 210, 214; Tom Moore: pp. 8, 10, 12, 16, 26, 30, 32, 34, 36, 38, 40, 42, 46, 50, 51, 52, 54, 56, 58, 66, 70, 76, 80, 82, 84, 86, 90, 92, 94, 96, 98, 102, 104, 106, 112, 118, 122, 124, 128, 130, 140, 146, 150, 160, 162, 164, 168, 170, 172, 176, 178, 180, 182, 184, 200, 202, 206, 212
Front Cover Photography: Scott Phillips

The following names/manufacturers appearing in *All New Fabric Savvy* are trademarks: Antron®, Armo® Weft, Axion®, Ban-Rol®, Bemberg™, Biz®, Clorox 2®, Coolmax®, Cordura®, Curve Runner™, Dacron®, Dawn®, Dritz®, Dry-Clean®, DuraPress®, E6000®, Elnapress®, Eucalan®, Facile®, Fairfield™ Poly-Fil Hi-Loft®, FrayBlock™, Gardens Alive®, Goop®, Gore-Tex®, Grandma's Secret Spot Remover™, Hobbs Heirloom® Premium Wool, Hobbs Thermore®, Hydrofil®, Hydroflex®, Ivory Snow®, Lite Steam-A-Seam 2®, Lube-A-Thread™, Lurex®, Lycra®, Metafil®, Moth-Away®, Murphy's Oil Soap®, Nature's Miracle®, Palmolive®, Pellon®, PerfectFuse™, Pilot®, Pledge®, Polartec®, Quilters Dream Cotton®, Rain-No-Stain®, Retayne™, Rit®, Rub 'n Buff®, Runaway®, Rustiban®, Scotch®, Scotchguard™, Seams Great™, Sensuede®, Sew-in Durapress™, Shout®, Signature™, Static Guard®, Stay Tape™, Steam-A-Seam®, Sulky®, SulkyTotally Stable® Stabilizer, Sunbrella®, Supplex®, Tactel®, Teflon™, Tencel®, Thermoloft®, Thinsulate™, Thread Heaven®, Ultrasuede®, Ultrex®, Velcro®, Velvaboard™, Viyella®, Warm & Natural®, Windbloc®, Wisk®, Woolfelt®, Woolite®, X-Acto®, YKK®

Library of Congress Cataloging-in-Publication data
Names: Betzina, Sandra, author.
  Title: All new fabric savvy : how to choose and use fabrics / Sandra Betzina.
  Description: Newtown, CT : The Taunton Press, [2017] | Includes index.
  Identifiers: LCCN 2017002586 | ISBN 9781631868412
  Subjects: LCSH: Textile fabrics. | Dressmaking materials. | Machine sewing.
  Classification: LCC TT557 .B478 2017 | DDC 646.4--dc23
  LC record available at https://lccn.loc.gov/2017002586

Dedication

To my high school sewing teacher, who taught me the joy of sewing. To my mother, who taught me the joy of life. To my father, who taught me an incredible work ethic. To my brother, who keeps challenging me. To my four children and my husband, who teach me every day the importance of loving and being loved.

Acknowledgments

I want to give thanks to my students, who challenge me every day to invent new methods to solve problems with old and new fabrics. I want to thank Marcy Tilton, Bernie Bacon for her vast sewing knowledge and lengthy discussions over the phone, Carol Arndt for brainstorming, Christine Groom for details, and Lisette Arroyo for endless computer input. And of course, thanks to my editor, Carolyn Mandarano, who worked around both of our busy schedules to make this vastly revised book happen.

Contents

Introduction

Sewing for ourselves or our home gives us wonderful creative opportunities. And never before have there been so many fabrics to choose from, ranging from your old favorites—like cotton, wool, knits, and silks—to new options, some of which you might never have heard of or sewn with—synthetics; those that resist water, sun, stains, and wrinkles; those made from animal hides (and, of course, their faux cousins); those regenerated from wood pulp; and many more.

Just as there have been changes in fabric, there have also been changes in sewing machine technology, as well as the notions used to sew with fabrics. Sewing has never been more exciting, yet some might also find it intimidating. It doesn't need to be, thanks to *All New Fabric Savvy*.

This latest revised edition of *Fabric Savvy*, my first reference book on fabrics, contains specifics for working with 107 different types of fabric, from preshrinking, layout, seam finishes, and pressing techniques to which needles and presser foot to use, and more. Fabrics are organized from A to Z, making this resource super-easy to use. More than just fabrics, *All New Fabric Savvy* also includes detailed information on how to determine fabric content, linings, presser feet, interfacing, knits, hand picking, closures, hems, seams, details, and stain removal. A glossary and index ensure you have all the information you need to be successful when sewing.

Use this book when you shop for fabric and when you sew, whether you are a beginner or have been sewing for years. It will be your essential guide for all things sewing.

African Mudcloth

Fabric Fact

African mudcloth is a rather firm ethnic fabric. It is woven in 6-in.-wide strips that are joined by hand to make up the fabric width. The fabric is sold by the piece rather than by the yard.

Suitable For

Vests, structured tops, jackets. Choose garment styles with minimum seaming to avoid breaking up fabric design. Avoid princess styling. Also makes great place mats and table runners.

Sewing Tips

Let fabric feed naturally.

Tip

What causes thread breakage? (1) Missing a guide in the threading process. (2) Using the wrong needle for the fabric. (3) Using the wrong thread cap to hold the thread on. To avoid these problems, match up the thread cap with the mouth of the spool. Fit the cap so that the spool of thread does not move. The thread feeds evenly when the spool is stationary.

WORKING WITH AFRICAN MUDCLOTH

Preshrink

Overlock crossgrain ends and machine-baste to prevent fabric from stretching during washing. Machine-wash in warm water and machine-dry at normal temperature to remove mud residue, which makes fabric somewhat stiff and odorous.

Layout

"Without nap" layout, single thickness. Position pattern pieces to make the best of motifs.

Marking

Clover Chaco Liner or Clover white marking pen for dark colors.

Cutting

Although it is okay to cut through a double fabric thickness, you save fabric by cutting single thickness. This also allows you to position patterns better on fabric to maximize fabric design features.

Interfacing

Sewers' Dream or Armo® Weft.

Thread

Good-quality polyester or cotton.

Needle

80/12 H.

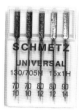

Stitch Length

2.5 mm.

Presser Foot

Standard.

Seam Finish

Flat fell or bind with double-fold bias. (See #9 on p. 216, #19 on p. 218.)

Pressing

Steam iron on cotton setting.

Topstitching

Doesn't show up.

Closures

For buttonholes use 70/10 HJ needle and water-soluble stabilizer between presser foot and feed dogs.

Hem

Hong Kong finish and hand-hem. (See #16 on p. 218, #13 on p. 230.)

Tip **Clover Chaco Liner**, a disappearing chalk, leaves no residue.

Alpaca

Fabric Fact

Alpaca, llamas, and camels are cousins, and the wool is a close relative to cashmere in its softness and luxury. It is also very warm to wear without being bulky, but if you get hot easily, this fabric is not for you. Vicuña is similar to alpaca only much finer and more costly since it comes from a smaller animal.

Suitable For

Woven alpaca makes beautiful jackets or coats and luxurious throws. Knitted alpaca makes a nice sweater, cardigan, clingy dress, or gored skirt. Since alpaca is available in both knits and wovens and is fairly costly, I suggest pretesting the pattern. Ripped stitches weaken the fabric.

Sewing Tips

Hand-baste the seams to minimize fabric slippage. Lift the fabric every 6 in. and smooth out. Stabilize neckline and shoulders with stay tape or ¼-in.-wide selvage strips. If you have difficulty sliding a jacket into position under the buttonhole foot, it will not feed properly for a flawless buttonhole. Consider alternatives such as button openings in a seam, button loops, or snaps. You can also face the opening in a lighter-weight fabric like wool jersey.

Preshrink

Hold steam iron ½ in. above fabric or preshrink at the dry cleaner. Pure alpaca can be hand-washed but must be dried flat.

> ✂ **Tip** A topstitching needle, labeled "N," has a larger eye to prevent the thicker thread from shredding as it passes through.

WORKING WITH ALPACA

Layout

Right side is obvious because it is the most hairy. To determine right side on single knits, where the hairy side is not as obvious, stretch the fabric. It will roll to right side. Press foldline to see if crease is permanent, and if so, cut around it. "With nap" layout, double thickness. Hairs go down.

Marking

Tailor tacks or safety pins.

Cutting

Rotary cutter or sharp scissors. Use pattern weights. Round off points from collars and pockets for a cleaner, smoother edge. Serge-finish pieces after cutting.

Interfacing

No fusibles; sew-in only. If you are making a tailored jacket, underline entire jacket with cotton batiste or voile. Armo Weft can then be fused to underlining before it is attached to the fashion fabric.

Thread

Silk thread is preferred for invisible seams. Good-quality polyester or cotton also can be used.

Needle

80/12 H on wovens, 75/11 HS on knits.

Stitch Length

Wovens: 2.5 mm straight stitch; knits: Tiny zigzag (0.5 mm width, 2.0 mm length).

Presser Foot

Wovens: Standard; knits: Walking.

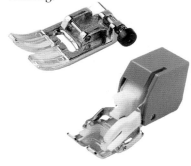

Seam Finish

Wovens: No seam finish if lined; otherwise pink or serge each piece separately with 3-thread overlock. Knits: Sew first with tiny zigzag, then serge seam allowances together. (See #2 and #3 on p. 216, #20 on p. 218.)

Pressing

Steam iron on wool setting, using press-and-lift motion. Place right side against needle board.

Topstitching

Not recommended. Hand-pick wovens with Sulky® rayon thread or buttonhole twist. Make stitches ½ in. from finished edge and ½ in. apart. (See #1 on p. 222.)

Closures

Wovens: Corded machine, hand, bound buttonholes, or button openings in a seam. (See #2 and #5 on p. 224, #10 on p. 225.) Knit cardigans: Press ¼ in. toward wrong side of front. Cover with grosgrain ribbon. Sew long sides of grosgrain with ribbon against presser foot and knit against feed dogs. Make machine buttonholes with 70/10 HJ needle and extra-fine thread. (See #7 on p. 225.)

Hem

Wovens: Hand-hem. (See #4 on p. 228.) Knits: Serge bottom of knit with differential feed or with finger behind presser foot to keep knit from stretching. Sew two rows of double-needle topstitching with woolly nylon thread hand-wrapped on bobbin and double-needle ZWI stretch. Topstitch using walking foot. Loosen top tension until stitches lie flat. (See #1 on p. 228.)

Batik

Fabric Fact

Batiks are created by a wax resist and overdyeing process. The base fabric is either 100% cotton or 100% rayon. Batiks make great travel fabrics since they breathe and the patterns tend to camouflage wrinkles.

Suitable For

Loose tops and dresses, full skirts, pull-on pants, and bathing suit cover-ups; also napkins and place mats.

Sewing Tips

Let fabric feed naturally.

> **Tip** **Check fabric drapability by gathering in your hand and draping it over the tummy. If fabric looks bulky now, it will not get any better.**

WORKING WITH BATIK

Preshrink

For cotton: Machine-wash in warm water on regular cycle. Machine-dry on regular cycle. For rayon: Rayon becomes unstable when wet, making it difficult to make lay flat after laundering. Wash alone on gentle cycle in warm water. Take out of dryer before bone dry.

Layout

"Without nap" layout, double thickness.

Marking

Clover Chaco Liner or Pilot® Frixion erasable ink pen.

Cutting

Rotary cutter or scissors.

Interfacing

Fusi-Knit.

Thread

Polyester or cotton.

Needle

80/12 H.

Stitch Length

2.5 mm.

Presser Foot

Standard.

Seam Finish

Flat fell or sewn with a plain seam and serged together. (See #4 and #9 on p. 216.)

Pressing

Steam iron on cotton setting.

Topstitching

Topstitch ⅛ in. from finished edge using a 3.0 mm stitch length (see #2 on p. 222) and a topstitching foot.

Closures

Machine buttonholes, loops, frogs, and zippers. (See #1 on p. 224, #9 and #12 on p. 225.)

Hem

Double-fold ¼-in. hem stitched once or double-needle topstitched using the red band double needle for wovens. (See #1 on p. 228, #10 on p. 229.)

Tip ✂ **Distressed about the color bleed on your brand-new blouse? Remove excess dye from fabrics with Rit® color remover.**

Batiste, Voile & Lawn

Fabric Fact

Batiste, voile, and lawn are very fine woven cottons. These have a very soft hand and smooth surface. Sometimes voile is combined with silk to give it a nice luster.

Suitable For

Batiste, voile, and lawn are typically used to back quilts. Voile and lawn are smooth and soft to touch and can be used for lightweight blouses, very full skirts, and full dresses. Consider underlining garment pieces for soft support and less transparency.

Sewing Tips

This fabric is very easy to sew; simply let it feed through naturally.

WORKING WITH BATISTE, VOILE & LAWN

Preshrink

Machine-wash in warm water and dry in a regular dryer. Pull out of dryer before it is completely dry to avoid wrinkles.

Layout

"Without nap" layout.

Marking

Pilot Frixion erasable ink pen or Clover Chaco Liner.

Cutting

Rotary cutter or scissors.

Interfacing

Silk organza or So-Sheer.

> **Tip** There are some new fabric markers in town. Frixion erasable ink pens by Pilot work like fine felt-tip pens that can be erased or pressed to disappear. Clover's Chaco Liner is the best for a fine chalk line. You can also try Clover's white marking pen for marking dark colors or Dritz® marking chalk, which disappears in three days or with pressing.

Thread

Fine cotton thread.

Needle

70/10 HM.

Stitch Length

2.5 mm straight stitch.

Presser Foot

Standard.

Seam Finish

French seams. (See #40 on p. 221.)

Pressing

Steam or dry iron on cotton setting.

> **Tip** **Buttonholes in fine fabrics such as cotton lawn, voile, and lightweight silks can be bulky if you use regular-weight thread. Instead, use a new 70/10 HJ needle and fine machine-embroidery thread or fine silk thread.**

Topstitching

Topstitch ⅛ in. from edge of finished seam using topstitching foot. (See #2 on p. 222.)

Closures

Buttonholes using fine thread in top and bobbin.

Hem

Hems in this fabric are often embellished with lace or trim. You also can simply use a double-fold ¼-in. hem followed by hand or machine stitching. (See #10 on p. 229.) On a skirt or dress, you also can add a 3-in.-wide strip of bias binding for a border.

Batting

Fabric Fact

Batting is a sheet of spun fibers that is used between two fabrics to add body and insulation. Batting is available in silk, polyester, wool, and cotton. Silk battings are the most luxurious—airy and lightweight while providing warmth. Wool batting provides the most warmth and is the easiest to hand-quilt. Polyester batting has more loft than cotton and can be too hot to wear or sleep under. Cotton batting is easy to machine-quilt, feels comfortable to wear, and softens with age.

Suitable For

Vests, jackets, quilts, place mats, and table runners.

Sewing Tips

Batting is sandwiched between two fabrics before quilting. The batting package will state minimum quilting distance for the batting to hold together.

Tip Use a pipe cleaner to clean lint from hard-to-reach places in your sewing machine.

WORKING WITH BATTING

Preshrink

Not necessary.

Layout

Single thickness.

Marking

Safety pins.

Cutting

Rotary cutter or scissors.

Interfacing

Not appropriate.

Thread

Polyester or cotton.

Needle

75/11 HQ on lightweight fabrics and 90/14 HQ on heavier fabrics will prevent batting from bearding (pulling through to the top side of the fabric).

Stitch Length

Experiment with stitch length to get the look you want.

Presser Foot

Quilting or walking/even feed.

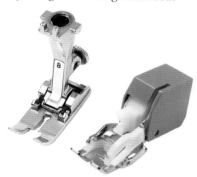

Seam Finish

Butt raw edges together and hand-overcast with basting thread to get the width you need.

Pressing

Use iron temperature to suit fabric being quilted. Do not use too much pressure, or the batting will lose much of its loft.

Topstitching

Topstitch quilted items ¼ in. from finished edges to flatten batting. (See #10 on p. 223.)

> **Tip** ✂ **Hobbs Thermore® is a thin, 100% polyester batting that drapes well and works equally well for garments and quilts. Quilters Dream Cotton® is a low-loft batting that adds warmth yet feels lightweight. Warm & Natural® cotton is a thin cotton batting that can get boardlike if overquilted. Hobbs Heirloom® Premium Wool is a low-loft batting that provides warmth. Fairfield™ Poly-Fil Hi-Loft® is a good choice for fluffy, warm quilts. Richland Silk's silk batting is available online. (See Sources on p. 250.)**

Closures

Faced buttonholes, button loops, and snaps. (See #6 on p. 224, #9 and #11 on p. 225.)

Hem

Bind edges with fold-over braid or unquilted self-fabric binding. (See #9 and #11 on p. 229.)

Beaded Fabrics

Fabric Fact

Since this fabric is expensive, think of it as part of a garment. It can be used for bodices or details, such as a collar and pocket flaps.

Suitable For

Tank tops, bodices, and jackets. Choose a pattern with as few seams and darts as possible. Consider eliminating straight side seams by overlapping seamlines and cutting all in one piece. Pretest the pattern.

Sewing Tips

Underline with silk tulle or georgette, which can be dyed to match the beaded fabric. Use an upholstery hammer or pliers to smash beads in the seam allowances. This makes them easier to remove and leaves threads intact. Wear safety goggles or sunglasses to protect eyes. Pull beads out of all seam allowances. (See #34 on p. 220.) Do not brush beads away with hands since many beads are glass, and crushed beads can have sharp edges. Pull beads from inside of dart legs as well. Using a zipper foot, staystitch around all edges of the beaded fabric at $5/8$ in. Run a bead of clear glue next to staystitch line on the seam allowance. With tulle sandwiched between the beaded fabric and the lining, hand-baste together. Stabilize shoulder seams with narrow lining selvage. Line entire garment with silk organza or charmeuse, depending on the crispness you want.

> ✂ **Tip** A loud rattling sound in your machine indicates a need for lubrication. A snapping sound as the needle hits the fabric indicates a need for a new needle.

WORKING WITH BEADED FABRICS

Preshrink

Not necessary.

Layout

"With nap" layout, single thickness, if the beaded design has a direction. Place beaded fabric, bead side up, against a surface of contrasting color so you can see the design. Consider design when placing the pattern pieces. Be careful when you take off the tape the store puts on the crossgrain. A sudden rip of the tape will start a lengthwise run in the beads.

Marking

Tailor tacks or safety pins.

Cutting

Don't use your best scissors, as beads will mar the blades. Pattern weights are preferred since pins tear the pattern tissue.

Interfacing

Tulle or silk organza.

Thread

Good-quality cotton or polyester.

Needle

90/14 HJ. Have plenty on hand since beads break and dull needles quickly.

Stitch Length

2.0 mm straight stitch.

Presser Foot

Zipper. Sew seams with the edge of the foot against the ridge of the beads and bottom of foot in seam allowance or dart area where beads have been removed.

Seam Finish

If you aren't lining, finish each side of seam allowance with Seams Great™ or bias lining strips in Hong Kong finish. (See #16 and #19 on p. 218.) Eliminate facings. Finish neck and armholes with bias silk charmeuse, or use separate lining attached at neck and armholes only. Examine right side of seams for bald spots. Hand-sew beads in bald spots.

Pressing

With low-temperature iron on wrong side, press seams open over towel.

Topstitching

Never. Hand-picking close to edge can help flatten seam. (See #1 on p. 222.)

Closures

Consider buttonhole alternatives like button loops or faced openings. Zipper must be hand-picked. (See #6 on p. 224, #9 on p. 225, #19 on p. 227.)

Hem

Face with 1½-in.-wide bias strips in smooth fabric so there are no beads on inside of garment to snag hose or scratch surface of nearby fabrics. Whipstitch drapery weights to the hem fold. Hand-hem garment and lining separately. (See #18 on p. 231.)

> **Tip** Check care instructions on the bolt of beaded fabrics at the time of purchase. Glass beads can be dry-cleaned, while others dissolve in the dry-cleaning fluid and therefore require hand washing. If bead content is not stated, snip off a piece of beaded fabric for a burn test. Glass beads will not melt.

Boiled Wool

Fabric Fact

Boiled wool is a felted knitted wool. It offers the flexibility of a knit along with great warmth. Boiled wool cardigans are sold by Jaeger. You can create your own version of boiled wool by using 100% wool jersey. Purchase double the fabric amount the pattern calls for, and you will have enough after shrinkage. Machine-wash in hot water and Ivory Snow®, agitating for 30 minutes. Machine-dry in a hot dryer. The fabric will shrink approximately 40% to 50% in both directions.

Suitable For

Fitted styles with princess seams in lieu of darts, or boxy styles. Think in terms of sweater garment construction. To reduce bulk, eliminate hems, facings, and linings. Finish the edges with fold-over knitted trim or self-made binding.

Sewing Tips

Stabilize neck, shoulders, and top edge of pockets and perimeter with Stay Tape™. Single-layer patch pockets are the least bulky. Finish top of pocket with trim. Sew pocket to garment with machine blanket stitch. Boiled wool is a good candidate for machine or hand embroidery. Pin tucking with the double needle creates an attractive raised design detail. Before sewing braid to a garment, preshrink in lukewarm water and air-dry. Braid that is not preshrunk will cause puckers at the first dry cleaning. Sewing braid or trim on curves is easier if it is shaped first with a steam iron.

Tip

Whenever binding is applied to an outside edge, trim fabric down to seamline or hem crease. Sew binding to edge with right sides together at ¼ in. Wrap binding to wrong side, enclosing seam. Turn under raw edge only if you intend to hand-stitch. Otherwise, enclose seam by stitching in the ditch. Trim close to the stitching.

WORKING WITH BOILED WOOL

Preshrink

Not necessary.

Layout

"Without nap" layout, single thickness.

Marking

Clover Chaco Liner or tailor tacks.

Cutting

Rotary cutter or scissors. Use pattern weights.

Interfacing

None—fabric has enough body without it except for stand-up collars. Cut interfacing collar size; then cut off ⅞ in. of interfacing before applying.

Thread

Good-quality cotton, silk, or polyester. Silk and rayon threads give a lustrous sheen.

Needle

90/14 H.

Stitch Length

3.0 mm.

Presser Foot

Teflon™ or standard.

Seam Finish

Sew seams. Clip curves. Press seam open. Topstitch on each side of seam from right side using the wide double-needle ZWI 4.0 mm, straddling the seam, or topstitch each side separately ⅛ in. to ¼ in. from seam. Trim seam allowances close to topstitching. (See #13 on p. 217.) Another option is to overlap seams, and sew close to cut edge and again ¼ in away. Trim underlayer close to the second stitching line. (See #38 on p. 221.)

Pressing

Steam iron on wool setting. Use press cloth when pressing on the right side.

Topstitching

Not recommended.

Closures

Corded buttonholes through a single layer. (See #5 on p. 224.) Use stabilizer between the fabric and the feed dogs. Since a corded buttonhole through a single layer is fragile, consider a faced buttonhole (see #6 on p. 224) or button loops (see #9 on p. 225) for garments that will be buttoned frequently. Back buttons on the inside of the garment with small buttons to prevent them from pulling away from the fabric.

Hem

Eliminate hem allowance. Stabilize all edges with stabilizer or sew in twill tape at edge to prevent stretching. There are several options for finishing edges: (1) Fold-over knitted braid sewn on by hand; (2) Strips of crossgrain-cut wool jersey or faux leather; (3) Decorative serger stitch using shiny rayon thread. (See #11 on p. 229, #29 on p. 232.)

Detailing

On collars and cuffs, interface between both layers with interfacing 1 in. from cut edge. With interfacing sandwiched between both collars and wrong sides together, sew around outside collar edges at ⅝ in. and ⅞ in. Trim off ⅝-in. seam allowance beyond rows of topstitching.

Brocade

Fabric Fact

Brocade has an allover design with slightly raised sections. Typical motifs are flowers, geometric shapes, animals, or plants. The surface contrast can be subtle or pronounced.

Suitable For

Jackets, vests, straight dresses or skirts, narrow pants with flat-front styling. Avoid gathers or pleats. Since this fabric is crisp, any style requiring drape will make you look heavy. It's a great fabric for pillows.

Sewing Tips

When trimming any seam, use pinking shears no closer than ¼ in. This fabric ravels!

Tip **Proper lubrication is very important if your sewing machine has a rotary hook. An oscillating hook can do without lubrication.**

WORKING WITH BROCADE

Preshrink

If you want the brocade to look as it did when you first bought it, don't preshrink. Dry-clean completed garment. For more drape, run through three washing machine and dryer cycles. Brocade can be preshrunk by machine washing in warm water and machine drying in a cool dryer. Brocade becomes more drapey and textured looking, but loses quite a bit of its sheen. Patterns get smaller, and you lose ¼ in. per yard lengthwise in the process. Try a sample.

Layout

"With nap" layout, double thickness. If fabric is very narrow, as with silk brocades, a single thickness may be more economical. Since brocade has no give, don't overfit jackets, or they will wrinkle and be uncomfortable to wear.

Marking

Pilot Frixion erasable pen, Clover Chaco Liner, or tailor tacks.

Cutting

Sharp scissors or rotary cutter. Overlock each piece separately after cutting.

Interfacing

Fusi-Knit, Sewers' Dream, or Armo Weft for tailoring.

Thread

Good-quality polyester, cotton, or silk machine twist.

Needle

70/10 H.

Stitch Length

2.5 mm straight stitch.

Presser Foot

Standard.

Seam Finish

Press open and overlock separately (even if garment is lined). Use Hong Kong finish with lightweight silk as binding, or bind separately with double-fold bias. (See #3 on p. 216, #16 and #19 on p. 218.)

Pressing

Dry iron on medium-high setting. Press on the wrong side of the fabric.

Topstitching

Not compatible.

Closures

For buttonholes, use 70/10 HJ needle with fine machine embroidery thread, such as Seralene.

Hem

Do not use a hem deeper than 1¼ in. or it will be too bulky. Finish hem edge with serger, double-fold bias, or Hong Kong finish, and then hand-hem. (See #4 on p. 228, #13 and #14 on p. 230.)

Burnout

Tip Simple styles in elegant fabrics can put more fun and ease into your sewing. How about a simple T-shirt in silk crepe de Chine or silk burnout?

Fabric Fact

Burnout is often referred to as wedding ring velvet because the width of the fabric can be slipped through a wedding ring. Burnout is made from two different yarns. The velvet yarn is burned out with a chemical in selected areas, leaving behind a pattern of velvet on silk chiffon.

Suitable For

Loose-fitting tops, pants, and skirts, tank- or slip-style dresses, and dresses with drape features.

Sewing Tips

Place a credit card at an angle in front of the presser foot as you sew to push the fabric into the machine. When joining burnout to other fabrics, always sew with burnout on the bottom.

WORKING WITH BURNOUT

Preshrink

If you plan to dry-clean, preshrink by passing steam iron ½ in. above the fabric surface. This fabric can be machine-washed and machine-dried on the gentle cycle, creating more sheen on the nap.

Layout

"With nap" layout, double thickness. Bias cuts are unstable for this fabric unless you have a lot of experience. To control fabric and cut accurately, cover table with tissue paper. Pin double thickness of fabric to paper with right side out. Pin pattern pieces with nap going down through all thicknesses. Keep pins in seam allowances.

Marking

Clover Chaco Liner or tailor tacks. Waxed chalk will stain silk. Clover white marking pen for dark colors.

Cutting

Using sharp scissors, cut through all layers, including tissue paper, for accuracy. Serrated shears are great for this.

Interfacing

Silk organza. For less transparency, silk georgette makes a great lining for this fabric.

Thread

Fine machine-embroidery cotton thread.

Needle

60/8 or 65/9 HM or HJ.

Stitch Length

2.0 mm. Sew long vertical seams with a tiny zigzag (0.5 mm width, 2.5 mm length) to allow seams to relax. (See #17 on p. 218.)

Presser Foot

Straight stitch foot and single-hole throat plate. Or use satin stitch foot and throat plate and switch needle to far left position for support on three sides.

Seam Finish

Narrow French seams. (See #10 and #11 on p. 217.)

Pressing

Dry iron on silk setting.

Topstitching

Not recommended.

Closures

Fabric loops or machine buttonholes using fine machine embroidery thread. (See #1 on p. 224, #9 on p. 225.) Interface zipper seam allowances with silk organza. Hand-picked zippers are the most compatible. (See #19 on p. 227.)

Hem

Thread bobbin with fusible thread and use fine thread on top. Trim hem allowance to ½ in. With the wrong side of the fabric against the feed dogs, staystitch along hemline. Press hem allowance to wrong side to dissolve fusible thread and form a sharp crease. Trim hem allowance to ⅛ in., close to stitching. Hand-roll hem, enclosing raw edge. Hand-sew or machine-sew with fine thread. Keep finger pressure on the back of the presser foot to prevent hem from stretching. (See #16 on p. 230.)

Camel Hair

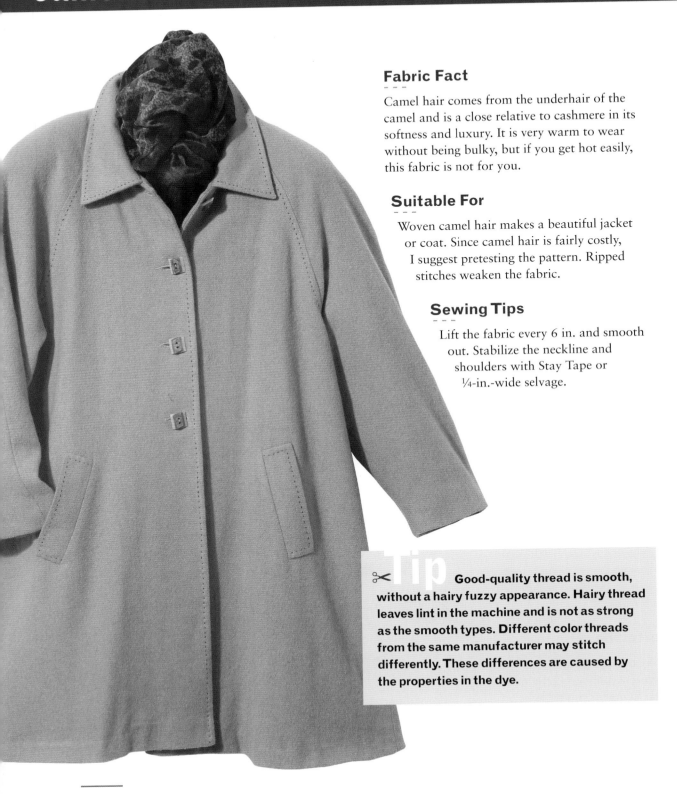

Fabric Fact

Camel hair comes from the underhair of the camel and is a close relative to cashmere in its softness and luxury. It is very warm to wear without being bulky, but if you get hot easily, this fabric is not for you.

Suitable For

Woven camel hair makes a beautiful jacket or coat. Since camel hair is fairly costly, I suggest pretesting the pattern. Ripped stitches weaken the fabric.

Sewing Tips

Lift the fabric every 6 in. and smooth out. Stabilize the neckline and shoulders with Stay Tape or ¼-in.-wide selvage.

> ✂ **Tip** Good-quality thread is smooth, without a hairy fuzzy appearance. Hairy thread leaves lint in the machine and is not as strong as the smooth types. Different color threads from the same manufacturer may stitch differently. These differences are caused by the properties in the dye.

WORKING WITH CAMEL HAIR

Preshrink

Hold steam iron ½ in. above fabric or preshrink at the dry cleaner.

Layout

"With nap" layout, double thickness. Right side is obvious since it is more hairy. Hairs go down. If crease at foldline does not press out, cut around it. Use pattern weights.

Marking

Tailor tacks or tailor's chalk.

Cutting

Rotary cutter or sharp scissors.

Interfacing

No fusibles; sew-in only. If you are making a tailored jacket, underline entire jacket with cotton batiste or voile. Armo Weft can then be fused to underlining before it is attached to the fashion fabric.

Thread

Silk thread is preferred for less visible seams. Good-quality polyester or cotton is suitable.

Needle

80/12 H.

Stitch Length

2.5 mm straight stitch.

Presser Foot

Standard.

Seam Finish

No seam finish if lined; otherwise pink or serge each piece separately with 3-thread overlock. (See #2 and #3 on p. 216.) Hong Kong seams give a nice finish to an unlined jacket. (See #16 on p. 218.)

Pressing

Cover pressing surface with a towel. Steam iron on wool setting using press-and-lift motion. Always use a self-fabric press cloth on the right side. Let fabric dry before moving off pressing surface or a poufy appearance results.

Tip

Before pressing outer edge of lapels, hand-baste from the top side, favoring the way you want the garment to look. Silk thread has elasticity and prevents thread imprint during pressing. Place right side of fabric against a towel. Cover wrong side with press cloth, spray for moisture, press, and pound flat with tailor's clapper. Towel prevents seam see-through.

Topstitching

Not recommended because it lessens the value. Instead, hand-pick with Sulky rayon or buttonhole twist, making stitches ½ in. from the finished edge and ½ in. apart. (See #1 on p. 222.)

Closures

Corded buttonholes machine or hand-stitched, or bound buttonholes. (See #5 on p. 224, #8 on p. 225.)

Hem

Hand-hem. (See #4 on p. 228.)

Canvas

Fabric Fact

Canvas is a firmly woven cotton. It is usually heavily sized but can be softened by preshrinking.

Suitable For

Home-dec projects, including upholstery, seat covers, window coverings, folding screens, and floor coverings. Canvas is too heavy for clothing, but it makes a great tote bag.

Sewing Tips

The main difficulty in sewing with canvas is the sheer bulk of it. Give yourself plenty of space to work in. Hand sewing on canvas and leather can be tough without a "glover's" needle, designed with a wedge point to pierce through the dense weave.

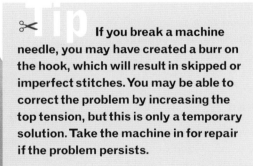

Tip ✂ **If you break a machine needle, you may have created a burr on the hook, which will result in skipped or imperfect stitches. You may be able to correct the problem by increasing the top tension, but this is only a temporary solution. Take the machine in for repair if the problem persists.**

WORKING WITH CANVAS

Preshrink

Not necessary if you plan to dry-clean. But if you want the fabric to have a softer hand, you may need to cut the fabric in lengths that can be preshrunk in an oversize washer and dryer at the Laundromat. Scotchguard™ spray works well on this fabric.

Layout

"Without nap" layout, single thickness, because it is easier to cut. Pattern weights will prevent pins from tearing pattern tissue.

Marking

Pencils or Pilot Frixion erasable ink pen.

Cutting

Rotary cutter or large shears.

Interfacing

None; fabric has enough body on its own.

Thread

Upholstery thread on top.

Needle

100/16 HJ or 110/18 HJ.

Stitch Length

3.5 mm.

Presser Foot

Standard.

Seam Finish

Not necessary if used in upholstery. For window coverings, press seams open. Clip at 2-in. intervals to prevent seam from drawing up as moisture from windows dries out, or serge separately. (See #1 and #3 on p. 216.)

Pressing

Hot steam iron on linen setting.

Topstitching

Topstitch ¼ in. from finished edge; lengthen stitch to 4.0 mm. (See #10 on p. 223.)

Closures

Oversize grommets, snaps, and Velcro®. Make sure snap has long enough stem to go through all layers. (See #11 on p. 225, #16 on p. 226, #18 on p. 227.)

Hem

Machine-hem or serge. (See #6 on p. 228.) On window coverings, a double-fold 2-in. hem will provide the needed weight for the panel to hang smoothly. For tote bags, cover raw edge with double-fold bias. (See #9 on p. 229.)

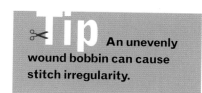

Tip **An unevenly wound bobbin can cause stitch irregularity.**

Cashmere

Fabric Fact

Cashmere is made from fine hairs taken from the underbellies of goats raised in extreme climates. Cashmere is the #1 luxury fabric for softness, warmth without bulk, and breathability. Banksville Designer Fabrics has the largest selection of 100% cashmere in the U.S. (see Sources on p. 250). Because of its cost, cashmere is often blended with other fibers. High-quality cashmere wrinkles the least. Pure cashmere has no sheen.

Suitable For

Woven cashmere makes a beautiful jacket or coat. Knitted cashmere makes a luxurious sweater, cardigan, clingy dress, gored skirt, or bathrobe. Since cashmere is available in both knits and wovens and is fairly costly, I suggest pretesting the pattern. Ripped stitches weaken the fabric.

Sewing Tips

Sew tautly, pulling the fabric until the seam allowance begins to curl. Do not stretch further. Lift fabric every 6 in. and smooth out. Stabilize neckline and shoulders with Stay Tape or selvage strips.

Preshrink

Hold steam iron ½ in. above fabric or preshrink at the dry cleaner.

Layout

"With nap" layout, double thickness. Right side on a woven is obvious because it is more hairy. Cashmere knits are tubular. To determine right side on a knit, stretch the knit; fabric will roll to the right side. If crease at foldline does not press out, cut around it. Straighten cut ends of fabric with a T-square.

WORKING WITH CASHMERE

Marking

Tailor tacks or tailor's chalk.

Cutting

Rotary cutter or sharp scissors. Use pattern weights.

Interfacing

Textured Weft or Armo Weft. If you are making a jacket, consider underlining the entire jacket with cotton batiste or voile. Interfacing can then be fused to underlining. The character of the fabric is maintained by not fusing directly onto the fabric and attaching all the hand stitches to the underlining.

Thread

Silk machine twist will yield the least visible seams. Good-quality polyester or cotton is suitable.

Needle

80/12 H on wovens, 75/11 HS on knits.

Stitch Length

Wovens: 2.5 mm straight stitch; knits: Tiny zigzag (0.5 mm width, 2.0 mm length).

Presser Foot

Wovens: Standard; knits: Teflon.

Seam Finish

Wovens: No seam finish if lined. Cashmere knits do not ravel so a plain seam pressed open is the least visible. (See #1 on p. 216.) Knits: First sew tiny zigzag, then serge together. (See #20 on p. 218.)

Pressing

Steam iron on wool setting, using a press-and-lift motion. Take care not to stretch cashmere. Always use a self-fabric press cloth on the right side. Do not move off the pressing surface until fabric is dry.

Topstitching

Not recommended. Instead, hand-pick wovens with Sulky rayon thread or buttonhole twist ⅜ in. from finished edge and ⅜ in. apart. (See #1 on p. 222.)

Closures

Wovens—use machine- or hand-stitched corded or bound buttonholes. (See #2 and #5 on p. 224, #8 on p. 225.) Knit cardigans—press ¼ in. toward wrong side of front. Cover with grosgrain ribbon. Sew long sides of grosgrain with ribbon against presser foot and knit against feed dogs. Make machine buttonholes with 70/10 HJ needle and extra-fine thread. (See #7 on p. 225.)

Hem

Wovens—hand-hem. (See #4 on p. 228.) Knits—use cover or flatlock hem stitch. (See #1, #2, and #5 on p. 228.) Or serge bottom of knit using differential feed or pushing behind presser foot with finger to keep from stretching. Press ½-in. strip of Steam-A-Seam® on wrong side of hem. Pull off paper. Turn up ½-in. hem and press. Topstitch with double-needle ZWI stretch and woolly nylon thread hand-wrapped on bobbin. Use a walking foot to keep knit from stretching. Loosen top tension until double row of stitches lies flat.

> ✂ **Tip** Cashmere sweaters do not need to go to the dry cleaner. Use warm water machine wash on the gentle cycle and the permanent-press cycle on the dryer. The sweaters come out fluffier and newer looking than dry cleaned, and there is no shrinkage if they are 100% cashmere.

Charmeuse

Fabric Fact

Silk charmeuse, a luxurious, supple silk, is a favorite for blouses and lingerie. It has a shiny satin face and dull back. Polyester charmeuse is also available, but it is almost impossible to get pucker-free seams since charmeuse must be cut on grain.

> **Tip** Eucalan® Delicate Wash liquid cleaner is superior for washing sweaters and silks because it does not leave a yellow cast. This product also works for machine washing wool crepe in cool water on the gentle cycle.

Suitable For

Blouses, full pants, lingerie, and piping. Bias strips of silk charmeuse make an attractive finish around the neck, sleeves, and hem edge on solid-color wool jersey, wool crepe, and velour. Use a bias maker to ease this task. Shape bias at iron and use spray starch to give memory.

Sewing Tips

Hold on to top and bobbin threads when you begin sewing to prevent fabric from pulling into the throat plate hole. Sew tautly, pulling the fabric equally from front and back.

WORKING WITH CHARMEUSE

Preshrink

For dark colors, hold steam iron ½ in. above fabric surface. Dry-clean completed garment. For light colors, hand-wash in warm water and 1 tablespoon of shampoo for color-treated hair or Eucalan Delicate Wash. Rinse with 1 tablespoon of hair conditioner. Air-dry. Press while damp. Completed garment can be hand-washed. To prevent color loss, use shampoo for colored hair or add 1 tablespoon of Epsom salt to regular shampoo.

Layout

"With nap" layout, double thickness. For cutting accuracy, tape tissue paper to table. Pin double thickness of fabric to tissue at 12-in. intervals. Pin pattern through fabric and tissue layers. Keep pins in seam allowances.

Marking

Clover Chaco Liner or Pilot Frixion erasable ink pen.

Cutting

Cut through all layers with sharp scissors; rotary cutter also acceptable.

Interfacing

Silk organza for a crisp finish; self-fabric for a drapey finish.

Thread

Fine machine-embroidery thread in cotton or silk gives the best stitch, is not bulky, and will not stretch.

Needle

60/8, 65/9, 70/10 HM or HJ.

Stitch Length

1.5 mm to 2.0 mm straight stitch.

Presser Foot

Single-hole throat plate. Or use satin stitch foot and throat plate and switch needle to far left position for support on three sides. Loosen top tension and bobbin tension ⅛ to ¼ turn.

Seam Finish

Flat-fell or French seam on the serger works well here. (See #9 on p. 216, #10 and #11 on p. 217.)

Pressing

Dry iron on silk setting. Steam will cause water spots unless fabric is prewashed.

Topstitching

Machine-stitch close to sewn edge with fine thread using a topstitch presser foot, or hand-pick with shiny Sulky rayon or silk thread. (See #1, #2, and #3 on p. 222.)

Closures

Machine buttonholes in silk thread are more flexible and less bulky than buttonholes in other threads, or use fine machine-embroidery thread on top and in bobbin. (See #1 on p. 224.)

Hem

Trim hem allowance to ½ in. Thread bobbin with fusible thread and use fine thread on top. With wrong side of fabric against the feed dogs, staystitch along hemline. Press hem allowance to wrong side to dissolve fusible thread and form sharp crease. Trim hem allowance to ⅛ in. Hand-roll hem, enclosing raw edge. Machine-sew with fine thread. (See #16 on p. 230.) On bias garments, serge finish with a rolled hem stitch, removing right needle so that the rolled hem takes a bigger bite out of the fabric.

Chenille

Fabric Fact

This fuzzy, soft-to-the-touch fabric wears better and does not stretch out of shape if it is fully interfaced with Fusi-Knit. If you prefer the soft drapeyness, choose a style where slight stretching is acceptable. When purchasing a sweater, buy a size smaller than normal. Chenille grows as it is worn.

Suitable For

Vest or jacket (must be fully interfaced); big shirt, loose top, or bathrobe (use as is).

Sewing Tips

Overlock all pieces separately right after fusing or cutting. Pushing the fabric toward the presser foot rather than letting the feed dogs move the fabric along prevents the fabric from stretching as you sew.

WORKING WITH CHENILLE

Preshrink

Turn wrong side out. Hand- or machine-wash on gentle cycle with warm water. Dry flat.

Layout

"With nap" layout, double thickness. Use pattern weights.

Marking

Tailor tacks or safety pins.

Cutting

Scissors or rotary cutter.

Interfacing

Fusi-Knit.

Thread

Good-quality cotton or polyester.

Needle

80/12 H.

Stitch Length

2.0 mm.

Presser Foot

Walking or Teflon.

Seam Finish

Sew seam with straight stitch. Press open. Serge each seam allowance separately or bind separately with a Hong Kong finish. (See #3 on p. 216, #16 on p. 218.)

Pressing

Cover pressing surface with fluffy towel. Place right side of chenille against towel. Press on cotton setting with steam. No pressing on right side of the nap—it flattens it.

Topstitching

Not recommended.

Closures

Corded buttonhole, faced buttonhole, bound buttonhole in contrasting fabric, buttonhole in a seam. (See #5 and #6 on p. 224, #8 and #10 on p. 225.)

Hem

Serge raw edge or finish with Hong Kong finish. Hand-hem. (See #13 on p. 230.)

Tip How can you determine the right side of the fabric? On some fabrics, such as plain weaves, the right and wrong side are the same. For others, look closely at the selvages. The smoother, more perfect side of the selvage is the right side of the fabric. The right side of the fabric is smoother. The wrong side of the fabric has more slubs and thread tails. Holes in the selvage poke up toward the right side.

Chiffon

Fabric Fact

Silk chiffon has the best drape and seam quality of the chiffon family. Rayon and polyester chiffon do not conform quite as well to the body. Chiffon has a mind of its own. Do not attempt to work with this fabric when you are under time pressure. You and the fabric will end up in a standoff.

Suitable For

Full pants, loose tops, and flowing dresses. Look for loose-fitting, simply styled garments with minimum seams and darts. Styles that are not full enough look skimpy. Garments should be one-third to one-half larger than your hip measurement and one-quarter to one-third larger than your bust measurement. If your hips are 40 in., full pants need to measure 53 in. to 60 in. For a 36-in. bust, the garment should measure 45 in. to 48 in.

Sewing Tips

You are going to get your best stitch if you place strips of tissue paper against the feed dogs and your work under the presser foot. Hold top and bobbin threads when you begin sewing to prevent fabric from pulling down into the throat plate hole. Sew tautly, pulling the fabric equally from the front and back. Do not backstitch. Tear off the tissue.

Preshrink

Not necessary. Dry-clean completed garment or hand-wash in 1 tablespoon shampoo. Air-dry flat.

> ✂ **Tip** **Eliminate static cling when wearing a chiffon skirt by rubbing a small amount of hand cream onto your legs through your hose or by spraying your legs with Static Guard®.**

WORKING WITH CHIFFON

Layout

"Without nap" layout, single thickness. To control fabric and cut accurately, cover table with tissue paper. Pin single thickness of fabric to paper. Make duplicate of any "cut on fold" pattern pieces. Tape duplicate to original at foldline so that entire pattern can be cut through single fabric thickness. Pin pattern through fabric and paper. Keep pins within seam allowances.

Marking

Clover Chaco Liner, Pilot Frixion erasable ink pen, tailor tacks. Do not use waxed chalk because it leaves stains.

Cutting

Using sharp scissors, cut through pattern, fabric, and tissue paper.

Interfacing

Skin-colored silk organza or self-fabric for more softness. Interface top collars and cuffs so that seam allowances won't show through.

Thread

Fine cotton thread is preferred because it doesn't stretch. Polyester thread causes chiffon to pucker.

Needle

60/8 or 65/9 HJ or HM, new needle only.

Stitch Length

2.0 mm.

Presser Foot

Straight stitch presser foot and single-hole throat plate. Or use satin stitch foot and throat plate and switch needle to far left position for support on three sides.

Seam Finish

Narrow French seams. On long vertical seams, sew with a tiny zigzag (0.5 mm width, 2.5 mm length) to prevent seam from drawing up. Include strip of tissue between fabric and feed dogs. Tear off tissue after first seam but include again as you sew the enclosed seam. (See #11 on p. 217, #40 on p. 221.)

Pressing

Clean, dry iron on silk setting. Steam will cause water spots unless fabric was prewashed. Chiffon is difficult to press without stretching.

Topstitching

Not recommended.

Closures

Machine buttonholes with fine machine-embroidery thread or fabric loops. (See #1 on p. 224, #9 on p. 225.) With zippers, interface seam allowances with organza and hand-pick. (See #19 on p. 227.)

Hem

Options: (1) Using 2.0 mm stitch length, sew along finished hemline. Press hem to wrong side, with stitching line on crease. Trim hem allowance to 1/8 in. Hand-roll hem, enclosing raw edge. Hand- or machine-sew with fine thread. (See #16 on p. 230.) (2) Serge rolled hem. Increase stitch width and remove right needle. Run staystitching line at 1/2 in. When serging, let rolled hem encase staystitching. Differential feed set at 0.7 helps here. Use fine thread in the serger. Pull off tissue.

Chirimen

Fabric Fact

Chirimen is a traditional Japanese kimono fabric and as such comes in Japanese prints and solids. It is available in rayon and polyester. This fabric is cherished and difficult to find. The rayon version is 49 in. wide. Rayon chirimen is very beautiful but does not have much drape. When you preshrink rayon chirimen, it comes out of the dryer crinkled to almost half its width. It returns to its full size once pleats are ironed out. Polyester chirimen is very drapey and comes out of preshrinking just the same as before it went in.

Suitable For

Blouses, dresses without too much fullness, yoke detailing, bias binding.

Sewing Tips

Once you have pressed the fabric after preshrinking, it is easy to sew; simply let it feed naturally.

WORKING WITH CHIRIMEN

Preshrink

Machine-wash in warm water and machine-dry. When you preshrink the rayon version of the fabric, it comes out of the dryer crinkled to almost half of its width. Once you iron out the pleats, it returns to its full size. Polyester chirimen comes out of the dryer the same as before it went in.

Layout

"Without nap," double thickness.

Marking

Clover Chaco Liner or Pilot Frixion erasable ink pen.

Cutting

Rotary cutter or scissors.

Interfacing

Sewers' Dream or Fusi-Knit.

Thread

Cotton or polyester.

Needle

70/10 H or HJ.

Stitch Length

2.5 mm straight stitch for seams, 1.8 mm for collar points and curves.

Presser Foot

Standard.

Seam Finish

Flat fell. (See #9 on p. 216.)

Pressing

Steam iron on rayon setting.

Topstitching

Topstitch ⅛ in. from seamed edge of details; a topstitching foot is useful here.

Closures

For buttonholes, use a 70/10 HJ needle and fine cotton thread to make ball buttons, frog closures, and button loops. (See #9, #12, and #13 on p. 225.)

Hem

Double-folded one-quarter shirttail hem. (See #10 on p. 229.)

Tip When sewing around curves, reduce your stitch length and slow down the machine. You have two hem choices: (1) A ¼-in. double fold followed by topstitching; (2) A serged raw edge, turned up ½ in., and topstitched. Clip out divots in the seam allowance before turning. (See #8 on p. 229.)

Corduroy

Fabric Fact

Corduroy is derived from the French *cordon du roi*, which means "cord of kings."

Suitable For

Vests, straight skirts, tailored shirts, structured jackets, jumpers, tailored pants, and children's clothes. Dark colors are especially flattering on adults. If you are heavy, avoid wide-wale corduroy since it adds bulk.

Sewing Tips

Sew in direction of pile.

Tip **Always thread the top of your machine with the presser foot up so that the thread can seat properly in the tension discs. The presser foot can then be lowered for easier needle threading.**

WORKING WITH CORDUROY

Preshrink

Dry cleaning keeps a corduroy garment new-looking longer. If you plan to dry-clean completed garment, hold steam iron ½ in. above surface. If not, baste fabric crossgrain edges together so nap is on the inside. Machine-wash in warm water and machine-dry on delicate cycle. Restore flattened pile by tumble drying, wrong side out, with damp towel for 10 minutes. Remove promptly and hang up. To avoid lint transfer, place a dark-colored towel in with dark corduroy, a light-colored towel with light corduroy.

Layout

"With nap" layout, double thickness, wrong side in. Pile wears better if pieces are cut with nap going down. For richer color, cut with nap going up. Use pattern weights instead of pins.

Marking

Clover Chaco Liner, Pilot Frixion erasable ink pen, tailor tacks. Use smooth cotton for facings to eliminate bulk.

Cutting

Rotary cutter or scissors.

Interfacing

Sew-in.

Thread

Good-quality cotton or polyester.

Needle

80/12 HJ or 80/12 H.

Stitch Length

2.5 mm straight stitch.

Presser Foot

Walking or roller. Loosen top tension slightly.

Seam Finish

Serge piece separately or enclose in flat-fell seams. (See #3 and #9 on p. 216.)

Pressing

Cover pressing surface with fluffy towel, self-fabric, Velvaboard™, or needle board. Iron on cotton setting with steam. Press with point of iron in seam allowance. Never press on right side of fabric. Rub fabric against itself to restore nap.

Topstitching

Not recommended.

Closures

For buttonholes, use 70/10 HJ needle and fine machine-embroidery thread to reduce bulk. Lengthen and widen stitch slightly. Apply FrayBlock™ to buttonhole, let dry, then cut open to control shredding. (See #4 on p. 224.) Place hanging loops inside waistband to avoid crushing pile with pinchers on hangers.

Hem

Serge raw edges. Hand-hem. (See #4 on p. 228.)

Cotton for Quilters

Fabric Fact

Because there are a lot more quilters than there are garment sewers, the choices in the fabric store for cotton are tremendous. A more casual lifestyle and the cost of dry cleaning make cotton a viable choice for garment sewing.

Suitable For

While most cottons do not drape, they make up well in blouses, dresses without too much fullness, pull-on medium-width pants, robes, napkins, pillow covers, and place mats.

Sewing Tips

Cottons are the easiest fabric to sew. Simply let the fabric feed naturally.

WORKING WITH COTTON FOR QUILTERS

Preshrink

Overlock crossgrain ends together to prevent stretching the fabric during washing. Treat the fabric the way you will treat the finished piece, which usually means a warm-water machine wash and regular temperature dryer.

Layout

"Without nap" layout, double thickness.

Marking

Clover Chaco Liner or Pilot Frixion erasable ink pen.

Cutting

Rotary cutter or sharp scissors.

Interfacing

Sewers' Dream, ShirtMaker's Choice for crisp collars and cuffs, non-woven Pellon® for purses and craft projects.

Thread

Good-quality cotton or polyester.

Needle

70/10 or 80/12.

Presser Foot

Standard.

Stitch Length

2.5mm straight stitch.

Seam Finish

Flat fell. (See #9 on p. 216.)

Pressing

Steam iron on cotton setting.

Topstitching

Topstitch ⅛ in. to ¼ in. from seamed edge of fabric. A topstitching foot helps here.

Closures

Buttonholes, snaps, any type of zipper. (See #1 and #4 on p. 224, #11 on p. 225, #19 on p. 227.)

Hem

Double-fold ¼-in. hem. Press on a ¼-in.-wide strip of Steam-A-Seam to wrong side of fabric. Pull off paper. Press up ¼-in. hem. Enclosing raw edge, press up another ¼ in. Machine- or hand-stitch hem. (See #10 on p. 229.)

Crepe de Chine

Fabric Fact

Silk crepe de Chine has a slightly crinkly surface formed by twisted yarns. It is available in three weights: 2-ply, the most common; 3-ply, the favorite of top-notch designers; and 4-ply, found in tailored pants and jackets of European designers. The Japanese unit of measurement of "momme" refers to fabric weight. The higher the momme, the thicker the fabric; 2-ply silk is 14–16 momme, 3-ply silk is 30 momme, and 4-ply silk is 40 momme. Unlike polyester crepe de Chine, silk crepe de Chine has a beautiful drape and pucker-free seams.

Suitable For

All three silk weights work for tailored shirts and blouses; 3-ply and 4-ply work for tailored jackets, pants, blouses, straight dresses, and semi-full pants; 2-ply works well in full pants, boxer shorts, loose tops, and full dresses. If you need a dressy coat to wear out in the evening, consider making a coat in black or taupe 4-ply silk underlined with flannel for warmth. Make it just above the knee in length, and you can wear it over anything.

Sewing Tips

To avoid seam ripping, hand-baste seams for fitting. Hold top and bottom threads when starting seam. Sew tautly. Don't overfit, which puts too much stress on seams.

Tip Underlining a pair of 2-ply silk pants can eliminate wrinkles. If you want the pant to be crisper, underline with silk organza. If you want the pant to be soft, underline in soft cottons such as lawn or voile.

WORKING WITH CREPE DE CHINE

Preshrink

If the completed garment will be dry-cleaned, preshrink by holding steam iron ½ in. above surface. Light colors can be hand-washed, saving a lot on dry-cleaning bills. Prewash in warm water and 1 tablespoon shampoo. Rinse until water runs clear. Add 1 tablespoon hair conditioner to last rinse. Air-dry and press while damp. To set dye in dark colors, add 1 tablespoon of Epsom salt to wash step. Some prints and solids do run during hand washing, so try a sample first.

Layout

"Without nap" layout, double thickness. To control fabric and cut accurately, cover table with tissue paper. Pin double thickness of fabric to paper. Pin pattern through fabric and paper. Keep pins within seam allowances.

Marking

Pilot Frixion erasable ink pen, Clover Chaco Liner, Clover white marking pen for dark colors.

Cutting

Using sharp scissors or rotary cutter, cut through all layers. Serrated shears also work great.

Interfacing

Underline straight skirts and fitted dresses with silk organza for crispness or to prevent wrinkling, cotton batiste for body without crispness.

Thread

Fine machine-embroidery silk or cotton thread gives the best stitch because it marries with the fabric, doesn't take up too much room, and doesn't stretch and cause puckers.

Needle

60/8, 65/9, or 70/10 HM or HJ.

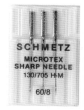 

Stitch Length

1.5 mm to 2.0 mm.

Presser Foot

Straight stitch foot or if using standard foot, switch needle to far left position for support on three sides. Loosen top and bobbin tension ⅛ to ¼ turn.

Seam Finish

French seams or flat fell. (See #9 on p. 216, and #10 on p. 217, #40 on p. 221.)

Pressing

Dry iron on silk setting.

Topstitching

Hand picking ¼ in. from edge and ¼ in. apart makes nice detailing. (See #1 on p. 222.)

Closures

For buttonholes, use 70/10 HJ needle and fine machine embroidery thread to reduce bulk. Loosen top tension slightly. (See #1 on p. 224.)

Hem

On straight garments, serge-finish or Hong Kong–finish raw edge. Turn up 1-in. hem allowance and hand-sew. (See #13 on p. 230.) For full skirts, circular ruffles, and curved edges on tailored shirts, trim hem allowance to ½ in. Using 2.0 mm stitch length, sew along finished hemline. Press hem to wrong side with stitching line on crease. Trim hem allowance to ⅛ in. Hand-roll hem, enclosing raw edge. Hand- or machine-sew with fine thread. Keep finger pressure on back of presser foot to prevent hem from stretching. (See #16 on p. 230.)

Crinkle

Fabric Fact

Crinkles are formed by tightening the fabric weft and heat setting. They are available in 100% cotton, 100% silk, and 100% polyester, sometimes called "laundered challis." Look for crinkled fabric with flat backing fabric, which helps hold the crinkle in. Cotton crinkle bags out at the seat and knees as you wear it. The crinkled appearance returns after washing, but who wants a baggy seat and knees?

Suitable For

Cotton crinkle works for loose tops and unstructured shirts. Wool crinkle works well for unstructured, unlined coats or jackets.

Sewing Tips

Before you cut out facings, press pleated fabric as flat as possible. Interface with fusible tricot. For all seams, push fabric into the presser foot as you sew. Do not pull fabric from front or back. Stabilize neck and shoulders with lengths of Stay Tape cut using the pattern as a guide. Natural-fiber crinkle fabric will not keep its crinkle unless it is underlined with silk organza cut to the exact size of the pattern. Baste the layers together and treat as one in construction.

> **Tip** **Since beeswaxed thread on a hem makes the hem too visible, run your thread through Thread Heaven®, a conditioner that prevents tangling.**

WORKING WITH CRINKLE

Preshrink

Polyester crinkle needs no preshrinking, but cotton and silk crinkle do. Silk crinkle is preshrunk by holding a steam iron ½ in. from fabric surface on the wrong side. To preshrink cotton crinkle, machine-wash in warm water and tumble-dry on a permanent press cycle. The fabric will lose width and length and appear very narrow and very pleated. Press slightly to remove some of the pleating so it looks more like it did when you bought it. Preshrinking without a follow-up pressing (if you like the tiny pleats) is a bad idea. The garment is very heavy and pleats release in places of stress (knee, seat, tummy) at the first wearing—most unattractive!

Layout

"Without nap" layout, double thickness. Use pattern weights instead of pins.

Marking

Clover Chaco Liner or Pilot Frixion erasable ink pen.

Cutting

Scissors or rotary cutter.

Interfacing

Fusi-Knit or Sewers' Dream on facings only.

Thread

Good-quality cotton or polyester.

Needle

80/12 H for cotton, 70/10 H or HJ for silk and polyester.

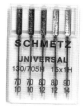

Stitch Length

Tiny zigzag (0.5 mm width, 2.5 mm length).

Presser Foot

Walking.

Seam Finish

Sew seam with tiny zigzag, then serge together with a 3-thread overlock stitch. (See #21 on p. 218.)

Pressing

For cotton or wool crinkle, use dry iron on cotton setting. For silk crinkle, use dry iron on silk setting. Steam removes too many crinkles. It is suitable for select polyester only.

Topstitching

Not recommended.

Closures

Button loops, button openings in a seam, frog closures, and snaps. (See #9, #10, #11, and #12 on p. 225.)

Hem

Serge raw edge using differential feed, or push behind presser foot as in easing. Turn up 1 in. Hand-hem, knotting every fourth stitch. (See #4 on p. 228.)

Damask

Fabric Fact

Damask is a jacquard similar to brocade, except the weave is flatter and looks the same on both sides. Shiny and matte threads, usually in one color, create a pattern on the surface.

Suitable For

Jackets, blouses, bias skirts, straight or semi-full dresses. Also curtains, draperies, and tablecloths.

Sewing Tips

Let fabric feed naturally.

Tip You will get the best-quality embroidery if you use a different bobbin case just for embroidery. Take your favorite thread along when you have your machine serviced, and your repairman will adjust your bobbin tension to accommodate that particular thread.

WORKING WITH DAMASK

Preshrink

Machine-wash in warm water and machine-dry on regular temperature.

Layout

"Without nap" layout, double thickness.

Marking

Clover Chaco Liner, Pilot Frixion erasable ink pen, tracing paper.

Cutting

Rotary cutter or sharp scissors.

Interfacing

Fusi-Knit.

Thread

Good-quality cotton or polyester.

Needle

80/12 H.

Stitch Length

2.5 mm.

Presser Foot

Standard.

Seam Finish

Flat fell. (See #9 on p. 216.)

Pressing

Cotton setting with steam. No press cloth necessary.

Topstitching

Topstitch ¼ in. from edge with regular thread. (See #10 on p. 223.)

Closures

Snaps, machine buttonholes. (See #1 on p. 224, #11 on p. 225.)

Tip Check the tension on your sewing machine. You don't know how to do that? Try this. Put a different color thread on the top than on the bobbin. Sew for a few inches. If the bobbin color shows on the top side of the fabric, loosen the upper tension by turning the tension knob to a lower number. If the top thread shows on the bottom of the fabric, tighten the tension by turning the tension knob to a higher number.

Hem

Double-fold ½-in. hem. Machine-stitch on blouse. (See #10 on p. 229.) Hand-hem on jacket, pants, or dress. (See #4 on p. 228.)

Denim

Fabric Fact

A twill weave makes denim the workhorse of 100% cotton fabrics. Stretch denims are also very popular. A rayon, polyester, and spandex blend is a bit stiffer than denim with the added property of stretch. Another stretch denim is a cotton and Lycra® blend that grows softer as it stretches.

Suitable For

Jeans, bomber jackets, straight skirts, semi-fitted shirtdresses, tailored shirts, upholstery, and pillows. Denim comes in two weights. Lightweight denim is better for shirts and dresses. Heavyweight denim is better for pants, straight skirts, and jackets. Denim weights can be referred to by ounce measurements for a yard of fabric. A good weight for jeans is 12 oz. to 14 oz.

Sewing Tips

Prevent skipped stitches by holding fabric taut whenever you are machine-sewing or serging through multiple layers. Hammer multiple layers flat before sewing. You will be rewarded with no skipped stitches.

Preshrink

Wash separately as colors bleed. Avoid detergents with brighteners. Machine-wash in warm water and machine-dry on regular temp. Preshrink twice to eliminate all shrinkage. After second drying, remove fabric while still slightly damp and iron dry to prevent crease lines from

> ✂ **Tip** Problems hemming jeans? Turn hem under and hammer seam joints. Use a 100/16 HJ needle and Gütermann gold-colored thread, topstitching weight, on top. Sew jeans hem from the right side, lengthening your stitch to 3.0 mm. Rub needle with needle lube occasionally.

WORKING WITH DENIM

forming. If you want a "faded" look, wash and bleach fabric three to five times.

Layout

"Without nap" layout for regular denim and "with nap" layout for brushed denim. Double thickness. Grainline is important. Off-grain cuts create problems like twisting pant legs. Cut facings from lighter-weight fabric, such as a coordinating cotton.

Marking

Clover Chaco Liner, Pilot Frixion erasable ink pen, Clover white pen for dark colors.

Cutting

Sharp scissors or rotary cutter.

Interfacing

Waistbands: Armo Weft; shirts: French Fuse or Fusi-Knit.

Thread

Good-quality polyester. Use upholstery thread on top if seams will be under stress.

Needle

90/14 HJ for lightweight or 100/16 HJ for heavyweight. Double HJ 4.0/100 for topstitching two parallel rows.

Stitch Length

2.5 mm on lightweight, 3.0 mm on heavyweight.

Presser Foot

Straight stitch.

Seam Finish

Few machines are capable of joining two flat-fell seams at the crotch. Instead, sew a straight seam. Serge one seam allowance and trim the other. Without turning under, overlap serged seam allowance onto trimmed seam allowance. Topstitch. This forms a fake flat fell that is less bulky and easier to sew. (See #27 on p. 219.)

Pressing

High-temperature steam iron.

Topstitching

Lengthen stitch to 3.5 mm and use heavy-duty or upholstery thread ¼ in. from edge. Gütermann, YLI, and Signature™ make threads that match the color and weight used in ready-to-wear jeans. Use regular thread on bobbin. Use a double-needle ZWI HJ 4.0/100 to topstitch two parallel rows. A triple stitch using regular thread can give the look of heavy topstitching. Do not do a triple stitch with a double needle. Instead, make two separate rows of stitching. Hammer bulky seams flat before topstitching, and you will not get skipped stitches. (See #6 on p. 216, #9 and #10 on p. 223.)

Closures

Snaps make the best closures. (See #11 on p. 225.) Also use buttons or bachelor buttons and keyhole buttonhole. (See #2 on p. 224.)

Hem

Use topstitching thread and a 100/16 HJ needle. Fold hem twice at ¾ in. Pound with a tailor's clapper or hammer to flatten before stitching. Sew one or two rows of parallel stitching with a single needle. (See #10 on p. 229.) On stretch denim, press on a ¾-in.-wide strip of interfacing cut in the non-stretch direction so that hem does not stretch as it is topstitched.

Embroidered Fabrics

Fabric Fact

Machine embroidery is used to decorate the surface of silk shantung, silk organza, and lightweight wool flannel.

Suitable For

Boxy jackets, flat-front pants, simple tops, straight skirts, vests, purses, pillows, dining chair covers. Choose simple styles for garment sewing so that the embroidered pattern is shown off to its best advantage and is not broken by seams.

Sewing Tips

Let fabric feed naturally.

Tip The life expectancy of a good-quality machine is 23,000 hours of sewing. If you sewed 20 hours a week and 52 weeks a year, you would only use up 1,040 sewing hours in a year.

WORKING WITH EMBROIDERED FABRICS

Preshrink

Not necessary. Steam iron can cause puckering around embroidery. Dry-clean completed garment.

Layout

"With nap" layout, since many embroideries have a direction for flowers and leaves. Single thickness, right side up, for better pattern placement on embroidered design.

Marking

Tailor tacks or safety pins.

Cutting

Sharp scissors or very sharp, new rotary blade if fabric is not too heavily embroidered.

Interfacing

Silk organza.

Thread

Good-quality 100% cotton.

Needle

70/10 HJ for light embroidery, 90/14 HJ to pierce dense embroidery.

Stitch Length

2.5 mm.

Presser Foot

Standard.

Seam Finish

Serge-finish cutout pieces. Sew conventional seams and press open. (See #3 on p. 216.) Other seam treatments are too bulky. For lined garments, initial serging can be eliminated and raw edges can be pinked. (See #2 on p. 216.)

Pressing

Cover pressing area with Turkish towel or Velvaboard. Press from wrong side using a dry iron on medium temperature. Do not use too much pressure on iron or embroidery will flatten.

Topstitching

Not recommended since topstitching will detract from embroidered design, but can be used if fabric refuses to flatten after pressing.

Closures

Machine buttonholes (see #1 on p. 224), button loops (see #9 on p. 225), corded buttonholes (see #5 on p. 224), buttonhole in a seam (see #10 on p. 225), frog closures (see #12 on p. 225), and invisible zippers (see #19 on p. 227).

Hem

Serge or Hong Kong finish raw edge. Turn up 1¼-in. hem allowance. Hand-hem. (See #13 on p. 230, #4 on p. 228.) Another option is to finish outside edges with foldover braid or bias binding. (See #9 and #11 on p. 229.)

Tip Always use the smallest hoop possible to accommodate your motif in embroidery. The hoop stabilizes the fabric and holds it taut during the embroidery process. The larger the hoop, the less stable the fabric.

Ethnic Fabrics

Fabric Fact

Ethnic fabrics are fabrics woven on the loop in the home by both men and women in different regions of the world. You do not have to be a world traveler to make garments from ethnic fabrics—you just have to know where to look for them. I have found treasures in consignment stores, flea markets, and stores that sell goods from around the world. I love to travel and I love to sew, so I am always on the lookout for a blanket, tablecloth, or bed cover that could be made into clothing.

Suitable For

Vests, long coats, jackets.

Sewing Tips

Let fabric feed into presser foot naturally.

> **Tip** If the fabric you are using has a border, consider cutting off the border and using it with the garment as a yoke, hem treatment, collar, or cuffs.

WORKING WITH ETHNIC FABRICS

Preshrink

Plan to dry-clean since dyes or weaves may not be stable.

Layout

"Without nap" layout.

Marking

Clover Chaco Liner.

Cutting

Rotary cutter or shears.

Interfacing

Fusi-Knit.

Thread

Cotton or polyester.

Needle

80/12 H.

Stitch Length

3.0 mm straight stitch.

Presser Foot

Standard.

Seam Finish

Flat-fell or Hong Kong finish. (See #9 on p. 216, #16 on p. 218.)

Pressing

Use steam and temperature compatible with fiber content. Try a sample.

Topstitching

Close to the edge with topstitching foot.

Closures

Buttonhole in seam, snaps, or buttonhole. (See #1 on p. 224, #10 and #11 on p. 225.)

Hem

Hong Kong Finish raw edge. Turn up 1¼ in. and hand-stitch. (See #13 on p. 230.)

Eyelet

Fabric Fact

Eyelet fabrics have small cutouts with stitching around them. Many fabrics can be used as a base for eyelet: cotton batiste, lawn, broadcloth, organdy, piqué, even faux leather.

Suitable For

Cotton eyelet is most often used for blouses, full skirts, and girls' dresses. It also can make a fun bathrobe.

Sewing Tips

Let fabric feed naturally.

> ✂ **Tip** **To avoid spray starch buildup on the soleplate of your iron, spray the garment, roll it up, and let it sit for 1 minute before ironing.**

WORKING WITH EYELET

Preshrink

Since eyelet designs can be made on a variety of fabrics, preshrink appropriate to base fabric. Machine-wash cotton and linen eyelet in warm water on regular cycle and machine-dry. Faux leather eyelet needs no preshrinking.

Layout

"Without nap" layout, double thickness.

Marking

Tailor tacks, safety pins, Pilot Frixion erasable ink pen.

Cutting

Sharp scissors or rotary cutter.

Interfacing

Silk organza in your skin tone.

Thread

Good-quality cotton or polyester.

Needle

70/10 HJ or HM.

Stitch Length

2.5 mm.

Presser Foot

Standard.

Seam Finish

Flat fell (see #5 and #9 on p. 216) or 4-thread serged.

Pressing

Suitable to base fabric.

Topstitching

Optional; sew very close to edge (⅛ in.) if at all. (See #2 and #3 on p. 222.)

Tip

Why does the thread keep breaking? Try this. (1) Rethread your machine top and bottom; the thread may have jumped out of a guide. (2) Put in a new needle compatible with your fabric. (3) Change thread. (4) Experiment on a different fabric. (5) Loosen the top tension—last resort! (6) If problem persists, take the machine to a repairman.

Closures

Snaps, zippers, button loops. Machine buttonholes not suitable because fabric does not feed evenly with the buttonhole foot. (See #9 and #11 on p. 225, #19 on p. 227.)

Hem

Serge raw edge. Turn up hem allowance. Machine- or hand-hem on skirt. (See #33 on p. 233.)

Faux Fur

Fabric Fact

Faux fur comes in two weights: a silky low-pile rayon or polyester fur, and a stiffer long-pile polyester variety, sometimes called craft fur. The silky fur is better for garments. Craft fur is suitable for costumes.

Suitable For

Simple styling shows off fur to the best advantage. Choose loose-fitting styles with a shawl collar (or no collar), raglan sleeves, and in-seam pockets. The low pile is the most slimming, but a boxy style in the long pile can fool many into thinking it is genuine fur. Whenever you make something in fur, cut the entire garment one size larger, unless the pattern was specifically designed for fur.

Sewing Tips

If the idea of trimming all seam allowances off the pattern and using the hinge technique for long-pile fur scares you, simply cut fabric with seam allowances on. Cut away excess bulk on seams with hair clippers. Stabilize neckline with Stay Tape or narrow selvage. Pin seams at 1-in. intervals with pins horizontal to seamline. When pinning, push hairs into fur with stick or pencil so that no hairs protrude from the seam. Catch as few hairs as possible. Cut out darts on stitching line and use zigzag to hinge together. From right side, pull fur out with a toothbrush or hair pick to hide seam. (See #28 on p. 219, #31 on p. 220.) On collars, shave seam allowances with an electric hair clipper.

Preshrink

Not necessary unless you plan to launder it later. Machine-wash in cold water. Machine-dry on no-heat fluff cycle or shake fur and air-dry. Store fabric on a roll.

> ✂ **Tip** When sewing fur to another fabric, such as a lining, sew with the more stable fabric on top. Sew with a Teflon presser foot, and finger-press layers flat in front of the needle.

WORKING WITH FAUX FUR

Layout

"With nap" layout, single thickness, wrong side up. For heavy fur, trim seam allowances completely off pattern. (See "Sewing Tips" on facing page.) For lighter fur, leave seam allowances on pattern. Leave hem intact. Use pattern weights or long flower-head pins to hold pattern pieces to fabric. Trace pattern onto fur backing with felt-tip pen on light backing, silver-point pen on dark backing. Cut through backing only. Fur trim can usually be cut on the crossgrain. Cut undercollars from a coordinating, less bulky fabric.

Marking

Clover Chaco Liner, safety pins, Clover white pen for dark colors.

Cutting

If allergic to hair, wear a face mask during cutting and vacuum frequently. Cut through backing only with short sharp scissors or an X-Acto® knife. Cut one layer at a time. Seam allowances are cut off heavy fur for hinged seams. Use cut on facings when possible.

Interfacing

No fusibles. Use woven interfacing, such as Sew-In Durapress™.

Thread

Good-quality polyester or cotton.

Needle

80/12 H for fur with flexible backing, 90/14 H for fur with stiff backing.

Stitch Length

Hinged seam for heavy fur: Large zigzag (4.5 mm width, 2.5 mm length), allowing needle to fall off edge. Test and adjust zigzag width to depth of fur; your goal is the flattest seam. (See #28 on p. 219.) If your serger has 2-thread capacity, a 2-thread flatlock can be used for seaming. Regular seam for thin fur: Straight stitch 3.0 mm length using 5/8-in. seams.

Presser Foot

Roller or walking. Reduce pressure on presser foot and top tension slightly.

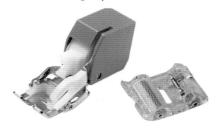

Seam Finish

None. Raw edges butt together on thick fur. Brush outside of seams in the direction of the fur with a toothbrush, or pull out hairs with a hair pick. (See #28 on p. 219, #31 on p. 220.) For thin fur, use plain seams pressed open.

Pressing

Press short-hair furs over a needle board with a cool iron. Never press right side of fur. On long-hair furs, finger-press only.

Topstitching

Not compatible. To help collars and cuffs lie flat, hand-pick through all layers from the right side 1/4 in. from finished edge. Stitches will disappear in the fur. (See #1 on p. 222.)

Closures

No machine buttonholes. Sew buttons on the outside and use covered snaps, large covered fur hooks for closures, faced buttonholes, or cord loops and buttons. (See #13 on p. 225, #14 on p. 226.)

Hem

On thicker furs face hem with 5-in.- to 7-in.-wide satin lining cut from pattern piece and hand-hem. On lightweight furs, turn up a 2-in. hem and hand-hem. (See #15 on p. 230.)

Faux Leather

Fabric Fact

Non-stretch leather looks, feels, and drapes like a high-grade leather, but it's actually man-made. Some faux leathers have no stretch; these are not my favorites because they can be board-like on the body. Stretch leather is my favorite because it has stretch in one or both directions and it also looks, feels, and drapes like a high-grade soft leather. It washes beautifully but breathes very little.

Suitable For

Pants, skirts, jackets, trench coats. Since stretch leather has a nice drape, it can be used on straight or slightly full styles. Since the fabric is waterproof, it is excellent for rainwear, but it is warm to wear because it does not breathe. Stretch leather is suitable for binding when cut in the stretch direction. Non-stretch leather works in boxy styles and makes good seat cushions, tote bags, purses, or rain hats.

Sewing Tips

Because stitches leave permanent holes, use fabric clips to hold seams together for sewing. Since this fabric has a tendency to stick to the body, consider lining with Ambiance Bemberg™ rayon. A polyester lining will prevent the fabric from breathing at all, making it very hot to wear. For more realistic leather-looking pants, create a seam at the knee. Legs are seamed at the knee. If you are trying to make a faux leather or suede garment look genuine, choose a pattern with small pieces or create seams in large pieces. Supple leather skins come in small sizes and cannot accommodate large pattern pieces.

WORKING WITH FAUX LEATHER

Preshrink

Cut off a strip of fabric to test stitch quality on a seam sample. If you experience skipped stitches, the fabric must be laundered to eliminate the coating that is causing the skipped stitches. This will not change the face of the fabric. Machine-wash in warm water on short cycle. Let hang to dry.

Layout

"Without nap" layout, double thickness, knit side out. Use pattern weights.

Marking

Clover Chaco Liner or Clover white marking pen for dark colors. Do not use tracing wheel with spokes, which will put holes in the fabric.

Cutting

Rotary cutter or scissors.

Interfacing

Fusi-Knit or Sewers' Dream.

Thread

Good-quality polyester.

Needle

75/11 HS for stretch leather and 90/14 H for non-stretch leather.

Stitch Length

3.5 mm straight stitch; shorter stitches weaken fabric.

Presser Foot

Teflon or roller foot.

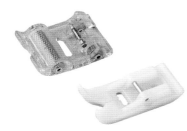

Seam Finish

Fake flat fell (see #27 on p. 219) or finger-press open and topstitch from right side straddling seam. Trim seam allowances close to stitching. (See #13 on p. 217.)

Pressing

Dry iron on high synthetic setting. Use a press cloth on both sides, or fabric will stick to iron.

Topstitching

Topstitch ¼ in. from finished edge with regular thread and a 3.0 mm stitch. (See #10 on p. 223.)

Closures

Buttonholes not suitable here since fabric will show wear. Snaps work well. (See #11 on p. 225.) Excellent candidate for invisible zippers, but stabilize seam allowance with fusible interfacing cut in the non-stretch direction. (See #19 on p. 227.)

Hem

Hold hem in place with Wonder Tape or fabric glue followed by topstitching in a long stitch, 3.5 mm. (See #7 on p. 229.)

Tip To make your own piping from synthetic stretch leather or wool jersey, cut on the crossgrain for maximum stretch. To prevent the jacket front and facing seam from shortening, hand-baste the piping to the facing. Lengthen stitch when piping is included in seam to accommodate extra fabric layers.

Faux Suede

Fabric Fact

Faux suede comes in two weights—one soft and drapey, and one firm. The heavier weight, referred to as Ultrasuede®, works well in home-dec projects but can be somewhat stiff and puffy on the body. Prewashing and machine drying five times helps to relax it and make it more flattering for garments. The lighter weight, referred to as Facile®, is softer and drapier and works well for garments.

Suitable For

Home-dec items such as pillows and valances. Fashion accessories such as purses, small containers, and belts. When using the heavier weight for garment sewing, choose a pattern with straight seams and a boxy silhouette like a jacket, straight skirt, or narrow pants that do not feature fabric drape. Since faux suede doesn't ease well, choose raglan or dolman sleeves. The lightweight variety works well in shirts and skirts with a bit of fullness. Faux suede strips do not make good binding on curves since the fabric has no give and will ripple going around corners.

Tip

✂ Would you like to eliminate the dimple at the end of the dart in gabardine, Ultrasuede, and other difficult-to-press fabrics? Cut a 2-in. square of linen with pinking shears. Place square under the small end of the dart as you sew. Let 1 in. of square protrude off end of dart. Sew dart from fat to skinny end, switching to small stitches ½ in. from dart point. To press, place dart over ham. Linen square fills in the space at the end of the dart. The result is a dart without a dimple. (See #7 on p. 223.)

WORKING WITH FAUX SUEDE

Sewing Tips

Use fabric clips to hold seams together for sewing. (See #7 on p. 223 to sew dart without dimple.)

Preshrink

Ultrasuede: To soften and create better drape, machine-wash in warm water and detergent, and machine-dry on a low setting with towel and tennis shoe five times. Facile: Machine-wash and dry alone once. Leave completed garment in dryer for a few minutes only. Remove and pull seams taut to remove puckers.

Layout

"With nap" layout, double thickness, cutting pieces in the same direction. Pieces can be angled up to 45 degrees without affecting color shading. Use pattern weights.

Marking

Pilot Frixion erasable ink pen or Clover white pen for dark colors.

Cutting

Rotary cutter works the best, but sharp scissors also work.

Interfacing

Fusi-Knit or Sewers' Dream.

Thread

Good-quality polyester.

Needle

75/11 HS or 70/10 HJ for lightweight; 80/12 HJ for heavyweight.

Stitch Length

2.5 mm.

Presser Foot

Roller, walking, or Teflon.

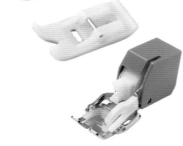

Seam Finish

Lightweight Ultrasuede seams can simply be pressed open. For other faux suedes, use double needle topstitching for less bulkiness or fake flat fell. (See #13 on p. 217, #27 on p. 219.)

Pressing

Use a press cloth and steam iron on medium-high temperature. Overpressing can be corrected with steam and a small brush.

Topstitching

Use 90/14 HS needle, lengthen stitch to 3.5 mm, and use a decorative or topstitching thread. (See #10 on p. 223.)

Closures

For buttonholes, use 70/10 HJ needle and Solvy between presser foot and fabric. For an even easier buttonhole, fuse facing and garment together with Lite Steam-A-Seam 2® in the buttonhole area. Sew a narrow rectangle ¼ in. longer than desired for buttonhole opening on the right side through both layers. Cut slit for buttonhole opening. (See #1 on p. 224, #8 on p. 225, #17 on p. 227.)

Hem

Fuse hem with Lite Steam-A-Seam 2 followed by topstitching or glue with fabric glue. (See #3 on p. 228, #7 on p. 229.)

Felt

Fabric Fact

Felt is a non-woven, non-knitted fabric created by sheets of fiber that tangle when needled or exposed to heat.

Suitable For

Acrylic felt is typically used for craft projects. Polyester felt, a bit loftier, is used for Christmas ornaments, stockings, and stuffed animals. Woolfelt®, which contains 20% to 35% wool, makes nice appliqués, handbags, hats, wall hangings, and interfacing behind heavily beaded collars and cuffs. Felted fabrics created by machine washing and drying make great vests, poodle skirts, and scarves.

Sewing Tips

Let fabric feed naturally. To care for items constructed from handmade felt, do not dry-clean. Hand-wash in cool water and mild soap. Rinse. Squeeze out excess moisture. Do not wring or twist. Block into shape. Air-dry.

Tip **Since wool felt is almost impossible to find, create your own by machine washing 100% wool fabric in hot water with Ivory Snow. Agitate for 30 minutes. Dry in a hot dryer.**

WORKING WITH FELT

Preshrink

Not necessary for craft projects that will not be laundered. For washable projects, machine-wash in warm water and tumble-dry. You may lose 2 in. to 4 in. per 36-in. width and 3 in. to 5 in. per 36-in. length. Wash different colors separately as some colors run more than others.

Layout

Any direction, double or single thickness. If felt is thin or a light color, use two layers to prevent color see-through.

Marking

Soap sliver or Pilot Frixion erasable ink pen.

Cutting

Rotary cutter or scissors.

Interfacing

Fusible interfacing of any weight can be used to give desired stiffness.

Thread

Polyester or cotton.

Needle

80/12 H, not needle particular.

Stitch Length

3.0 mm.

Presser Foot

Standard.

Seam Finish

Straight seams, pressed or topstitched open. No finish necessary since fabric does not ravel. (See #1 on p. 216.)

Pressing

Steam iron on medium temperature.

Topstitching

In craft projects, shapes are usually topstitched to a felt base. When topstitching, line up cut edge of shape with edge of the topstitching foot. Keep the same alignment, sewing close to the edge, so that spacing of topstitching will be uniform throughout the project.

Closures

Zippers or faced buttonholes. (See #6 on p. 224, #19 on p. 227.)

Hem

Raw edges are acceptable or cut with pinking shears or a rotary cutter with a wave blade.

Flannel

Fabric Fact

Flannel is 100% cotton and can be recognized by a soft-brushed look on one or both sides.

Suitable For

Pajamas, pull-on pants, men's shirts, baby receiving blankets. Many quilters use flannel between fabric layers as a batting substitute; can also be used as underlining in jackets and coats for warmth or to give the fabric more dimension.

Sewing Tips

Let fabric feed naturally.

✂ Tip **100% cotton flannel makes a warm interlining for a silk jacket. Preshrink the flannel. Fuse the interfacing to the flannel interlining. Then line the entire jacket. Since the flannel takes up room in the jacket, sew vertical seams at ½ in. rather than ⅝ in.**

WORKING WITH FLANNEL

Preshrink

Machine-wash in hot water and machine-dry on a hot cycle. This fabric shrinks a lot!

Layout

"With nap" layout, double thickness.

Marking

Pilot Frixion erasable ink pen or Clover Chaco Liner.

Cutting

Scissors or rotary cutter.

Interfacing

Fusi-Knit or Sewers' Dream.

Thread

Polyester or cotton.

Needle

80/12 H.

Stitch Length

2.5 mm.

Presser Foot

Standard.

Seam Finish

Flat-fell seams for unlined garments. Plain seams pressed open when used as lining or underlining. (See #1 and #9 on p. 216.)

Tip Not all fabrics have a right or wrong side, but in certain lights the sides may look different. Pick one side to be the wrong side and identify it with blue painter's tape. You will never regret it.

Pressing

Steam iron on cotton setting.

Topstitching

Topstitch ¼ in. from edge. (See #10 on p. 223.)

Closures

Machine buttonholes or snaps. (See #1 on p. 224, #11 on p. 225.)

Hem

Double-fold ½-in. hem and topstitch. (See #10 on p. 229.)

Fleece

Fabric Fact

Synthetic fleece is a knit fabric that stretches on the crossgrain. It sheds water and holds body heat but allows perspiration to escape. Polar fleece by Malden Mills is the best-quality fleece since it pills and stretches the least. It also feels denser and has a deeper pile. In generic brand fleece, look for the "anti-pill" factor. Some stores carry a fleece that is 80% silk, 13% polyester, and 7% viscose for about $25 per yard. This fleece is denser with a deeper pile.

Suitable For

Sweatshirts, pull-on pants, short cropped jackets, vests, and even A-line skirts. To prevent a skirt from sticking to thighs, line with lingerie nylon tricot. Fleece is comfortable and warm and survives years of abuse.

Sewing Tips

Staystitching stretches fleece. Stabilize necklines with ¼-in.-wide Stay Tape cut to size from the pattern tissue. Stabilize crotch and shoulder seams with ¼-in.-wide clear elastic. Hand-baste. If you notice any seam stretching as you sew, place finger behind presser foot as with easing. Finger-press darts to one side and topstitch to flatten.

Preshrink

Not necessary. After construction, machine-wash inside out, alone or with other fleece garments in cool water, gentle cycle, using liquid (not powdered) detergent. Machine-dry on low setting or let hang dry. Do not dry-clean.

> ✂ **Tip** **On high-loft fabrics such as fleece, fake fur, and mohair, pattern weights are far more effective than pins in securing the pattern to the fabric. In addition, they preserve the tissue pattern.**

WORKING WITH FLEECE

Layout

"With nap" layout, double thickness. To determine right side of fabric, pull on crossgrain; fabric curls to wrong side. Be consistent with which side of the fabric you use, as the pile height may differ; use pattern weights.

Marking

Identify wrong side with painter's tape.

Cutting

Scissors or large rotary cutter. If you are using a pattern not specifically designed for fleece, cut top collar ¼ in. bigger and round off collar points so it can be turned smoothly. Cut with a ¼-in. seam allowance, or cut a regular-width seam allowance and trim it down after sewing.

Interfacing

None, except for zippers and behind closures. Use nonfusible interfacing such as silk organza in the seam allowance since the pressing required to fuse a fusible will crush the nap.

Thread

Good-quality polyester.

Needle

70/10 H, 80/12 H, 75/11 HS. Fleece is not needle particular.

Stitch Length

3.0 mm straight stitch or long serger stitch. Use stretch stitch in crotch seams.

Presser Foot

Satin stitch foot (also known as embroidery foot) eliminates wavy, stretched seams where regular construction is used.

Seam Finish

For a durable, attractive finish, finger-press seam open and topstitch with a double needle ZWI stretch 4.0 mm from the right side, straddling seam as you topstitch. Trim seam allowances close to stitching. Or construct with 4-thread overlook and lengthen stitch slightly. Use differential feed if you have it.

If not, sew with finger behind presser foot as with easing. (See #13 on p. 217.)

Pressing

No pressing; fabric melts.

Topstitching

Topstitch ¼ in. from edge. Lengthen stitch to 4.0 mm or longer. (See #10 on p. 223.)

Closures

YKK® plastic zippers. Use sew-in interfacing on zipper seam allowance. Snaps must also be reinforced with sew-in interfacing between layers to prevent them from pulling out of the fabric. (See #11 on p. 225, #19 on p. 227.) Machine buttonholes stretch out unless you hand-baste a strip of clear elastic on the wrong side and make the buttonhole through it.

Hem

Since fleece does not ravel, edges can be left as is. Other options include pinking, topstitching with double needle, overlocking with decorative thread on needles and woolly nylon on loopers, binding with faux leather or a knit cut on the crossgrain, or blanket stitching on the serger or by hand. Ribbing is also popular. (See #31 on p. 233.)

Fur & Fur Pelts

Fabric Fact

Fur pelts come in long and short hair. The pelts vary in size and have a fur side and a sueded side. If you are making a collar and cuffs, it will not be necessary to convert yardage into square feet because you will only need a pelt or two, depending on the size of the pelts and the size of your pattern pieces. But if you want to make a short vest or coat, you will need to be able to convert the yardage measurement into a square foot measurement. Multiply the yardage needed by 11.25, then multiply again by 1.25, resulting in square feet. If the pelts are small, you may need to buy an extra. If you are buying the pelts at a place that sells leather, suede, and fur skins, I would simply take your pattern pieces to the shop with you so you can measure out what you need. My favorite furs are Mongolian lamb and beaver. Something

like cowhide is large but way too stiff for clothing; some people use it for rugs.

Suitable For

Collars, cuffs, vests, short jackets, slippers.

Sewing Tips

If making a short vest or short jacket, try to avoid as many seams as possible by overlapping the seamlines. In the case of Mongolian lamb, you can probably get a short vest out of one pelt, eliminating the side seams. If you are larger than a size 12, you will need two pelts of Mongolian lamb.

Preshrink

Not needed.

WORKING WITH FUR & FUR PELTS

Layout

Start by making mirror images of pattern pieces since you will not be able to place pieces on the fold or cut double. Fold up the hem allowance and fold down the shoulder seam allowances since you will be using hinge technique on shoulders and will not need a seam allowance. Get rid of any seam allowances, such as side seams, where you can use the hinge technique to sew. Position the pelt on the table fur side down, suede side facing you. Place pieces with grainline parallel with backbone. They do not have to be perfectly straight. Hold pattern pieces in place with pattern weights.

Marking

Mark around pattern pieces with a marking pen, Pilot Frixion erasable ink pen, or Clover white marking pen for dark skins. Trace around dart markings.

Cutting

Using small sharp scissors, cut through the suede side, leaving fur intact. Cut the lines you used to outline pattern and dart sewing lines. Cut out dart center, since it will be sewn with hinge technique. Once backing is cut, fur pieces will separate.

Interfacing

None necessary.

Thread

Polyester only, since the tannins used to process the leather will rot cotton thread.

Needle

90/14 NTW. Use glover's needle for hand sewing.

Stitch Length

Since using hinge technique, set machine to a zigzag of 3.0 mm width and 3.0 mm length. Loosen top tension.

Presser Foot

Roller.

Seam Finish

Place seam with fur right sides together. Push fur into pelt with scissors or a pick, out of the way for the zigzag. With machine set at wide zigzag, sew on and off edges of fur. One side of the stitch will catch the edge of fur and the second side will be along the edge of fur. Adjust width of zigzag to accommodate fur. Sew darts in same way. Pull layers apart so seam flattens out and there is no seam allowance. After the seam is sewn, use pick or knitting needle to pull fur hairs out of seam on right side of fur so seam is almost invisible. When sewing fur to another fabric such as lining or a thinner fabric for the under collar, sew with fur pelt on bottom, next to feed dogs. (See #28 on p. 219, #31 on p. 220.)

Pressing

No pressing needed.

Topstitching

You cannot press on the fur and topstitching doesn't work either, so stabstitch along edges ½ in. away to hold layers together along finished seam. (See #39 on p. 221.)

Closures

Fur hooks, snaps, and zippers will not work unless you sew fur to added front plackets, cut in coordinating fabric or leather. Place snaps or zipper in placket. Otherwise, zipper will get caught in the fur hairs, or you will not be able to find the snap in the fur.

Hem

To finish at the hem, face with medium-weight silk. Or eliminate hem allowance, leave pelt raw, and let fur hang down, covering raw edge.

Gabardine

Fabric Fact

Gabardine is a twill weave that has a beautiful drape and is highly wrinkle-resistant. While wool gabardine is the most common, gabardine also comes in silk, cotton, and rayon. Polyester gabardine, called "gabardreme," is anything but a dream. Seams pucker and it does not press well.

Suitable For

Tailored styles, trench coats, tailored jackets, tailored pants, straight skirts, or loose shirts. Styles with drape do very well in gabardine. Since gabardine does not ease well, choose raglan or dolman sleeves unless you are a very experienced sewer.

Sewing Tips

Very easy to sew but not so easy to get a good press. If a fabric is difficult to ease, such as wool gabardine, remove all but ½ in. of ease in sleeve cap or try running an ease line all around the sleeve cap, from underarm to underarm. (See #7 on p. 223 to sew a dart without a dimple.)

Preshrink

If the completed garment will be dry-cleaned, hold steam iron ½ in. above surface or preshrink at the dry cleaner. Wool gabardine can be hand-washed in the bathtub. Serge ends together. Hand-wash with shampoo in cold water. Do not wring—merely squeeze out water. Spin in no-heat dryer to take out excess moisture. Stretch if off grain. Air-dry flat. If garment is not worn for long periods of time, steam-press to raise diagonal weave.

WORKING WITH GABARDINE

Layout

"With nap" layout, double thickness.

Marking

Tailor tacks, Pilot Frixion erasable ink pen, Clover white pen for dark colors.

Cutting

Rotary cutter or scissors. Cutting seam allowances ¼ in. wider than normal enables seams to press flatter.

Interfacing

Hymo hair canvas for tailoring. Armo Weft does not give a long-term fuse, lifting off gabardine's surface after several dry cleanings. Another option for a place that needs interfacing is to underline with a soft cotton and fuse Armo Weft to the cotton.

Thread

Good-quality silk, cotton, or polyester.

> ✂ **Tip** Many trips to the machine repair shop can be avoided by simply changing the needle, rewinding a new bobbin, and rethreading the top of the machine.

Needle

80/12 H.

Stitch Length

3.0 mm.

Presser Foot

Standard. Loosen top tension slightly.

Seam Finish

Options: (1) Pressed open and serged separately. (2) Flat fell. (3) Hong Kong bound. (See #3 and #9 on p. 216, #16 on p. 218.)

Pressing

Steam iron on wool setting. Press as you sew. To prevent seam allowance show-through, place seam over a seam roll, seam stick, or half-round, dribble a bead of water in the valley of the seam, and press. Use no more pressure than the weight of the iron on wrong side. Turn seam over, cover with self-fabric press cloth, and press again. Let fabric

> ✂ **Tip** While the sheen of rayon thread is beautiful, save it for decorative work. It is not strong enough for seams.

cool and dry before moving from pressing surface. If fabric becomes overpressed and shines, hold steam iron ½ in. above right side of fabric. Brush with tailor's brush.

Topstitching

Topstitch ¼ in. from the finished edge using topstitching foot. Hand picking ¼ in. from the edge with stitches ¼ in. apart using pearl cotton thread or rayon thread results in a beautiful detail. (See #1 on p. 222, #10 on p. 223.)

Closures

For buttonholes, use 70/10 HJ needle and cord to prevent stretching. Rayon thread on top and a 90/14 HJ needle make incredible buttonholes on this fabric. Snaps are also suitable. (See #5 on p. 224, #11 on p. 225.)

Hem

Hand-sewn, or multiple rows of topstitching parallel to each other and ¼ in. apart. (See #4 on p. 228, #23 on p. 231.)

Georgette

Fabric Fact

Georgette is a drapey woven fabric with tightly twisted yarns that result in a pebbly weave. The look is transparent with slightly more coverage than chiffon. Silk georgette is drapier than polyester georgette.

Suitable For

Full pants, loose tops, and flowing dresses. Look for loose-fitting, simply styled garments with a minimum amount of seams and darts. Garments that are not full enough look skimpy. Full pants should be one-third to one-half larger than your hip measurement and one-quarter to one-third larger than your bust measurement. If your hips are 40 in., full pants need to measure 53 in. to 60 in. Georgette makes beautiful scarves and works well as a lining in burnout velvet. Line printed georgette with plain georgette lining.

Sewing Tips

Hold top and bobbin threads when you begin sewing to prevent fabric from pulling into the throat plate hole. Let fabric feed naturally. Lift presser foot periodically, leaving the needle in the fabric, to release bubble buildup. No backstitching.

> ✂ **Tip** The majority of garment construction is done with 3-ply thread, sometimes called "all purpose" or "sew all." A lighter-weight 2-ply thread called "embroidery thread" is not just for embroidery. Seams in chiffon and georgette are less visible if sewn with 2-ply thread.

WORKING WITH GEORGETTE

Preshrink

Good-quality georgette can be hand-washed in warm water with 1 tablespoon of shampoo. Dry flat. Press lightly with steam. This treatment will cause poor-quality georgette to lose its crispness. Try a sample before you commit to it. If the sample gets wimpy, do not preshrink.

Layout

"Without nap" layout, double thickness. Use glass-head silk pins. To control fabric and cut accurately, cover table with tissue or medical examining paper. Pin or staple double thickness of fabric to paper. Pin pattern through fabric and paper.

Marking

Clover Chaco Liner, tailor tacks, Pilot Frixion erasable ink pen. Do not use waxed chalk as it leaves stains. Mark wrong side of cut pieces with tape.

Cutting

Using rotary cutter or sharp scissors, cut through pattern fabric and tissue paper.

Interfacing

Skin-colored silk organza or self-fabric for more softness. Interface top collars and cuffs so that seam allowances won't show through.

Thread

Fine machine-embroidery thread in silk or cotton. Polyester threads cause georgette to pucker.

Needle

New 60/8, 65/9 HM or 70/10 HJ.

Stitch Length

1.5 mm to 2.0 mm straight stitch.

Presser Foot

Straight stitch foot and single-hole throat plate. Or use satin stitch presser foot and throat plate and switch needle to far left position for support on three sides.

Seam Finish

French seams. (See #10 and #11 on p. 217, #40 on p. 221.)

Pressing

Dry iron on silk setting. Make sure iron is clean. Spritz area to be pressed.

Topstitching

Not recommended. Hand-pick close to edge. (See #1 on p. 222.)

Closures

Self-fabric button loops. Machine buttonholes with fine machine embroidery thread; place Solvy between presser foot and fabric. For zippers, interface the seam allowances with organza. Hand-picked zipper. (See #1 on p. 224, #9 on p. 225.)

Hem

Options: (1) Trim hem allowance to 1/8 in. Roll again, enclosing raw edge. Hand-sew or machine-sew with fine thread. Keep finger pressure on back of presser foot to prevent hem from stretching. (2) Serge rolled hem. Run a line of staystitching at 1/2 in. with finger behind presser foot to prevent fabric from stretching. When serging, remove right needle and let rolled hem encase staystitching. The differential feed set at 0.7 mm helps here. Use fine serger thread. (See #16 on p. 230.)

Glitter

Fabric Fact

Glitter, a fabric in stretch velour or satin, has beads, sequins, or glitz glued instead of sewn to the fabric itself. Glitter fabrics are not the easiest to work with since the decorations cannot simply be pulled off the fabric at seams. In addition, the glue builds up on the machine needle, causing skipped or missed stitches. Still, this fabric can be tamed. See "Sewing Tips" below.

Suitable For

Tops, evening dresses, pull-on skirts, full pants, and decorative throw pillows.

Sewing Tips

Coat the sewing needle and thread with a silicone product such as Sewers Aid or Lube-A-Thread™. A lubricant will allow the needle to glide through the fabric and the glued sections for a seam or two. As the glue builds up on the needle and the sewing stops or stitches become irregular, clean the needle with rubbing alcohol and reapply silicone product. Substitute bias binding for neckline and armhole facings or purchase a coordinating plain fabric for facing since the beads or sequins will be scratchy against your skin. Sew slowly, and you will break fewer needles. If a needle will not pierce through a beaded section, move the fabric under the presser foot back 1/16 in. and turn the hand wheel forward for the next stitch.

Tip When doing decorative stitching, use two strands of thread in the needle if you want your design to be filled in closer.

WORKING WITH GLITTER

Preshrink

Check care instructions on end of bolt. If dry cleaning is suggested and the faux sequins or beads are synthetic, they will dissolve in the dry-cleaning fluid. Glass beads are safe to dry-clean, but since these are expensive, I have not seen these used on the glue-on glitter fabric. Since this fabric cannot be dry-cleaned because the sequins or beads dissolve, hand-wash the completed garment in cool water and allow to air-dry flat. This works well for velour but not for satin, because you cannot iron in between the beads or sequins. If this piece is for a one-night event and you are not going to worry about cleaning it later, forget any preshrinking and get right to it. If you would like to launder after wearing (possible on stretch velours), Scotchguard before wearing. Hand-wash the fabric in cool water and run quickly through the dryer on the low-heat cycle.

Layout

"With nap" layout, double thickness, with right side in.

Marking

Clover Chaco Liner or Pilot Frixion erasable ink pen.

Cutting

Old scissors since you will be cutting through the glue and the beads.

Interfacing

Silk organza, since the high heat needed to set fusible interfacing will melt the glued-on glitter.

Thread

Cotton or polyester.

Needle

I have found that using a titanium needle works best on fabrics with glued-on decorations. The needle does not gum up as badly, which is what causes thread breakage.

Stitch Length

2.5 mm.

Presser Foot

Standard, roller, or even feed/walking.

Seam Finish

Sew knits with a tiny zigzag (0.5 mm width, 2.5 mm length), wovens with a 2.5 mm straight stitch. Do not serge or needles will break. (See #1 on p. 216, #17 on p. 218.)

Pressing

Dry iron on synthetic setting. Press on wrong side of fabric.

Topstitching

Not recommended.

Closures

Invisible zipper. (See #19 on p. 227.)

Hem

Face hem with a coordinating fabric since the glued-on elements will ruin your hose. (See #18 on p. 231.)

Guatemalan Cotton

Fabric Fact

Guatemalan cottons are 100% cotton, woven in ethnic designs originating from Guatemala. These fabrics are crisp but soften after washing. Air-dry or machine-dry alone to prevent an aged appearance caused by abrasion. To retain crispness, dry-clean the finished garment.

Suitable For

Wrap skirts, vests, unstructured jackets, tops, napkins, and placemats. Pants and straight skirts in this fabric tend to stretch out in the seat and knee.

Sewing Tips

Let the fabric feed naturally.

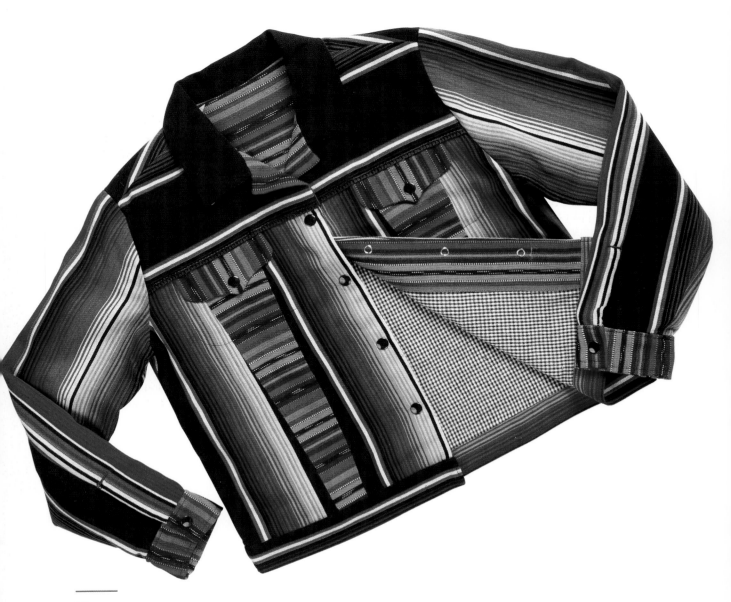

WORKING WITH GUATEMALAN COTTON

Preshrink

Machine-wash in cold water, adding Retayne™, a dye fixative, or ¼ cup of Epsom salt to lessen color loss. You will lose some color but not nearly as much as in a plain wash. Fabric softens after prewashing. Machine-dry on regular cycle. Air-dry dark colors to maintain color crispness. For better color retention, skip preshrinking and send completed garment to the dry cleaner.

Layout

"Without nap" layout, double thickness. (See tip below.)

Marking

Clover Chaco Liner, tailors tacks, Clover white marking pen for dark colors.

Cutting

Rotary cutter or scissors.

Interfacing

Fusi-Knit or Sewers' Dream.

Thread

Polyester or cotton.

Needle

80/12 H.

Stitch Length

2.5 mm.

Presser Foot

Standard.

Seam Finish

This fabric is prone to raveling, so flat-fell seams give the best protection. (See #9 on p. 216.)

> ✂ **Tip** Stabilize shoulders and waistlines of unstable fabric with straight-grain fusible tape or ¼-in.-wide selvage cut from lining fabric.

Pressing

Steam iron on cotton setting.

Topstitching

Topstitch ⅛ in. to ¼ in. from finished edge using a 3.0-mm stitch length. (See #2 and #3 on p. 222, #10 on p. 223.)

Closures

Corded buttonholes, faced button openings, loops, snaps, and invisible and exposed zippers. (See #5 and #6 on p. 224, #9 on p. 225, #19 on p. 227.)

Hem

Double-fold ½-in. hem. Topstitch from the right side of the fabric using a red band double needle for wovens. (See #23 on p. 231.)

> ✂ **Tip** For identical pieces in stripes and plaids, never cut through both layers at the same time. Cut the first piece through one fabric thickness. Then lay the cutout piece on the fabric, right sides together, and match the designs exactly. Use the cutout piece as a template to mark and cut the second piece.

Handwoven

Fabric Fact

Handwoven fabrics are made by hand on a loom. The best handwovens for garment sewing are a combination of rayon and cotton or rayon and wool. Rayon makes the fabric drapier, and natural fiber makes it more serviceable.

Suitable For

Loose, unstructured jackets, coats, vests, or garments with a minimum number of seams. Pull-on pants and skirts stretch out of shape and add weight to the wearer. Pretest pattern or hand-baste side seams for fit since machine stitches are difficult to remove in loose weaves.

Sewing Tips

Stabilize neckline and shoulders with Stay Tape or narrow selvage strip. Cut stabilizer length from pattern piece. Force garment piece to conform. Staystitching is not enough to stabilize these fabrics. If you want a crisp look for a jacket or vest, or if the fabric is unstable, fuse the back of the fabric with Sewers' Dream or Fusi-Knit.

> ✂ **Tip** If you cannot control presser foot tension and are working on a heavy-pile fabric, try this. From the front, pull on the underside layer of fabric (the side against the feed dogs) while pushing the top layer of fabric into the presser foot.

WORKING WITH HANDWOVEN

Preshrink

Most handwovens have been machine-washed and machine-dried, so preshrinking is unnecessary. Fabric for tops can be hand-washed in cold water. Don't wring. Squeeze out moisture between towels. Air-dry flat. Dry-clean completed garment.

Layout

"Without nap" layout, single thickness for fabric economy and possible matching. Make duplicates of all pattern pieces, creating a left back, right back, etc., so that the most economical layout can be used by not cutting the fabric on the fold. Flower-head pins will not get lost in the fabric.

Marking

Tailor tacks, small safety pins.

Cutting

Do not cut out notches as they will be overlocked off. Overlock cutout pieces right away. For jackets and vests, fuse all pieces to Fusi-Knit or Sewers' Dream and then overlock. Fusing stabilizes handwovens and gives them more body.

Interfacing

French Fuse or Fusi-Knit.

Thread

Good-quality cotton or polyester.

Needle

80/12 H.

Stitch Length

2.5 mm.

Presser Foot

Walking or roller foot.

Seam Finish

Bind each side of seam allowance with double-fold bias tape or Hong Kong finish, or serge each side of seam separately and press open. Topstitch seam flat on each side ¼ in. from the seamline from the right side of the fabric. (See #3 on p. 216, #16 and #19 on p. 218.)

Pressing

Steam iron on medium-high setting. Use a press cloth on dark colors or if metallic threads are present.

Topstitching

Use decorative thread and an HE needle to topstitch ¼ in. from finished edge if desired. Hand picking close to the edge can help flatten seam. (See #1 on p. 222, #10 on p. 223.)

Closures

Machine buttonholes will pull away from fabric in time. Use alternative closures: faced buttonholes, button loops, frogs, or button openings in a seam. (See #6 on p. 224, #9, #10, and #12 on p. 225.) Long pronged snaps available at www.SnapSource.com.

Hem

Finish hem edge with double-fold bias or a Hong Kong finish. Hand-hem. (See #13 on p. 230.) To allow for relaxation of the handwoven fabric over time, lining and garment should be hemmed separately and allowed to hang free at bottom.

Hemp Cloth

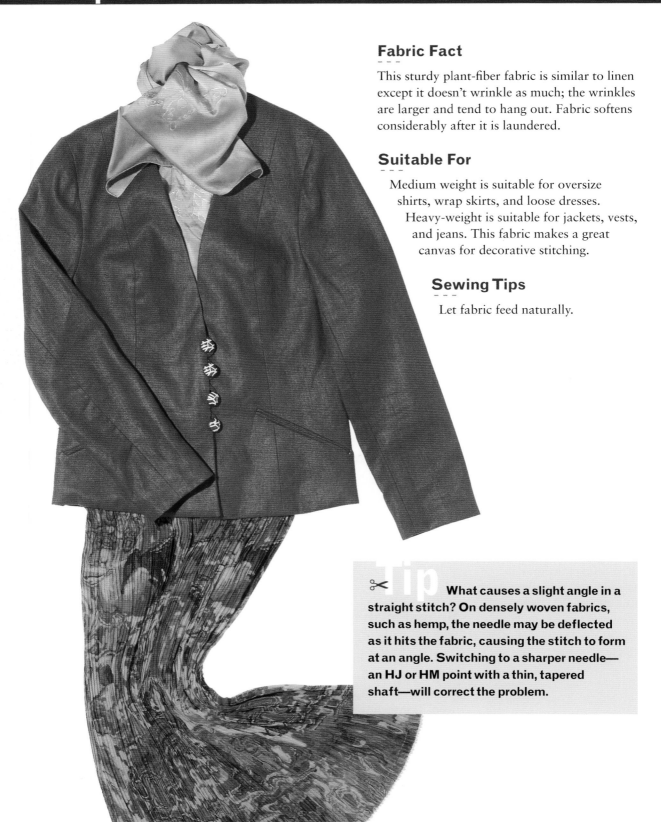

Fabric Fact

This sturdy plant-fiber fabric is similar to linen except it doesn't wrinkle as much; the wrinkles are larger and tend to hang out. Fabric softens considerably after it is laundered.

Suitable For

Medium weight is suitable for oversize shirts, wrap skirts, and loose dresses. Heavy-weight is suitable for jackets, vests, and jeans. This fabric makes a great canvas for decorative stitching.

Sewing Tips

Let fabric feed naturally.

Tip

What causes a slight angle in a straight stitch? On densely woven fabrics, such as hemp, the needle may be deflected as it hits the fabric, causing the stitch to form at an angle. Switching to a sharper needle—an HJ or HM point with a thin, tapered shaft—will correct the problem.

WORKING WITH HEMP CLOTH

Preshrink

Hemp will get softer with machine washing and machine drying on the permanent press cycle, but take it out of the dryer before completely dry to make ironing easier. Dark colors lose dye, so add ¼ cup Epsom salt or Retayne, a dye fixative, to rinse water. If you decide to dry-clean, preshrink by holding steam iron ½ in. above fabric surface.

Layout

"Without nap" layout, double thickness.

Marking

Clover Chaco Liner or Pilot Frixion erasable ink pen.

Cutting

This fabric is rather difficult to cut. Use long, sharp scissors to get better leverage or a rotary cutter.

Interfacing

Except for a jacket, fabric has enough body so that interfacing is not necessary. For jackets, use Armo Weft on front facing and collar.

Thread

Good-quality cotton or polyester.

Needle

90/14 H.

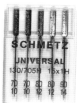

Stitch Length

2.5 mm.

Presser Foot

Standard.

Seam Finish

Serged fake flat fell. (See #27 on p. 219.) On unlined jacket, finish seams with Hong Kong finish. (See #16 on p. 218.)

Pressing

Use lots of steam on a high-heat, linen setting. Use spray starch to crispen details such as collars and pockets.

Topstitching

Results are excellent. Topstitch close to finished edge or ¼ in. from finished edge. Topstitching foot is helpful here. Lengthen stitch to 3.5 mm. (See #3 on p. 222, #10 on p. 223.)

Closures

For buttonholes, use 70/10 HJ needle and fine machine-embroidery thread to reduce bulk. Widen, don't lengthen, buttonhole stitch if possible. (See #4 on p. 224.)

Hem

Hand-hem or topstitch with double needle. (See #1 and #4 on p. 228.)

Fabric Fact

Good examples of double knits are wool double knit, ponte double knit in a variety of fabrication, and ribbing, where both sides of the fabric look the same. Look for knits that return to original size when stretched on the crossgrain and released.

Suitable For

Unstructured jackets, pull-on pants, cardigans, T-shirt dresses, gored or wrap skirts. To prevent knit tops from clinging to the high hip, make or buy a nylon tricot tank top that extends over the high hip, preferably with slits on the sides. Wear under clingy knits, and your problem is eliminated.

Sewing Tips

Stabilize shoulders and waistline seams with ¼-in. clear elastic using a walking foot. Do not stretch fabric as you sew, as this results in wavy seams. Eliminate facings whenever possible. On necklines, cut off ⅜-in. allowance from seam. Stabilize with ¼-in. Stay Tape. Finish with crossgrain strips in a lightweight fabric.

Preshrink

When using cotton knits, buy an additional ¼ yd. for every 2 yd. cut. Fabric has progressive shrinkage, which means it must be machine-washed in warm water and dried at low heat two times before cutting out. Prevent fabric from stretching out of shape by machine basting raw edges together. Preshrink wool

✂ **Tip**   To check the stretch on knit fabrics, fold down the crossgrain of the fabric 4 in. Place two pins 4 in. apart on either side of the crossgrain fold. Stretch fabric on the crossgrain. A good stretch fabric will double in size to 8 in. without the edge rolling. If the knit does not return to its original shape, choose your pattern carefully and do not use where it will receive stress, such as knees and seats.

WORKING WITH DOUBLE KNITS

double knits by holding a steam iron ½ in. above the surface. Dry clean completed wool garment. Preshrink other knits the way you plan to treat the finished garment. Hand- or machine-wash. Machine- or air-dry.

Layout

"With nap" layout, double or single thickness, as many fabrics shade differently in opposite direction. Straighten ends with T-square. Check for runs and snags. If lengthwise crease is visible after preshrinking, cut around it. If selvage is crooked, follow rib in fabric for straight of grain. Use greatest stretch of knit around the body. Use pattern weights or ballpoint pins in seam allowance to secure pattern.

Marking

Pilot Frixion erasable pen, Clover Chaco Liner.

Cutting

Rotary cutter or scissors, pattern weights.

Interfacing

Fusi-Knit.

Thread

Good-quality polyester is the best choice since it has some stretch. Wind bobbin slowly.

Needle

75/11 HS.

Stitch Length

Tiny zigzag (0.5 mm width, 2.5 mm length) or stretch stitch.

Presser Foot

Standard.

Seam Finish

Sew seams first with a tiny zigzag or lightning stitch if the garment is close-fitting. Double knits can be pressed open and topstitched or serged. Another option is to serge seams together with a 3- or 4-thread overlock with woolly nylon on the loopers. Use differential feed or your finger behind the presser foot to prevent stretching. Use triple stitch in areas of stress such as crotch and underarm seams. (See #6 on p. 216, #12 on p. 217, #22 on p. 218.)

Pressing

Steam iron on cotton setting. Use iron shoe or press cloth. On wool double knit, reduce iron temp to wool setting. Do not overpress or it will look flat and shiny.

Topstitching

Lengthen stitch to 3.0 mm and topstitch ¼ in. from finished edge with topstitch foot. (See #10 on p. 223.) Prevent curling at hem on topstitched seams by backstitching two stitches from bottom of seam to give weight.

Closures

Stabilize buttonhole with lengthwise grain of interfacing parallel to buttonhole. Baste clear elastic on facing side of buttonhole. Wrap with Solvy. Corded buttonholes. (See #5 on p. 224.) Stabilize zipper seam allowances with ½-in. strips of fusible interfacing. Hand-picked or invisible zippers. (See #19 on p. 227.)

Hem

Press up 1¾-in. hem and run two rows of parallel double stitching ¼ in. and 1¼ in. from hem crease. Use double-needle ZWI stretch with woolly nylon hand-wrapped on bobbin and Teflon or roller presser foot to prevent stretching as you topstitch. Trim close to stitching. Coverlock machine does great job. (See #5 on p. 228.)

Knits, Lycra

Fabric Fact

Lycra is combined with nylon, cotton, linen, and wool to give stretch in one or both directions. Spandex and Lycra mean the same thing. Cotton/Lycra is matte and often used for exercise wear. Nylon/Lycra is shiny and often used for swimsuits and biking shorts.

Suitable For

Nylon/Lycra and cotton/Lycra are good choices for activewear and anything that needs freedom for movement. Lycra comes in different weights. Less than 5 oz. is good for lingerie, 5 oz. to 6 oz. is good for biking shorts, 5 oz. to 8 oz. is good for a cross-country ski suit, 12 oz. to 14 oz. is good for a downhill ski suit. For nylon/Lycra and cotton/Lycra, use patterns specifically designed for Lycra. This fabric makes good skating costumes. The best fabric for bathing suits is Lycra blended with Antron®, Supplex®, or Tactel®.

Sewing Tips

Pretest pattern because ripped stitches leave holes, which turn into runs. Do not stretch fabric as you sew. Use triple stretch stitch in areas of stress such as crotch and underarm seams. Woolly nylon is not strong enough for seams under stress. Test seams by stretching them as much as possible. Loosen tension until no stitches break. After sewing on conventional machine, serge seams together. Never use the 5-thread overlock when sewing knits, since it has no elasticity. The 4-thread overlock is the best choice because it is strong and can stretch. Try on leg elastic and test for comfort. It should be snug but not binding. Zigzag (4.0 mm width, 4.0 mm length) elastic to right side of fabric. Pull in elastic the most on back of leg. Turn elastic to wrong side and sew narrow, long zigzag (1.0 mm width, 4.0 mm length) to wrong side of fabric.

WORKING WITH LYCRA KNITS

Preshrink

Machine-washing brings out the best in Lycra. Never bleach any fabric containing Lycra. Bleach will discolor fabric and break down the fibers. Preshrinking is not necessary for nylon/Lycra but mandatory for cotton/Lycra. Baste crosswise edges together to prevent stretching during washing. Machine-wash on gentle cycle with Ivory liquid. Machine-dry on low heat or air-dry. To preshrink wool/Lycra, hold steam iron ½ in. above fabric surface.

Layout

Check fabric for defects. Crease marks at fold are often permanent. Even crossgrain ends with T-square. Use fabric with the greatest stretch direction going around the body. Eliminate facings, and bind neck and armholes with self-fabric. With four-way stretch fabrics, check your body measurement against the pattern from front shoulder through the legs and up the back to the same shoulder. Pattern should measure 4 in. less than body measurement. Pattern length may need to be adjusted.

Marking

Make ⅛-in. snips in seam allowance or Pilot Frixion erasable ink pen.

Cutting

Rotary cutter or scissors. Use sharp, fine pins and ¼-in. seam allowances.

Interfacing

Not necessary.

Thread

Good-quality polyester is ideal because it has stretch.

Needle

For nylon/Lycra, use 70/10 SUK ballpoint. For all other Lycra blends, use 75/11 HS Stretch.

Stitch Length

For exercise or dancewear, use a 2.5 mm length or triple stitch, short-length overlock stitch, or small zigzag (0.75 mm width, 2.5 mm length). (See #6 on p. 216, #17 on p. 218.)

Presser Foot

Standard.

Seam Finish

Serge with the 4-thread overlock with woolly nylon in both loopers. Stabilize stressed seams in crotch and underarm with triple stretch stitch or small zigzag done on conventional machines. Sew details like neckline and casings with small zigzag. (See #5 and #6 on p. 216.)

Pressing

Steam or dry iron at a medium to low setting.

Topstitching

Use double-needle ZWI HS stretch with woolly nylon hand-wrapped on bobbin and regular thread on top. Lengthen stitch to 3.0 mm. (See #6 on p. 223.) Coverlock works well here.

Closures

Buttonholes are rarely necessary, but if so, cord and stabilize with clear elastic to prevent stretching. Invisible zippers are good. Stabilize zipper area with fusible interfacing on seam allowances. (See #3 and #5 on p. 224, #19 on p. 227.)

Hem

Coverlock or flatlock hem. Use good-quality ⅜-in. cotton bathing suit elastic in casings using 3-step zigzag. (See #26 on p. 232.) Bind with self-fabric for hems and facings. Use bias binder attachment. (See #2 and #5 on p. 228, #9 on p. 229.)

Knits, Scuba

Fabric Fact

Scuba knit got its name because it feels a lot like wetsuit fabric used for scuba diving, but it's a lot lighter and more flexible than the neoprene in a wetsuit. Scuba is a double knit, a blend of polyester and spandex with a spongy character. Draper scuba has some rayon added. Scuba gets softer after it is preshrunk. If the fabric has a pattern repeat, you may have to buy more yardage to do some matching.

Digital printing on fabric, done from an actual photograph, is used on a lot of scuba fabrics.

Suitable For

You will love working with and wearing this fabric. It does not wrinkle or stretch out of shape. Scuba makes great straight skirts, shift dresses, and skinny pants. While it has great recovery, it does not drape.

Sewing Tips

Scuba must be preshrunk or you may experience stitch skipping problems. Scuba acts a lot like a good double knit. Do not stretch seams as you sew—let the fabric feed naturally.

Preshrink

Machine-wash in warm water. Spin out water in dryer but pull out of dryer as soon as excess water is out. Let hang to finish drying.

Layout

Straighten cut ends with a T-square. Before layout, study the repeat of the pattern. You will probably have to cut a single thickness to get the pattern to match. Use pattern weights to hold pattern to fabric.

Marking

Frixion erasable ink pen or Clover Chaco Liner.

Cutting

Rotary cutter or sharp scissors.

Interfacing

Fusi-Knit.

WORKING WITH SCUBA KNITS

Thread

Use good-quality polyester since it has some stretch. Wind bobbin slowly.

Needle

75/11 HS.

Stitch Length

3.0 mm.

Presser Foot

Single-hole presser foot.

Seam Finish

Since the fabric does not press well, a lapped seam works best. On each seam, lap front over back. Trim off front seam allowance. Overlap cut edge onto back seamline. Topstitch close to cut edge of seam and then another row ¼ in. inside of the first. Traditional seaming also works if you topstitch seam allowances flat from the right side of the fabric. (See #38 on p. 221.)

Pressing

Use press cloth when pressing on the right side of the fabric.

Topstitching

On details, topstitch ⅛ in. from the seamed edge. A topstitching foot is helpful here. (See #2 on p. 222.)

Closures

For buttonholes, hand-baste a strip of clear elastic on the facing side in the buttonhole location. Wrap area with Solvy. Make buttonhole through elastic so it will not stretch. (See #3 on p. 224.) For snaps, add ribbon between fabric layers so that snap parts have something to grab on to that will not stretch. (See #11 on p. 225.) Invisible zipper works well, but interface the seam allowances behind the zipper for stability. (See #19 on p. 227.)

Hem

Hold up hem allowance with double sided tape like Wonder Tape. Coverlock or double-needle-stitch the hem. (See #1 on p. 228.)

Knits, Single

Fabric Fact

Wool jersey, rayon jersey, silk jersey, and nylon tricot are good examples of single-knit jersey. Fabric has a fair amount of stretch and curls to the right side when stretched on the crossgrain. Single knits do not have quite the recovery power of a double knit. Right side of fabric shows a knit stitch and wrong side shows a purl stitch.

Suitable For

Lingerie, tops, loose dresses, full skirts, full pull-on pants, and wrap garments.

Sewing Tips

Do not staystitch neck or it will stretch. Instead, stabilize neck and waistline with fusible or sew-in ¼-in.-wide Stay Tape. For horizontal seams, sew with a small zigzag, then use 4-thread serger. Stabilize horizontal seams such as shoulders or diagonal seams such as front neck on a wrap by serging through ¼-in. clear elastic. (See #35 on p. 220.) For long vertical seams, sew with tiny zigzag or lightning stitch and use 4-thread serger with woolly nylon in both loopers right next to it with seam allowances together. This will prevent seams from drawing up. (See #22 on p. 218.) Use differential feed or push behind presser foot to prevent knit from stretching.

Preshrink

Hold steam iron ½ in. away from wool jersey. Dry-clean completed garment when needed. Other jerseys can be hand-washed and dried flat.

Layout

"Without nap" layout, double thickness. Do not allow fabric to drape off table, as it stretches. If edges are curling, use spray starch and press edges before layout. Starch will flatten them. Use greatest stretch of the fabric around body. Even crosswise edges with a T-square. Eliminate

> ✂ **Tip** **Always check the width of seam allowances on patterns designed for knits. Sometimes they have been reduced to ¼ in. at the neck or elsewhere.**

WORKING WITH SINGLE KNITS

facings whenever possible. Measure pattern on neckline seam to see if it will slip over the head without a zipper. Necklines smaller than 21 in. will not slip over the head. Use pattern weights or ballpoint pins in seam allowances.

Marking

Pilot Frixion erasable ink pen or Clover Chaco Liner.

Cutting

Rotary cutter is more accurate than scissors since unstable knits stretch slightly as scissors lift them off the table. If fabric is slippery, cut it as you would silk crepe de Chine with tissue paper.

Interfacing

Fusi-Knit.

Thread

Fine machine-embroidery thread such as Seralene, a finer thread, on silk jerseys. Polyester thread on others.

Needle

75/11 HS.

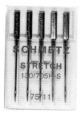

Stitch Length

Small zigzag (0.5 mm width, 2.5 mm length) or stretch stitch. (See #7 on p. 216.) If seam is wavy, lengthen stitch. If seam puckers, shorten stitch.

Presser Foot

Teflon or walking.

Seam Finish

For lightweight knits, sew seam, press to one side, and topstitch ¼ in. from seam. Trim away extra seam allowances. For invisible seams on wool jersey, seam with lightning or tiny zigzag and press open. (See #12 on p. 217.) For seams on full garments without stress, sew 4-thread overlock stretch, omitting the initial zigzag seam on the conventional machine. (See #5 on p. 216.)

Tip Knits require a stretch double needle for topstitching.

Pressing

Use steam iron temperature suited to your fabric content. Use press-and-lift motion when ironing. Back-and-forth ironing movements will stretch the fabric.

Topstitching

Use Teflon or walking foot ¼ in. from edge or hand-pick. (See #1 on p. 222, #8 and #10 on p. 223.)

Closures

Buttonholes are not recommended; any stress will distort them. Use snaps, faced buttonholes, or button loops. (See #6 on p. 224, #9 and #11 on p. 225.) Stabilize zipper seam allowances with ½-in. strips of interfacing. Hand-picked or invisible zippers look the classiest. (See #19 on p. 227.) For snaps, insert ribbon between fabric layers so the snap will not pull out.

Hem

Allow garment to hang for a half day before hemming. Prevent stretching as you topstitch by fusing a strip of Lite Steam-A-Seam 2 in the hem before you begin. Turn up a ¼-in. hem. Double-needle topstitch with 4.0 mm stretch double needle, flatlock hem, coverstitch. (See #1, #2, #3, and #5 on p. 228.) Lite Steam-A-Seam 2 is not necessary if using coverstitch.

Fabric Fact

Sweater knits are often sold in a kit that includes a pattern. When purchasing sweater knits by the yard, you may need to find a suitable ribbing or choose a style that doesn't need it. Look for 100% wool ribbing since it is the strongest and retains its shape the longest.

Suitable For

Tops, cardigans, and sweater coats with simple lines. If pattern is designed for regular fabric, use one size smaller since sweater knits grow. If sweater knit comes with ribbing knitted on, a straight hemline allows you to use the ribbed edge as the finished hem.

Sewing Tips

To prevent the back of knits from riding up in the skirt, cut back of skirt ½ in. longer than the front. Sew seams with the back against the feed dog so the feed dogs can ease in the extra ½ in. to fit the front. Lower the top tension to prevent fabric from stretching. Staystitching stretches the fabric. Instead, stabilize neck with fusible stabilizer tape or sew in ¼-in.-wide Stay Tape. Push fabric into presser foot—never pull it from front or back.

Preshrink

Hand-wash in baby shampoo. Dry flat.

Tip Want to "unshrink" a wool sweater? Gently boil the sweater in a solution of 1 part vinegar to 2 parts water for 30 minutes. Rinse with cool water and squeeze out excess. Dry flat. Despite the horrible smell while cooking, it works!

WORKING WITH SWEATER KNITS

Layout

"Without nap" layout, double thickness. If fabric fold is visible, cut around it. Use pattern weights since pins tear pattern tissue when used with sweater knits. Straighten ends with a T-square. To determine the right side of a knit, pull the fabric on a crosswise end. A knit will curl to the right side.

Marking

Safety pins or tailor tacks.

Cutting

Rotary cutter or sharp scissors.

Interfacing

Fusi-Knit.

Thread

Good-quality polyester is ideal because it has stretch.

Needle

75/11 HS.

Stitch Length

Small zigzag (0.75 mm width, 2.5 mm length).

Presser Foot

Walking or roller.

Seam Finish

Stabilize horizontal seams and neckline with ¼-in.-wide clear elastic. Sew seams with small zigzag (0.75 mm width, 2.5 mm length), then serge together with 4-thread serger. Adjust differential feed to a positive setting to avoid wavy seams, or keep finger behind presser foot. If you don't own a serger, sew seams with lightning stitch and bind seams with a Hong Kong finish using stretch mesh as binding. (See #12 on p. 217, #16 and #21 on p. 218.)

Pressing

Use a steam iron set to the right temperature for your fabric content. Use press-and-lift motion to avoid stretching the fabric. Use a press cloth on dark colors or if metallic yarns are present.

Topstitching

Not recommended. Hand picking close to edge can help flatten seam. (See #1 on p. 222.)

Closures

Substitute grosgrain ribbon for front facing on cardigans if buttonholes will be used. Interface with stable grain of interfacing parallel to buttonhole. Place strip of Lite Steam-A-Seam 2 between sweater fabric and grosgrain ribbon in buttonhole area. Press to fuse before machine buttonhole process. Wrap area around buttonhole location with Solvy. Cord buttonhole to prevent stretching. (See #5 on p. 224, #7 on p. 225.)

Hem

Allow garment to hang for a half day before hemming to lengthen. As you apply ribbing with the serger, include unstretched ¼-in. strip of clear elastic to prevent ribbing from stretching out. (See #30 on p. 232.) On cardigans, cut ribbing 1 in. shorter than garment front measurement from collarbone to hem on each side. Cut ribbing a third smaller than neckline measurement from collarbone to collarbone around back neck or around entire neckline on a plain neck. Stretch ribbing to fit neckline. All edges can also be finished with woven or braided foldover trim. Stabilize edge first with ¼-in. press-on Stay Tape. Be careful not to stretch the edge as you apply fold-over trim or edges will curl. (See #11 on p. 229.)

Lace

Fabric Fact

Lace is a porous material in which several yarns or twisting of the material creates surface effects. Lace is available in wool, cotton, and rayon. Nylon lace is the least expensive and good for pretesting a garment that will be made in a re-embroidered or beaded lace. Stretch lace should be treated as a stretch mesh (see p. 160).

Suitable For

Simple silhouettes with minimum seams to showcase fabric. Pretest pattern. Seams are permanent! Also use to accent lingerie. Since lingerie fabric comes in a wider variety of colors than lace, dye the lace to match.

Sewing Tips

Stabilize shoulders and waistline seams with Stay Tape or ¼-in.-wide selvage cut from lightweight lining fabric or flesh-toned silk organza. On very fine lace, use a 1-in. square of Solvy between the lace and feed dogs at start of seam to prevent the lace from being pulled down into the bobbin thread hole. (See #25 on p. 219.) Hold both threads as you start seam. Consider lining stretch lace with stretch mesh.

Preshrink

Most laces are washable. To preshrink, hand-wash in warm water and air-dry. Even polyester lace can shrink. If you plan to dry-clean a lace garment, steam the wrong side of the lace with a towel underneath to prevent flattening design. Never touch lace with the iron. Hold iron ½ in. above the surface. Store lace in a rolled towel.

> **Tip** **Cotton lace can be dyed with coffee, tea, and purchased dyes to get the color you want. Always test-dye a small piece first, keeping track of the dyebath time. When you want to stop the lace from getting darker, submerge in cold water. Wrap lace in a towel to remove excess moisture, and allow to dry flat. Never wring or hang dry. Sequins do not take dye. Pearls take color but remain lighter.**

WORKING WITH LACE

Layout

"With nap" layout, single thickness. Spread lace on a contrasting cutting surface so you can see motifs. Position pattern pieces so prominent motifs are balanced. Try to position scalloped edges at neck or hem. If this is not possible, scalloped edges can be cut off and reapplied after garment is completed. If lace doesn't have definite motifs that need matching, simply cut out along the pattern cutting lines.

Marking

Tailor tacks or safety pins. Thread-trace actual seamlines and motif outlines in different colors that extend beyond seamline for accurate seam overlap.

Cutting

Flower-head pins do not get lost in the fabric. Cut out along motif line or pattern cutting lines if lace has allover pattern that doesn't require matching. Eliminate facing whenever possible by using edge of lace or binding with bias satin or bridal tulle.

Interfacing

Tulle gives body and retains transparency. Flesh-toned silk organza or stretch mesh as underlining looks the most natural.

Thread

Good-quality cotton or polyester.

Needle

75/11 HS unless heavily embroidered, in which case a 70/10 HM or HJ will give a better stitch.

Stitch Length

Tiny, short zigzag (0.5 mm width, 1.5 mm length).

Presser foot

Presser foot with flattest bottom.

Seam Finish

To avoid cutting through prominent motifs, superimpose seamline of one piece onto seamline of another. Zigzag over prominent motif on top piece. Trim away excess lace underneath and on top so that pattern is single layer and motifs flow uninterrupted. For allover pattern lace, use a 4-thread serger on seams. No seam finish is necessary if garment is lined. (See #5 on p. 216, #25 on p. 219.)

Pressing

Cover pressing surface with towel. Place lace facedown. Hold steam iron ½ in. above fabric. Steam and pat flat. Never touch lace with an iron.

Topstitching

Not recommended. You can flatten necklines and armholes with hand picking. (See #1 on p. 222.)

Closures

Consider alternate closures like button loops or button openings in a seam (See #9 and #10 on p. 225.) Invisible or hand-picked zippers. (See #19 on p. 227.)

Hem

Since lace does not ravel, a decorative cut edge can become a hemline. Cut pieces of lace can be applied as trim by hand or machine; use a satin stitch with tightened tension (3.5 mm width, 1.0 mm length) or finish raw edge with 4-stitch serger stitch. (See #27 on p. 232.)

Lamé & Lurex

Fabric Fact

Nylon lamé contains traces of copper, aluminum, or gold and is available in about a dozen colors. Most easily found are tricot-backed lamé and tissue lamé. Lurex® is a fine metallic yarn that produces a textured knit. The wider and flatter yarns are made into wovens. Lurex knits are more stable and easier to sew. Shimmer by Martin & Savage has a similar look but contains no metallic threads. Luster is created with a blend of polyester and rayon.

Suitable For

Appliqué, trim, loose tops. Allow enough ease. Fabric is fragile and tears easily. Attractive for table runners and silver displays.

Sewing Tips

Hold top and bottom threads as you start seam. Pull fabric with equal pressure from front and back as you sew.

Tip

✁ **Avoid loosely woven Lurex fabrics since they do not wear well. Lining will increase durability and decrease discomfort from the scratchy fabric. Metallic yarns do not breathe, can tarnish if pressed with steam, and tend to fray on worn spots.**

WORKING WITH LAMÉ & LUREX

Preshrink

Hand-wash then air-dry tissue lamé. Machine-wash tricot-backed lamé in warm water on delicate cycle and air-dry.

Layout

"With nap" layout, double thickness. Fabric snags easily, so remove jewelry when working on it. Tricot lamé can be cut on any grain; tissue lamé is more particular and should be cut with "with nap" considerations. Pin in seam allowances only or use pattern weights.

Marking

Pilot Frixion erasable ink pen or snips in seam. No waxed chalk or tracing wheels, which will snag fabric.

Cutting

Rotary cutter or scissors. Ravels like crazy. Seal edges with FrayBlock, which will bleed and darken fabric, ¼ in. into seam allowance. Serging pulls off fabric. If the fabric is synthetic, try a hot stencil cutter, which cuts and seals at the same time.

Interfacing

Sewers' Dream or So-Sheer. Consider fusing all cutout pieces to make fabric easier to handle and less scratchy; a must for appliqué. Test iron temperature on a scrap piece.

Thread

Good-quality cotton.

Needle

70/10 HJ. Needles dull quickly on a conventional machine or serger, so have plenty on hand. Watch sewing closely as dull needles will snag the fabric.

Stitch Length

2.5 mm.

Presser Foot

Use straight stitch foot or flattest bottom presser foot you have. If you don't have these feet, switch needle to far left position for support on three sides.

Seam Finish

3-thread-serge seam allowances together after initial seam is sewn. (See #4 on p. 216.)

Pressing

Dry iron on synthetic setting. Use a press cloth.

Topstitching

Not recommended.

Closures

Buttonholes not recommended. Consider alternate closures like button loops and frogs. (See #9 and #12 on p. 225.) Invisible zipper. (See #19 on p. 227.)

Hem

Rolled hem on serger. Widen the bite and lengthen the stitch so that more fabric is rolled under to prevent hem from pulling off fabric. (See #17 on p. 230.) Another option is ½-in. pressed-under hem stabilized with Lite Steam-A- Seam 2. (See #3 on p. 228.)

Laminated Fabrics

Fabric Fact

Laminated fabrics are fabrics that have a light layer of plastic laminate to make them water-resistant. I have sewn with both cotton and linen laminates. The cotton laminate tends to be lighter-weight. Stitches cannot be ripped out without leaving holes, so pretest your pattern. Without linings, these coated fabrics can breathe a bit and are less bulky to pack.

Suitable For

Rainwear and shopping bags. Since the fabric does not ease well, consider styles such as raglan, where no ease is required, or reduce ease in the sleeve cap of a set-in sleeve. Avoid voluminous styles since fabric does not drape well.

Sewing Tips

These fabrics are easy to sew—just let fabric feed into the machine naturally. Use roller or Teflon foot when topstitching.

> **Tip** **Use colorful linings in dark-colored coats, and you will never leave the coat in a theater or restaurant. Plus, colorful linings are beautiful to look at.**

WORKING WITH LAMINATED FABRICS

Preshrink

Not necessary or recommended, as laminate will be compromised. Wipe off scuff or food stains.

Layout

Double thickness with laminate side out without nap. Hold pattern pieces in place with fabric weights to avoid pin holes.

Marking

Clover Chaco Liner or pencil.

Cutting

Serrated scissors.

Interfacing

Sew-in only; midweight Pellon works well since the garment will not be laundered.

Thread

Cotton or polyester.

Needle

80/12 H.

Stitch Length

3.0 mm.

Presser Foot

Teflon or walking.

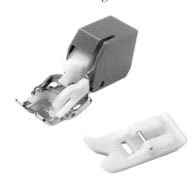

Seam Finish

Flat-fell seams assisted with Wonder Tape to hold in place while stitching. (See #9 on p. 216.)

Pressing

No steam on synthetic setting. Press on wrong side without press cloth but on right side with press cloth.

Topstitching

Lengthen stitch to 3.0 mm. Use either a roller or Teflon presser foot to topstitch with two rows, ⅛ in. away from edge and ¼ in. away from first row. (See #9 on p. 223.)

Closures

Snaps, zippers, decorative closures. (See #11 and #12 on p. 225, #19 on p. 227.)

Hem

Turn up raw edge of hem ¼ in. and hold in place with Wonder Tape. Turn up another 1 in. and topstitch in place.

Leather

Fabric Fact

Leather is available in all weights. Buy soft, drapey skins like plongé, lamb nappa, nubuck, and cabretta for flattering garment results. Goatskin is soft and water repellent. Plongé are thin, drapey, big leather skins but aren't

available in all colors. Leather is sold by the square foot, not by the yard. To calculate how much to buy, multiply the yardage needed for 45-in. fabric by 11.25, then multiply again by 1.25. This will give you the amount in square feet. For example, if 3 yd. of 45-in. fabric is needed, 3 x 11.25 = 33.75 x 1.25 = 42.19 or 42¼ sq. ft. Make sure all hides come from the same dye lot.

Suitable For

Straight skirts, fitted pants, jackets, and coats. Look for raglan sleeves or reduce sleeve ease to ½ in. Pretest pattern since stitches leave permanent holes. The best leathers for garments are plongé, lamb nappa, and goat because they drape. Leather also makes good trim on woolen or tapestry fabrics.

Sewing Tips

Hold fabric layers together with fabric clips. Hold top and bottom threads as you start seam. Do not backstitch. This weakens the skin and will cause the leather to rip under stress. Fit snugly—leather stretches as it is worn. Fit lining looser or lining seams will be stressed. Sew lining seams at ⅜ in. instead of ⅝ in.

Preshrink

Not necessary. Store rolled or perfectly flat. Do not wrap in plastic. To keep garments soft and supple, rub with leather balm twice a year.

> ✂ **Tip** **When layers become thick, you need a long-prong snap to go through all layers. Long-prong snaps are available from www.snapsource.com.**

WORKING WITH LEATHER

Layout

Most leather and suede skins are small and oddly shaped, so plan seams for large pattern pieces. Pants are pieced at the knee. Skirts are pieced within panels. Duplicate all pattern pieces so that you can have left and right sides. Grainline runs along the backbone of the hide. Examine hides for flaws and circle with chalk on wrong side so the areas can be avoided. Place hide wrong side up, single thickness. Use pattern weights.

Marking

Clover Chaco Liner, Pilot Frixion erasable ink pen, Clover white marking pen for dark colors.

Cutting

Scissors or rotary cutter. Since leather follows body curves, cut sleeves ⅜ in. longer and pants ¾ in. longer. Create seams at knees on pants for strength and to prevent baggy knees. Since leather doesn't turn well, round off corners on collars.

Interfacing

Fusi-Knit with no steam. Lining will reduce stretch in close-fitting garments and prevent dye from bleeding onto underwear. Attach lining only at waist for skirts and pants.

Thread

Polyester only. Tannins will rot cotton thread.

Needle

70/10 HJ for fine skins, 90/14 NTW for heavier skins. Use glover's needle for hand sewing.

Stitch Length

3.0 mm.

Presser Foot

Roller or Teflon. A walking foot can scratch skins as you slide leather under it. If leather is sticking to throat plate, cut an opening the size of the feed dogs in a Teflon pressing sheet and tape it to the throat plate.

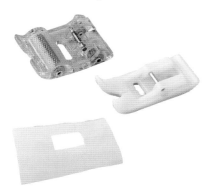

Seam Finish

Use fabric clips to hold seams together; cross-pin only at seam joints. Sew plain seams. Use Stay Tape on stress areas such as shoulders and pockets. Use leather scrap for table padding. Use a padded hammer or rubber mallet to tap open seams. Keep seams open with double-sided leather tape or topstitch seams to one side, ¼ in. from seamline.

Pressing

No steam. Dry iron on medium-heat setting. Use press-and-lift motion to avoid stretching the hide. Use brown bag as a press cloth.

Topstitching

On details, stitch very close to edge to flatten. (See #2 and #3 on p. 222.) Use Teflon or roller foot to prevent rippling.

Closures

Snaps, eyelets and lacing, button loops, or faced buttonhole. (See #6 on p. 224, #9 and #11 on p. 225, #15 on p. 226.) For zippers, use exposed zipper insertion to reduce bulk. (See #19 on p. 227.)

Hem

Double-sided leather tape is less messy than Barge rubber cement and leaves hem more flexible. (See #7 on p. 229.)

Linen

Fabric Fact

Linen is a crisp fabric that is made from fibers that grow in the flax plant and doesn't drape. It is extremely cool to wear in hot weather. Linen comes in four weights: gauge, handkerchief, medium, and heavy. The biggest mistake people make with linen is using the wrong weight for their project, such as heavy-weight linen for a blouse or tissue weight for pants. Observe linen weights used in ready-to-wear and choose the weight for your project accordingly. If the linen you bought seems a bit heavy for your project, cut it on the bias for a better drape. Handkerchief weight is beautiful cut on the bias.

Suitable For

Loose shirts and pants, boxy jackets, and dresses.

Sewing Tips

To reduce wrinkling in pants, consider underlining the entire garment with Sewers' Dream. Another option is to underline with silk organza. Although this reduces wrinkles slightly and makes the garment easier to wear, the garment must then be dry-cleaned.

Preshrink

To minimize wrinkling, press a fabric before preshrinking with a high-temperature dry iron to set the formaldehyde. Then machine-wash in warm water with a bit of

> ✂ **Tip** If silk and linen are washable, why do care labels on ready-to-wear say "dry-clean only"? Because neither the fashion fabric nor the interfacing has been prewashed.

WORKING WITH LINEN

Dawn® dishwashing detergent. Don't overpack washer since linen absorbs twice its weight in water. Add 1 tablespoon of bleach to white and off-white linens to soften more. To set dark or bright colors, use Retayne, which sets dye. Machine-dry at regular temperature but take out of dryer while damp. Linen softens with repeated washings. Press well before layout. If you prefer a very crisp look or do not want any color change, do not preshrink.

Layout

"Without nap" layout, double thickness.

Marking

Pilot Frixion erasable ink pen, tracing wheel, Clover Chaco Liner.

Cutting

Rotary cutter or scissors. On handkerchief linen, the lightest weight in linen, cut blouse fronts double and eliminate front facings. This will give more coverage in front and eliminate facing show-through.

Interfacing

Sewers' Dream or Fusi-Knit. Interface handkerchief linen only with itself.

Thread

Good-quality cotton or polyester.

Needle

70/10 H for handkerchief weight, 80/12 H for other weights.

Stitch Length

2.5 mm.

Presser Foot

Standard.

Seam Finish

Flat fell on light to medium weight. For an unlined jacket, Hong Kong seams are preferred. (See #9 on p. 216, #16 on p. 218.)

Pressing

Steam iron at highest setting. Spritz fabric with water and press on the right side. Has a natural luster when pressed.

Topstitching

For beautiful topstitching on heavier weights, use buttonhole twist on top, regular thread in bobbin, and N needle. Use edge foot or edge-joining foot as guide.

Closures

For buttonholes, use 70/10 HJ needle and fine machine embroidery thread. Loosen top tension slightly. Linen is a great candidate for snaps. Use 1-in. circle of stiff interfacing between layers for snap support. (See #1 on p. 224, #11 on p. 225.)

Hem

For a beautiful hemstitch finish, like the one on linen napkins, use double needle ZWI-HO, which has an H needle on the right side and a wing needle on the left side to create a hole. Apply spray starch to hem area and choose a machine stitch that goes into the hole more than once. Double-fold machine hem on shirts. On jackets, interface hemline with bias-cut strips of fusible interfacing 1 in. narrower than hem. Hong Kong finish and hand-hem on jackets. Hand- or machine-hem on pants and skirts. (See #13 on p. 230.)

Loose Weaves

Fabric Fact

Loosely woven fabrics, sometimes called "novelty weaves," offer interesting textures but must be stabilized with interfacing to avoid snagging and sagging later.

Suitable For

Loose, unstructured jackets and vests with minimum number of seams. Pretest pattern or hand-baste side seams for fit since stitches are difficult to remove in loose weaves.

Sewing Tips

For jackets and vests, block-fuse each piece separately. Cut to size from pattern piece, then overlock each piece on all sides. For drapey tops, do not fuse; merely overlock pieces right away. Stabilize neckline and shoulders with Stay Tape or narrow selvage strip from lining material. Cut stabilizer length from pattern piece. Force garment piece to conform to Stay Tape by positioning tape under the presser foot and fabric next to the feed dogs.

Preshrink

If your fabric is a loose weave but not handwoven, preshrink by holding steam iron ½ in. above surface. On loose weaves, dry-clean completed garment.

> **Tip** When changing thread on a serger using the tie-on technique, don't let the knot go through the tension discs. Lift the knot out of the discs, then pull the thread forward so that the thread that will go into the discs is past the knotted section.

WORKING WITH LOOSE WEAVES

Layout

"Without nap" layout, double thickness. Square up selvages and crossgrain threads. Pin selvages together. If pattern must be matched, use single thickness instead. Cut pieces larger than pattern so that you can block-fuse. Loose weaves tighten when fused.

Marking

Tailor tacks or safety pins.

Cutting

Rotary cutter or scissors. Flower-head pins will not get lost in the weave. Do not cut out notches since they will be serged off.

Interfacing

Underline each piece with Sewers' Dream or Fusi-Knit, then cut to size from pattern piece. Serge-finish each piece after cutting. Additional interfacing is not necessary. Interfacing reacts differently to different fibers and different dyes. Always try a sample before committing yourself.

Tip Since lining fabric has little or no give, cut the sleeve lining for a coat or jacket on the bias and you will find your sleeves more comfortable.

Thread

Good-quality cotton or polyester.

Needle

80/12 H. Use 80/12 HJ or HM if fabric has slubs or metallic yarns.

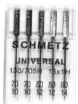

Stitch Length

2.5 mm.

Presser Foot

Walking or roller.

Seam Finish

Press seam open. Serge each side separately. On right side, topstitch ¼ in. from seam on each side. (See #3 on p. 216.) Loose weaves last longer if they are lined.

Pressing

Steam iron on medium-high setting. Cover pressing surface with a towel. Press on the wrong side to avoid flattening nubby surfaces. Use press cloth and no steam on dark colors or if metallic threads are present.

Topstitching

Use decorative thread and an HE needle to topstitch ¼ in. from finished edge if desired. (See #10 on p. 223.)

Closures

No buttonholes. Machine buttonholes and snaps will pull away from fabric in time. Use alternative closures such as button loops made from lighter-weight fabric or braid, frogs, or button openings in a seam. Bound buttonhole is an option if lips are made in a contrasting, more stable fabric. (See #8, #9, #10, and #12 on p. 225.)

Hem

Lining and garment should be hemmed separately and allowed to hang free at bottom. Finish garment hem edge with double-fold bias. Hand-hem. (See #14 on p. 230.) Decorative fold-over bindings can be attractive around the perimeter of unlined garments instead of traditional hems. Cut off seam and hem allowances, and apply fusible Stay Tape along the edge to stabilize edges. Clip halfway into Stay Tape width to allow it to conform to curves. (See #9 on p. 229.)

Matte Rayon Jersey

Fabric Fact

Matte rayon jersey is a designer's best friend. Of all of the knits, it has the most beautiful drape. Its characteristic weight and density make it stand out from other knits. It is simply the best.

Suitable For

Because this fabric drapes so well, it works in almost any style. Simple styling shows off the fabric to its best advantage in tops, dresses, skirts, and full pants with an elastic waist.

Sewing Tips

To prevent fabric from drawing into the throat plate hole, slip a folded 1-in. square of Solvy between the presser foot and the feed dogs at the beginning of the seam. Tear off Solvy after seam is sewn.

Tip To keep matte rayon jersey garments from stretching, store garments flat instead of on hangers. Dry-clean soiled garments.

WORKING WITH MATTE RAYON JERSEY

Preshrink

Preshrink at dry cleaner or hold steam iron ½ in. above fabric and steam well on both sides.

Layout

"With nap" layout, double thickness. For cutting accuracy, tape tissue to table. Overlay double layer of fabric onto tissue. Pin pattern through fabric and tissue layers. Since matte rayon jersey lengthens as it is worn, shorten bodice ½ in. between waist and crotch. Shorten sleeves ½ in.

Marking

Pilot Frixion erasable ink pen, Clover Chaco Liner, smooth tracing wheel only.

Cutting

Rotary cutter or sharp scissors. Cut through all layers including tissue.

Interfacing

Fusi-Knit. Stabilize necklines, shoulders, and waistlines with fusible straight-grain tape.

Thread

Polyester.

Needle

75/11 HS.

Stitch Length

Tiny zigzag (0.5 mm width, 2.5 mm length).

Presser Foot

Walking or Teflon.

Seam Finish

Small zigzag on conventional machine followed by 3- or 4-thread serging through both layers. (See #20 on p. 218.)

Pressing

Steam iron on synthetic setting. Press only on wrong side to avoid shine.

> **Tip** Silesia is a fine cotton fabric used by men's tailors for the inside of pockets. If you do not have access to Silesia, you can substitute handkerchief linen or lightweight stable cotton.

Topstitching

Causes rippled edges. Not recommended.

Closures

Invisible zipper. Stabilize zipper seam allowances with ½-in. strips of interfacing to prevent stretching. (See #19 on p. 227.) Button loops, faced button openings. (See #6 on p. 224, #9 on p. 225.)

Hem

Rolled hem on the serger for full skirts. Coverlock other garments, use cover stitch or press up ½-in. hem with a strip of Lite Steam-A-Seam 2, followed by double-needle stitching with finger pushing behind presser foot as when easing unless your machine has differential feed. (See #3 and #5 on p. 228, #17 on p. 230.)

Microfiber

Fabric Fact

Microfiber refers to the size of the thread, an average thread being as fine as a hair on your head. Microfiber can be spun from polyester, nylon, rayon, or acetate. The finest-quality polyester microfiber has 200 threads per inch. Microfiber comes in different weights, with the heavier weight giving the best seam results. This weight is sometimes called stretch moleskin, stretch suiting, or sueded microfiber. Fabric might be labeled peachskin, micro twill, or micro sandwashed. Microfiber is very drapey and makes a great travel fabric, but it does not breathe.

Suitable For

Loose unstructured styles with minimum seams such as full coats, tailored or full pants, full or wrap skirts in medium weight, nightgowns or pajamas in lightweight. Fabric does not ease well, so raglan or dolman sleeves give better results. Since microfiber is difficult to achieve a sharp press on, choose style accordingly.

Sewing Tips

Let fabric feed naturally.

> **Tip** ✂ **A microfiber measures 0.01 denier in size compared to a fine silk at 1.25 denier in size.**

WORKING WITH MICROFIBER

Preshrink

Machine-wash in warm water and machine-dry at normal temperature. Use only liquid fabric softener; dryer sheets leave oily spots. Remove completed garment from dryer before bone-dry, and pull seams taut to prevent puckering. Garment can also be air-dried.

Layout

"With nap" layout, double thickness on grain. Cut lightweight microfibers 10% or more off-grain to avoid puckered seams.

Marking

Clover Chaco Liner or Pilot Frixion erasable ink pen.

Cutting

Sharp scissors or rotary cutter.

Interfacing

Fusi-Knit.

Thread

Fine machine-embroidery thread such as Seralene, a finer thread.

Needle

60/8 HM or 70/10 HM. Have several on hand because fabric dulls needles quickly. Most sergers have needles that are interchangeable with conventional sewing machines. Changing serger needles to match fabric is especially important on microfibers.

Stitch Length

1.5 mm straight stitch.

Presser Foot

Straight stitch foot and single-hole throat plate.

Seam Finish

On lightweight microfibers, press open and pink or 3-thread overlock each side of seam allowance with super-fine serger thread such as Janome overlock polyester thread #80. (See #2 and #3 on p. 216.) On heavier microfibers, 3- or 4-thread overlock can be used with normal-weight thread. (See #5 on p. 216.)

Pressing

Dry, moderate-heat iron. Press seam as stitched before pressing open. Use a press cloth when ironing on the right side. Press over rounded seam stick to prevent serger stitches from making ridges on the right side.

Topstitching

Topstitch very close to edge using topstitch foot. Farther away causes ripples. (See #2 and #3 on p. 222.)

Closures

For buttonholes, use 70/10 HJ needle with fine machine-embroidery thread and Solvy between fabric and presser foot. (See #1 on p. 224.)

Hem

No double-needle topstitching since puckers often form between rows. For the most invisible hems, fuse with Lite Steam-A-Seam 2. Hand- or machine-stitch. (See #3, #4, and #6 on p. 228.)

Fabric Fact

Minky, a microfiber, is a very soft 100% polyester knitted fabric. It feels similar to fleece, but it's softer and thicker.

Suitable For

Minky is most often used for children's blankets, pillows, and stuffed animals. It is sometimes used as a quilt backing because of its incredibly soft touch.

Sewing Tips

Because Minky is so slippery, it slides all over the place. When joining layers together, you will need to do a lot of pinning fairly close together and maybe hand-baste as well. Double-sided adhesive tape does not work to hold seams together because of the hairy surface. This is not an easy fabric to work with.

Tip

If working with a long-pile Minky, shave the area in the seam allowance to make it easier to sew.

WORKING WITH MINKY

Preshrink

Cold-water wash, regular-temperature dry cycle. Take out of dryer right away. While the fabric does not shrink, preshrinking results in a better stitch quality.

Layout

"With nap" single thickness, pattern weights.

Marking

Safety pins or tailor tacks.

Cutting

This fabric makes a big mess when you cut it out, so lay a sheet under the cutting and sewing areas. Cut with rotary cutter or sharp scissors.

Interfacing

No fusibles. If you want to put in snaps or grommets, add a piece of ribbon between fabric layers so that the snaps or grommets do not pull out.

Thread

Polyester or cotton.

Needle

75/11 HS.

Stitch Length

The best seaming for this fabric is a 4-thread overlock. Seaming with overlock results in less slippage. If you do not have an overlock, sew seams with a zigzag (1.0 mm width and 3.0 mm width). Push seams into the presser foot or use differential feed.

Presser Foot

Walking.

Seam Finish

Sewing against the direction of the nap gives you the most control. Sew seams with the 4-thread serger; the seam allowance is serged off and therefore finished. On a regular machine, sew seam against the nap with the zigzag, then finger-press open. Topstitch on either side of seam, ¼ in. away from seam joint. Trim off excess seam allowance. (See #5 on p. 216.)

Pressing

No pressing—the heat will cause the fabric to melt.

Topstitching

Since you cannot press this fabric, you will have to topstitch the seamed edges to make them flat. Topstitch using 3.5 mm length stitch, followed by brushing up the nap.

Closures

Zipper only. (See #19 on p. 227.)

Hem

Hand-baste hem allowance. Coverlock or double-needle the hem in place. (See #5 on p. 228.)

Tip It is not necessary to presew clear elastic in place before stitching a seam before serging. Simply feed the elastic through the serger foot, from the top of the foot, under the foot, and out the back. Serging will hold it in place and provide the amount of stretch you need.

Mohair

Fabric Fact

Mohair is made from the soft, silky hair of the Angora goat. Mohair is lightweight to wear while providing warmth.

Suitable For

Unlined sweaters, coats, or jackets. Don't choose an oversize style, or you will just look big. This fabric makes a terrific travel garment because it is lightweight, warm, and never wrinkles. A wonderful lap robe can be made with 1½ yd.

Sewing Tips

Sew in the direction of the pile. To stabilize seams and prevent them from stretching, sew with a 2-in. strip of organza between the presser foot and the mohair. Underlining is not recommended because mohair will sag over the underlining in time. Lining is optional, but it must hang free at the hem.

✂ **Tip** **Never iron a soiled garment. The heat will set the stain.**

WORKING WITH MOHAIR

Preshrink

Hold steam iron ½ in. above fabric.

Layout

"With nap" layout, pile down, single thickness.

Marking

Tailor tacks or safety pins.

Cutting

Rotary cutter or scissors. Use pattern weights.

Interfacing

Organza on straight of grain or Veri-Shape on the bias for crisper detailing.

Thread

Silk machine twist or good-quality cotton.

Needle

70/10 H or 80/12 H.

Stitch Length

3.0 mm straight stitch.

Presser Foot

Walking.

Seam Finish

If garment is unlined, use stabilizing organza strip to bind seams together. (See #15 on p. 217.) If garment is lined, leave stabilizing strip in the seam and merely press plain seams open. (See #1 on p. 216.)

Pressing

Cover pressing surface with Velvaboard. On the wrong side, press only in the seam allowance with the tip of a dry iron on medium temperature. No pressing on the right side. Details such as pockets and lapels can be flattened with the right side against the Velvaboard. Cover mohair with press cloth. Press with steam on the wool setting. A tailor's clapper can be used gently. Render seams almost invisible by brushing pressed-open seams against the nap from the right side with a toothbrush.

Topstitching

Not necessary, but can help flatten edges if done ⅜ in. from finished edge. Walking foot should be used when topstitching. (See #9 on p. 223.) Loosen top tension slightly.

Closures

Consider other buttonhole options such as a faced opening, button loops, or openings in a seam. If you are an expert sewer and prefer an unlined piece, face front edge with grosgrain. Make buttonholes through grosgrain and mohair. (See #6 on p. 224, #7, #9, and #10 on p. 225.)

Hem

Hong Kong finish raw edge. Hand-hem twice. (See #13 on p. 230, #32 on p. 233.)

Moleskin

Fabric Fact

If you are looking for a good travel fabric, this is it! This fabric does not wrinkle or stretch out of shape and drapes very well. Sensuede® by Logantex is 97% microfiber and 3% spandex. Stretch moleskin is slightly heavier and does not stick to itself.

Suitable For

Stretch moleskin, sometimes referred to as stretch suede, works in any style pant from tailored to narrow pull-on. Moleskin works for unstructured tops and shift dresses as well. Sensuede is cozy to wear and works well in loose shirts or full pull-on pants. Stretch suedes are polyester, so if you tend to get warm, stay away from tailored jackets or tops with close-fitting, set-in sleeves.

Sewing Tips

Let fabric feed naturally.

WORKING WITH MOLESKIN

Preshrink

Not necessary.

Layout

"With nap" layout, double thickness.

Marking

Tracing wheel, Clover Chaco Liner, Pilot Frixion erasable ink pen.

Cutting

Rotary cutter or scissors.

Interfacing

Sewers' Dream, Fusi-Knit, Shirt-Crisp for crisp collar and cuffs.

Thread

Cotton or polyester.

Needle

70/10 HM.

Stitch Length

Tiny zigzag (0.5 mm width, 2.5 mm length) prevents vertical seams from shortening.

Presser Foot

Standard.

Seam Finish

Plain seams pressed open and pinked. Or serge seam allowances together after seam is sewn using lightweight serger thread in a 3-thread stitch. (See #2 and #4 on p. 216.)

Pressing

Steam iron on synthetic setting. Press on wrong side only. Do not overpress seams, which will leave seam imprint.

Topstitching

Not recommended. Topstitching on this fabric creates drag lines between the stitching rows and causes seams to shorten unless it is done very close to the edge.

Closures

Stretch buttonholes, loops, snaps, and zippers. (See #3 on p. 224, #9 and #11 on p. 225, #19 on p. 227.)

Hem

For shirts, double-fold ¼ in. and machine-stitch with one row of stitching. (See #10 on p. 229.) For dresses, skirts, and pants, use 1¼-in. hem allowance. Hand-hem, taking only one thread from the garment, skipping forward ¼ in., and taking one thread from the hem allowance. (See #4 on p. 228.)

> **Tip** Buttonholes a problem? Sandwich garment between layers of water-soluble Solvy. Use a 70/10 HJ needle and lightweight thread in the bobbin. Stitch around the buttonhole twice for durability (once if fabric is lightweight).

Ottoman

Fabric Fact

Ottoman is a ribbed fabric with cotton crosswise threads and rayon lengthwise threads, which have some sheen. Ottoman is a great fabric to have on hand to use for contrast trims, collars, and cuffs. Keep ½ yd. in black and off-white in your fabric stash.

Suitable For

Collars, cuffs, piping, and lips on bound buttonholes.

Sewing Tips

Ottoman is sometimes referred to as faille. The best ottoman has pronounced ribs in the fabric. Let fabric feed naturally.

Tip ✂ **Always iron dark solid colors on the wrong side to avoid shine.**

WORKING WITH OTTOMAN

Preshrink

Steam well on both sides of fabric with iron ½ in. above fabric surface. This fabric shrinks a lot!

Layout

"With nap" layout, single thickness. Can be cut lengthwise or crosswise.

Marking

Pilot Frixion erasable ink pen, Clover Chaco Liner, Clover white marking pen for dark colors.

Cutting

Rotary cutter or scissors.

Interfacing

Cotton or wool flannel gives a soft appearance with some heft; silk organza gives a crisp appearance.

Thread

Cotton or polyester.

Needle

80/12 H.

Stitch Length

2.5 mm.

Presser Foot

Standard.

Seam Finish

Plain. (See #1 on p. 216.)

Pressing

Dry iron on medium setting. Finger-press seams open; then press open on the wrong side with a light touch so that the ribs will not flatten.

Topstitching

Not recommended.

Closures

Bound buttonholes, button loops, and buttons in a seam. (See #8, #9, and #10 on p. 225.)

Hem

Not applicable when used as trim.

Piqué

Fabric Fact

Piqué is medium-weight cotton with a raised, pebbly weave that looks almost like a small check.

Suitable For

Vests, jackets, fitted blouses.

Sewing Tips

Let fabric feed naturally.

> ✂ **Tip** If you love a fabric but don't know how much to buy, 2½ yd. gives you the option of making pants, a blouse, some skirts, or a simple jacket. If you like to double fronts on blouses and jackets, 3 yd. is safer.

WORKING WITH PIQUÉ

Preshrink

Machine-wash in warm water and machine-dry on regular cycle. If using black piqué, hand-wash in cold water and air-dry to maintain the black and prevent graying.

Layout

"Without nap" layout, double thickness.

Marking

Clover Chaco Liner, tracing wheel, Pilot Frixion erasable ink pen.

Cutting

Rotary cutter or scissors.

Interfacing

Sewers' Dream, Fusi-Knit, Suitmaker on a vest or jacket.

Thread

Good-quality cotton or polyester.

Needle

80/12 H.

Stitch Length

2.5 mm.

Presser Foot

Standard.

Seam Finish

Flat fell or sew with a straight seam, press open, and overlock each side of seam separately. No seam finish if lining. (See #3 and #9 on p. 216.)

Tip Durable seam finishes such as flat fell or faux flat fell are better for a garment that will be frequently machine-washed and -dried.

Pressing

Steam iron on cotton setting.

Topstitching

Not recommended since it detracts from fabric's surface.

Closures

Buttonholes, snaps, button loops. (See #1 on p. 224, #9 and #11 on p. 225.)

Hem

Serge raw edge. Sew by hand or topstitch with double needle. (See #1 and #4 on p. 228.)

Polyester Silky

Fabric Fact

While polyester silky is very seductive on the bolt, it is difficult to get seams that don't pucker unless you cut fabric on the crossgrain or bias. If the polyester has a busy print, cutting lengthwise is okay since any seam puckering will be hidden in the print. Polyester silky is a good candidate to have pleated since polyester will hold pleats indefinitely. Polyester is warm to wear unless the style is loose; it tends to be hot and clingy. Don't layer clothing over polyester because it will trap the heat.

Suitable For

Blouses, nightgowns, tops, pants, and camisoles. Polyester as a lining is pretty but hot to wear.

Sewing Tips

Hold top and bottom threads when starting seam. Use taut sewing technique of pulling the fabric with equal pressure from both directions.

Tip

To prevent fabric from shifting when making buttonholes, position a small strip of fusible web between the facing and garment in the buttonhole area. The web locks the fabrics together during this crucial process.

WORKING WITH POLYESTER SILKY

Preshrink

Not necessary. Completed garment can be hand- or machine-washed in warm water. Air-dry. Machine drying creates too much static electricity.

Layout

Cut on the crossgrain or the bias to prevent puckered seams. If fabric will be pleated, cut on lengthwise grain since pleat will hide any seam puckering. Cut lengthwise on prints since puckered seams will be hidden.

Marking

Pilot Frixion erasable ink pen or Clover Chaco Liner.

Cutting

Rotary cutter or scissors.

Interfacing

So-Sheer or silk organza.

Thread

Fine machine embroidery in cotton, silk, or polyester.

Needle

60/8 or 65/9 HM or 70/10 HJ.

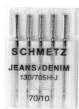

Stitch Length

2.0 mm straight stitch.

Presser Foot

Straight stitch foot and single-hole throat plate. Or use your flattest bottom presser foot and switch needle to the far left position.

Seam Finish

French seam. (See #10 on p. 217, #40 on p. 221.)

Pressing

Medium-temperature steam iron. Test sample.

Topstitching

Close to the edge helps flatten edges. Topstitching foot helps here. (See #2 and #3 on p. 222.)

Closures

Buttonholes using 70/10 HJ needle and fine machine-embroidery thread. Also thread loops. (See #1 on p. 224, #9 on p. 225.)

Hem

Options: (1) Thread bobbin with fusible thread and fine thread on top. With wrong side of fabric against feed dogs, staystitch along hemline. Press to the wrong side to dissolve the fusible thread and form sharp crease. Trim hem allowance to ⅛ in. Roll again, enclosing raw edge. Hand-sew or machine-sew with fine thread. Keep finger pressure on back of presser foot to prevent hem from stretching. (2) Serged rolled hem works well on full styles. Run a line of staystitching at ½ in. with finger behind presser foot to prevent fabric from stretching. When serging, remove right needle, and let rolled hem encase staystitching. The differential feed set at 0.7 mm helps here. Use a fine serger thread. (See #17 on p. 230.) A beautiful hem for lingerie is the blind hem stitch, which gives a scalloped appearance. (See #35 on p. 233.)

Prepleated Fabrics

Fabric Fact

Fabric is sold stretched and unstretched (4 yd. to 5 yd. of fabric pleat down to 1¼ yd.). Sunburst pleating is the most beautiful, with its small pleats at the top and large pleats at the bottom. You need two panels to make a skirt, if sold by the panel. Prepleated fabrics are usually all polyester or a polyester blend because the polyester helps hold the pleat.

Suitable For

Simply styled, close-fitting tops, tube skirts, and full pants with elasticized waists. Look for simple shapes with as few seams as possible. Eliminate pattern detailing when using pleated fabric. Other uses might be for details such as collars, ruffles, cuffs, sleeves, or godets used in conjunction with a smooth fabric.

Sewing Tips

Hand-baste seams for fitting. When sewing, flatten out vertical pleats at side seams by pulling fabric flat with fingers on each side of stitching line to avoid catching folds of nearby pleats. After seam is sewn, pleats will cup up around it, rendering it invisible. Eliminate facings.

Tip **Check the fabric on the bolt to determine the right side of cottons and wools. Cottons are folded right side out on the bolt, wools are folded right side in.**

WORKING WITH PREPLEATED FABRICS

Preshrink

Store fabric rolled. Preshrinking is not necessary. Completed garment can be hand-laundered and air-dried. Never put in a dryer or pleats will disappear.

Layout

Straighten crossgrain with a T-square. "With nap" layout, single thickness. Let fabric relax on the table. Do not bunch up or stretch out. Align pleats with lengthwise grainline on pattern. Use pattern weights, as pins will tear pattern tissue. Cut duplicate of any pattern piece labeled "cut on the fold." Tape duplicate to foldline of pattern piece so that entire piece can be cut through a single thickness.

Marking

Safety pins. Nothing else shows.

Cutting

Cut garment at least one size smaller as pleats will release as needed for ease. Before moving off the table, Scotch® tape pleats within the seam allowance at neck, shoulder, and armhole. Stabilize all three areas with twill tape before removing Scotch tape.

Interfacing

Not recommended. Pleats can be underlined in certain areas with cotton batiste. Hand-tack pleats to underlining.

Thread

Good-quality polyester or cotton.

Needle

70/10 H, HJ, or HM.

Stitch Length

2.5 mm.

Presser Foot

Walking.

Seam Finish

Serge seam allowances together with 4-thread overlock. (See #5 on p. 216.)

Pressing

None. Pressing will remove pleats.

Topstitching

Not recommended.

Closures

Consider buttonhole alternatives such as fabric loops or frogs. (See #9, #12, and #13 on p. 225.)

Hem

Ready-to-wear garments are hemmed before pleated. Whenever possible, let selvage be finished hem edge. (See #24 on p. 231.) If selvage hem is not possible, serge using differential feed and narrow stitch. Push fabric into the back of the serger foot so that hem edge is not stretched. After hemming, roll up hem and stuff into the ribbed part of a cotton sock. Steam well with steam iron. Let dry before pulling out of sock. For fluted hem, turn under ¼ in. twice and zigzag, use picot stitch, or serge wide rolled hem. (See #28 on p. 232.)

Puckered Fabrics

Fabric Fact

The three-dimensional effect in a puckered fabric is created by elasticized threads on the fabric back. Textured fabrics camouflage wrinkles, making them great travel fabrics.

Suitable For

Details such as collars or pocket flaps, or part of a garment, such as the bodice of an empire-styled dress. Puckered fabrics make interesting bustiers, vests, simply styled fitted tops, short bolero jackets. For long body-conscious dresses, side seams must be stabilized with narrow clear elastic.

Sewing Tips

To eliminate all hassles and seam stretching, sew with strips of Solvy between the presser foot and the fabric. Push fabric into presser foot. Tear off Solvy after sewing. Face neckline, armholes, and front edge with lightly interfaced non-puckered fabric.

Tip When sewing through any elastic other than narrow clear elastic, use a ballpoint needle to prevent elastic threads from damage and from coming through to the right side of the fabric.

WORKING WITH PUCKERED FABRICS

Preshrink

Not necessary.

Layout

"With nap" layout, single thickness. Make duplicate of any pattern piece labeled "cut on the fold." Tape duplicate to original along foldline so that all pattern pieces can be cut through a single thickness. Use pattern weights; pins will tear tissue.

Marking

Clover Chaco Liner, Pilot Frixion erasable ink pen, safety pins.

Cutting

Rotary cutter or scissors. Cut and sew 1-in. seam allowances to keep elastic threads from working out as the seam is sewn.

Interfacing

Silk organza. No fusible interfacing. Stabilize neck and shoulders with narrow, clear elastic. Prestretch elastic once before using. Do not stretch elastic as you apply it; feed the elastic through the slot on the presser foot. Stitch through as you are seaming. Lining is not necessary, but if desired, use swimsuit lining or Lycra in areas where stretch is needed. If fabric is used only for textural effect and no stretch is needed, line with cotton batiste or silk.

Thread

Good-quality polyester or cotton.

Needle

70/10 H.

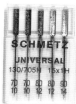

Stitch Length

Tiny zigzag (0.5 mm width, 2.5 mm length).

Presser Foot

Walking or Teflon.

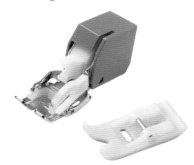

Seam Finish

Small zigzag stitch with seam allowances serged separately. (See #3 on p. 216.)

Pressing

Cover pressing surface with towel and press with low-temperature steam iron. An iron that is too warm will melt elastic threads. Finger-press after steaming.

Topstitching

Not recommended. Hand picking close to edge can help flatten seam. (See #1 on p. 222.)

Closures

Snaps with extra-long prongs, button loops, frogs. (See #9, #11, and #12 on p. 225.) Invisible zippers. (See #19 on p. 227.)

Hem

Serge raw hem edge. Do not allow hem edge to stretch. Use differential feed or push fabric into the back of presser foot as you serge, just as you would for easing. Turn hem under ½ in. Hand-sew, stretch fabric before every fourth stitch, and knot. (See #4 on p. 228.) Another option is to bind edges with crossgrain knit or bias binding. Stabilize all rounded edges with selvage or twill tape, clipped to enable it to conform to curves. Do this before binding so that no stretching occurs as the binding is applied. (See #11 on p. 229.)

Quilted Fabrics

Fabric Fact

Quilted fabrics are made by sandwiching batting in between two fabrics and sewing the layers together on a quilting machine. Quilted fabrics are available in polyester satin, cotton, and even Ultrasuede. If you own a long-arm quilting machine, you can create your own quilted fabrics.

Suitable For

Unlined jackets and vests with simple styling, double-sided placemats, and floor cushions.

Sewing Tips

Push fabric layers into the presser foot to prevent shifting.

Tip Combining different thread weights is a bad idea since a balanced stitch requires the same tension on top and bottom. Two exceptions to the rule: machine embroidery and machine buttonholes. Both are less bulky if a lightweight thread is used on the bobbin.

WORKING WITH QUILTED FABRICS

Preshrink

Not necessary for Ultrasuede, which doesn't shrink, or quilted satins, which must be dry-cleaned. To preshrink quilted cotton, machine-wash in warm water and machine-dry on regular cycle.

Layout

"With nap" layout, single layer. Use pattern weights.

Marking

Pilot Frixion erasable ink pen or tailor tacks.

Cutting

Rotary cutter or scissors. Use left hand to flatten layers as you cut with your right. Reverse if left-handed, of course. If you plan to flat-fell seams, cut seams ¼ in. wider so they can wrap around sufficiently.

Interfacing

Pull off batting behind facing pieces to eliminate bulk, then stabilize with Fusi-Knit or Sewers' Dream.

Thread

Polyester or cotton.

Needle

75/11 HQ on lightweight fabrics and 90/14 HQ on heavier fabrics to prevent batting from bearding through to the topside of the fabric.

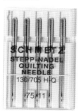

Stitch Length

3.0 mm.

Presser Foot

Teflon or walking.

Seam Finish

Flat fell for a reversible garment. (See #9 on p. 216.) Bind seams if garment is unlined and one-sided. (See #19 on p. 218.)

Pressing

Use a medium heat steam iron. Press on wrong side without too much iron pressure or you will flatten the quilted appearance.

Topstitching

Topstitching ¼ in. from edge helps flatten details and outer edges. A topstitching foot helps here. (See #10 on p. 223.)

Closures

Faced buttonholes, loops, button openings in a seam, zippers, and snaps. (See #6 on p. 224, #9, #10, and #11 on p. 225, #19 on p. 227.)

Hem

Bound edges give the cleanest finish and the least bulk. Use self-made trim or fold-over braid (see #9 and #11 on p. 229) or simply serge-finish, turn under, and hand-hem. (See #4 on p. 228.)

Rayon Viscose

Fabric Fact

Rayon viscose is a regenerated fabric produced from wood pulp. Rayons are cool to wear and take dye well. Technological improvements have removed many of the drawbacks of rayon. Today's rayons retain their shape, shrink and wrinkle less, and drape better than their predecessors. Cuprammonium rayon, found in Switzerland and Germany, is more refined and has more weight than some of the domestic rayons; it feels more like 3-ply silk.

Suitable For

Full pants, full or A-line skirts, and boxy shirts or full dresses. Avoid close-fitting styles. Look for flowing lines.

Sewing Tips

Despite your best efforts at accurate cutting, seam lengths seem to differ when you pin together. Pin with shorter seam on top, matching top and bottom of both pieces, letting feed dogs ease in longer side to match shorter one.

> ✂ **Tip** **Overpressing can cause fabric shine. Run the shiny surface against self-fabric. If the shine does not disappear, your iron was too hot and you have melted the fibers.**

WORKING WITH RAYON VISCOSE

Preshrink

Machine-wash alone in cold water gentle cycle with Ivory liquid on gentle cycle. Too much agitation when wet distorts the fabric. Machine-dry on permanent-press cycle. Remove from dryer while slightly damp and iron dry. By pretreating alone, fabric grains get less distorted.

Layout

"Without nap" layout, double thickness. For cutting accuracy, tape tissue paper to table. Pin double fabric thickness to tissue at 12-in. intervals. Pin pattern through fabric and tissue layers.

Marking

Pilot Frixion erasable ink pen, Clover Chaco Liner, tracing wheel.

Cutting

Scissors or rotary cutter. Cut through all layers including tissue.

Interfacing

Fusibles adhere well but come loose after laundering. Silk organza works the best.

Thread

Use cotton only. Polyester thread can cause shredding on any seam with stress.

Needle

70/10 HJ or 70/10 HM, new needle only. Needle will snag fabric if dull.

Stitch Length

For long side seams, sew with a tiny zigzag (0.5 mm width, 2.5 mm length). This will allow seams to relax as the fabric relaxes.

Presser Foot

Standard.

Seam Finish

Flat fell or pressed open, and serged separately with fine serger thread. (See #3 and #9 on p. 216.) Use small zigzag on both steps. (See #17 on p. 218.)

Pressing

Dry iron on medium temperature. Moisture stretches fabric. Since some dye may transfer in pressing, use a disposable press cloth such as a paper towel. Some rayons need to cool on the pressing surface before being moved or wrinkles will develop.

Topstitching

Achieve beautiful results topstitching 1/8 in. from the finished edge using topstitching foot. (See #2 and #3 on p. 222.)

Closures

For machine buttonholes use 70/10 HJ needle and fine thread. (See #1 on p. 224.)

Hem

Serge raw edge. Turn up 1 in. Hand-hem. (See #4 on p. 228.) For unstable rayons, use Lite Steam-A-Seam 2 in a 1/2-in. hem allowance to prevent stretching. Topstitch with double needle. (See #1 and #3 on p. 228.)

Ripstop

Fabric Fact

Ripstop is a lightweight, wind-resistant nylon that is more wind resistant than nylon taffeta. The heavier version is called Trailpack. Some ripstops have a durable finish that makes them water repellent as well. Ripstop does not breathe.

Suitable For

Lightweight jackets, ponchos, wind pants, shopping bags, and garment bags. Heavier weight used for backpacks.

Sewing Tips

Puckered seams can be avoided with taut sewing, pulling with equal pressure from front and back. Slower sewing gives more control over the fabric. If puckering persists, put in a new needle and position strips of tissue paper between fabric and feed dog. If you want a truly watertight garment, seal seams with seam-sealant glue.

Preshrink

Not necessary. Completed garment can be machine-washed in warm water and machine-dried on permanent press cycle. Straighten ends with T-square. Trim off selvages to prevent seam puckering later. Store rolled.

Tip Don't sew over pins. When the machine is forced to jump over a pin, the stitch is weakened, causing an area of the seam to be susceptible to breaks.

WORKING WITH RIPSTOP

Layout

"Without nap" layout. Single thickness if using stencil cutter, double thickness for rotary cutter or scissors. Pin only in the seam allowances or use pattern weights.

Marking

Clover Chaco Liner or snips in seam allowance.

Cutting

If you use a hot stencil cutter and cut single fabric thickness, fabric can be cut and sealed in one operation. Rotary cutter and scissors are also suitable. Seal edges with a candle flame right after cutting to prevent raveling.

Interfacing

Use sew-in interfacing like DuraPress behind zippers or snaps.

Thread

Polyester.

Needle

70/10 HM or 70/10 HJ.

Stitch Length

2.5 mm.

Presser Foot

Teflon or walking.

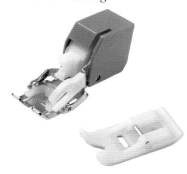

Seam Finish

Edges must be sealed during cutting or immediately after with a candle flame. Seam with 4-thread overlock. If desired, pull seams to one side and topstitch or sew French seams and then topstitch. (See #5 on p. 216, #40 on p. 221.)

Pressing

Medium-temperature iron with steam.

Topstitching

Seams and details can be topstitched at ⅛ in. to flatten. (See #2 and #3 on p. 222.) Use topstitching foot.

Closures

Nylon cord and nylon toggles will not melt in dryer. Or use Velcro or coil zippers, which are self-mending. With snaps, use non-fusible interfacing or ribbon between fabric layers, or snaps will pull away from the fabric. (See #11 on p. 225, #16 on p. 226.)

Hem

Narrow casing with shock cord drawstring or elastic or ¾-in. double-fold machine hem. (See #31 on p. 233, #10 on p. 229.)

> **Tip** If you love to make garments from patterns that have oddball shapes when cut out, identify the neck, armholes, shoulder, and hem before taking off the pattern pieces. Medical adhesive tape works well for this since you can write on it easily, and it adheres a bit better than blue painter's tape.

Satin

Fabric Fact

While all satins have a sheen, their drapability and stitch performance vary with the fiber content. Rayon is the drapiest, followed by silk and polyester. Both rayon and silk give better stitch results than polyester. Polyester and rayon tend to water-spot, while silk does not. Satin is most often used for bridal or special-occasion garments as well as coat and jacket linings.

Suitable For

Fitted blouses, full dresses, bridal gowns, coat linings.

Sewing Tips

Puckered seams reduce the value of the finished garment. Use a brand new fine needle for satin. Sew tautly, pulling fabric from front and back with equal pressure as you sew. On long seams, curl up bottom layer in front of presser foot. If you are getting skipped stitches, rub needle with Sewers Aid, a needle lubricant. Also run a bead of Sewers Aid on thread cone.

✂ **Tip** **If you do not have a perfect thread match and you need to do some handwork or hand-hemming, pull lengths of thread from the fabric scraps. Hand-sew with those threads for a perfect color and fiber match.**

WORKING WITH SATIN

Preshrink

Not necessary unless you are planning to launder completed garment. Prewash in warm water and mild detergent without water softener; line-dry. This eliminates skipped stitches caused by chemical residue. Completed garment can be hand-washed and line-dried. If static is a problem, spray with Static Guard.

Layout

"With nap" layout, double thickness. Shiny fabrics shade differently in different directions.

Marking

Snips in the seam allowance or Clover Chaco Liner. Don't use fabric markers, which bleed into fabric and are hard to remove, or waxed chalk, which leaves spots.

Cutting

Sharp scissors or rotary cutter.

Interfacing

Silk organza. Fusible interfacing causes puckers and gives fabric a stiff, board-like appearance. Underlining with organza is recommended since the only way to hem invisibly is to attach hem to underlining.

Thread

Cotton or silk fine machine embroidery.

Needle

70/10 HJ or HM.

Stitch Length

2.0 mm straight stitch.

Presser Foot

Straight stitch foot and single-hole throat plate. Or use satin stitch foot and switch needle to far left position for support on three sides. Flat underside of the straight stitch foot holds slippery fabrics against feed dogs, reducing puckered seams and skipped stitches.

Seam Finish

Pressed open and serged separately or French seams. (See #3 on p. 216, #40 on p. 221.)

Pressing

Dry iron on synthetic setting. Don't use too much pressure as this fabric overpresses easily.

Topstitching

Hand picking is the best choice. Or topstitch close to the finished edge. (See #3 on p. 222.) Parallel topstitching is easier if you leave the presser foot in one place and move the needle position.

Closures

For buttonholes, use 70/10 HJ needle and fine embroidery thread to reduce bulk. (See #1 on p. 224.)

Hem

Options: (1) Hem stitching can be invisible only if garment is underlined. Attach hem to underlining. Topstitched hems tend to pucker. (2) Serged rolled hem with woolly nylon on both loopers, using a longer and wider serger stitch. Remove right needle on serger to allow more fabric to be rolled into hem.

Seersucker

Fabric Fact

The puckers on the surface of this fabric are made by changes in the weave, so they are permanent. Check fabric content: Some are 50% cotton and 50% polyester and some are 100% cotton. 100% cotton breathes better, but the polyester combo is quite comfortable to wear as well. You may even find some seersuckers that are combined with Lycra; treat these as a stretch woven.

Suitable For

Because of its textured surface, this fabric makes a fine travel garment since it never shows wrinkles. Makes up well in camp shirts, shorts, summer bathrobes, and loose-fitting dresses and skirts.

Sewing Tips

Easy to sew since it acts just like a cotton. Textures not only hide wrinkles in wearing but also hide mistakes in sewing.

> **Tip** **Traditional seersucker fabric is blue and white, but it's readily available in a variety of colors and designs.**

WORKING WITH SEERSUCKER

Preshrink

Warm-water wash and machine-dry at normal temperature.

Layout

"Without nap," double thickness.

Marking

Pilot Frixion erasable ink pen.

Cutting

Rotary cutter or scissors.

Interfacing

Sewers' Dream, Shirt-Crisp for crisp collars and cuffs.

Thread

Cotton or polyester.

Needle

80/12 H.

Stitch Length

2.5 mm straight stitch.

Presser Foot

Standard.

Seam Finish

Flat fell. (See #9 on p. 216.)

Pressing

Steam iron on cotton setting.

Topstitching

⅛ in. from seamed edge. Topstitching foot works well here.

Closures

Buttonholes, snaps, invisible zippers. (See #1 on p. 224, #11 on p. 225, #19 on p. 227.)

Hem

Double-fold ¼-in. hem. Press a ¼-in.-wide strip of Steam-A-Seam to wrong side of fabric. Pull off paper. Press up ¼-in. hem. Enclosing raw edge, press up another ¼ in. Machine- or hand-stitch hem. (See #10 on p. 229.)

Sequins

Fabric Fact

Sequined fabrics are made by machine sewing shiny discs to a backing fabric. Sequins sewn to chiffon make the nicest tops since they drape well. Allow three times longer to work on sequins than any other fabric. Less-expensive sequin fabric has smaller sequins widely spread on a knit backing.

Suitable For

Simple collarless jackets, tops, straight skirts, or strapless dresses. Stick to simple styles; avoid gathers, pleats, and pockets.

Sewing Tips

With a standard presser foot, staystitch along the seamline and on dart sewing lines. Just outside of the seamline on the seam allowance, run a line of FrayBlock or clear glue right on the staystitch line. This stabilizes the thread that holds sequins to the fabric. Options: (1) Pull sequins out of seam allowances. Do not cut threads. Save some loose sequins. Sew seams along staystitching line, using a zipper foot that rides flat in the seam allowance. Replace damaged sequins or bald spots near seamline. (2) If taking sequins out of the seam allowances is just too much hassle for you, Karen Howland suggests folding back seam allowances on each side of the seam butting the folds, and joining them by hand with a ladder stitch. Letting sequins from each piece overlap one another forces the seam allowances open and helps camouflage the seam. If you use this method, add a stable lining, sewn just a bit smaller than the sequin fabric, to take the stress off the seams.

WORKING WITH SEQUINS

Preshrink

Not necessary. Store rolled.

Layout

To make cleanup easier, place sheets under cutting table and machine table before you begin. Single thickness. Place pattern pieces with the sequin nap down, even if this means laying the pieces on the crossgrain. Use pattern weights. Pins are useless here.

Marking

Tailor tacks, safety pins, Pilot Frixion erasable ink pen.

Cutting

Allow for 1-in. seam allowances. Cut out with old scissors, as sequins will nick the blades. Cut facings in coordinating satin.

Interfacing

Silk organza. No fusibles.

Thread

Good-quality cotton or polyester.

Needle

90/14 HJ or 100/16 H. Have plenty on hand, as sequins dull needles.

Stitch Length

3.0 mm.

Presser Foot

Zipper.

Seam Finish

With standard presser foot, staystitch along seamlines and dart sewing lines with matching thread. Run FrayBlock or glue right on stitching line. Pull sequins out of seam allowances and inside of dart sewing lines. Sew seams and darts with zipper foot. Finger-press open. Hand-whip seam allowance to back side of fabric. (See #24 on p. 219, #37 on p. 221.) Not necessary if fabric backing is knit.

Pressing

Finger-press only. Pressing with an iron will tarnish the sequins.

Topstitching

Never. Hand picking close to seam can help flatten seam. (See #1 on p. 222.)

Closures

Bias loops made from a coordinating smooth, shiny fabric such as satin lining or silk charmeuse. (See #9 on p. 225.) Hand-picked zippers are suitable for fitted garments. (See #19 on p. 227.)

Hem

Face hems in skirts or dresses with a smooth woven fabric or the sequins will run your hose. (See #18 on p. 231.)

> **Tip** Carry fabric swatches of garments you have made or have in progress. You never know when you will see that perfect shoe or pair of earrings to complete the outfit. Shopping with fabric swatches can help you make good accessory purchases.

Shearling

Fabric Fact

Shearling is a lambskin that has been tanned without removing the wool. It has a suede surface on one side and a clipped fur surface on the other. Usually the suede side is worn outward. Real and faux shearling fabrics are available. Real shearling breathes, faux shearling does not, but the cost difference is significant. Real shearling skins come in different weights and are about 5 ft. square. (See formula on p. 96 to calculate how many square feet of shearling you will need.) Lightweight skins are preferable since they are more comfortable to wear and easier to work with. Real shearling is more flexible than faux shearling. The fur on the curly clipped side can be long or short. For tips on working with real shearling, see the facing page.

Suitable For

Jackets and vests. Princess seaming provides shaping since the fabric has no drape. Also popular for slippers and gloves.

Sewing Tips

Use single fabric thickness for collars and cuffs. Reduce ease in sleeve caps, since fabric does not ease well. Never backstitch. Machine-knot on the threads to conceal seams. Sew facings to garment sueded sides together, with $7/8$-in. seam. Trim seam allowance to $1/4$ in. so that it has the same finish as the seams. Trim width of facing to $3/4$ in. Cut out fabric between dart lines. With wrong sides together, zigzag dart sides together. (See #28 on p. 219.)

> ✂ **Tip** **Always buy one extra button for your project. Sew it on the inside side seam and you will never have to search for a lost button.**

WORKING WITH SHEARLING

Preshrink

Not necessary.

Layout

Place shearling single thickness with suede side up. "With nap" layout, hold pieces in place with fabric weights. Outline shape of pieces with Pilot Frixion erasable ink pen. Remove pattern pieces before cutting.

Marking

Pilot Frixion erasable ink pen or ¼-in. clips in seam allowance.

Cutting

Mark ¼ in. inside of pattern cutting line, which will be your cutting line for overlap seams on faux shearling. Small sharp scissors, cutting through the skin only, not the fur. Cut one size bigger if the pattern is very fitted and not designed for shearling.

Interfacing

Not needed; fabric has enough body on its own.

Thread

Polyester.

Needle

90/14 NTW for machine sewing, glover's needle for hand sewing.

Stitch Length

3.0 mm. Reduce pressure on presser foot if possible.

Presser Foot

Teflon.

Seam Finish

Lapped seams are the least bulky and show off the curly side at seam joints. Since you cut ¼ in. off all seam allowances, overlap one piece over the other, aligning the seam lines. Hold fabric layers together with oversize fabric clips. Topstitch along the seam line through both layers. (See #38 on p. 221.)

Pressing

On suede side only, use press cloth and dry iron. Flatten seam joints and detail edges by pounding with rubber mallet.

Topstitching

Topstitch ¼ in. from edge, or hand-lace, using an upholstery needle and yarn. (See #10 on p. 223.)

Closures

Snaps, toggles, faced buttonhole openings, exposed zippers. (See #6 on p. 224, #11 on p. 225, #19 on p. 227.)

Hem

Turn under hem allowance. Sew ½ in. from hem edge. Trim off hem fold so hem edges look like a seam with fur edge showing.

Shirting

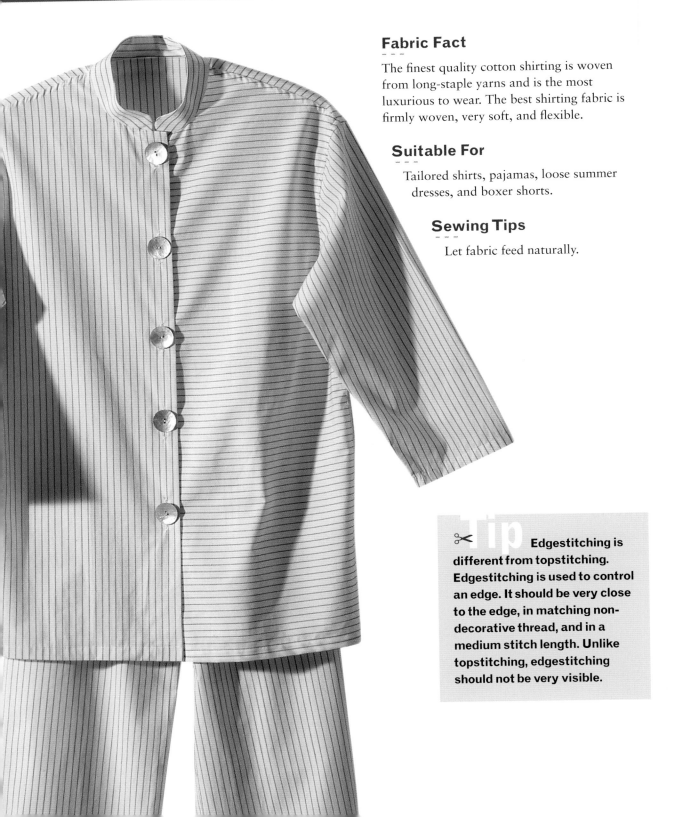

Fabric Fact

The finest quality cotton shirting is woven from long-staple yarns and is the most luxurious to wear. The best shirting fabric is firmly woven, very soft, and flexible.

Suitable For

Tailored shirts, pajamas, loose summer dresses, and boxer shorts.

Sewing Tips

Let fabric feed naturally.

> ✂ **Tip** Edgestitching is different from topstitching. Edgestitching is used to control an edge. It should be very close to the edge, in matching non-decorative thread, and in a medium stitch length. Unlike topstitching, edgestitching should not be very visible.

WORKING WITH SHIRTING

Preshrink

Serge crossgrain ends to prevent excess raveling. Machine-wash in warm water and machine-dry on regular temperature. Remove while slightly damp. Iron dry, stretching slightly in lengthwise direction only to prevent puckered seams.

Layout

"Without nap" layout, double thickness.

Marking

Pilot Frixion erasable ink pen, tracing wheel, Clover Chaco Liner.

Cutting

Rotary cutter or scissors.

Interfacing

Sewers' Dream or Suitmaker for very crisp collar and cuffs. Interface both layers of collar and cuffs.

Thread

Good-quality cotton.

Needle

70/10 H, HJ.

Stitch Length

2.5 mm straight stitch for seams, 1.8 mm for collar points and curves.

Presser Foot

Standard or flat fell.

Seam Finish

Flat fell or French. (See #9 on p. 216, #40 on p. 221.)

Pressing

Steam iron on cotton setting. For crisp details, use spray starch.

Topstitching

Topstitch close to the edge using a 70/10 HJ needle and topstitching foot. (See #3 on p. 222.)

Closures

For buttonholes, use 70/10 HJ needle with extra-fine thread. (See #1 on p. 224.) Snaps. (See #11 on p. 225.)

Hem

¼-in. double-fold hem with topstitching. Easestitch curves. (See #8 and #10 on p. 229.)

Fabric Fact

China silk is a lightweight plain weave silk. Its breathability makes it a good choice for linings. China silk is unsuitable for garments because it wrinkles too much and is too lightweight.

Suitable For

Linings only; too thin for garments.

Sewing Tips

Hold on to top and bottom threads as you begin seam. Pull fabric taut from front and back as you sew.

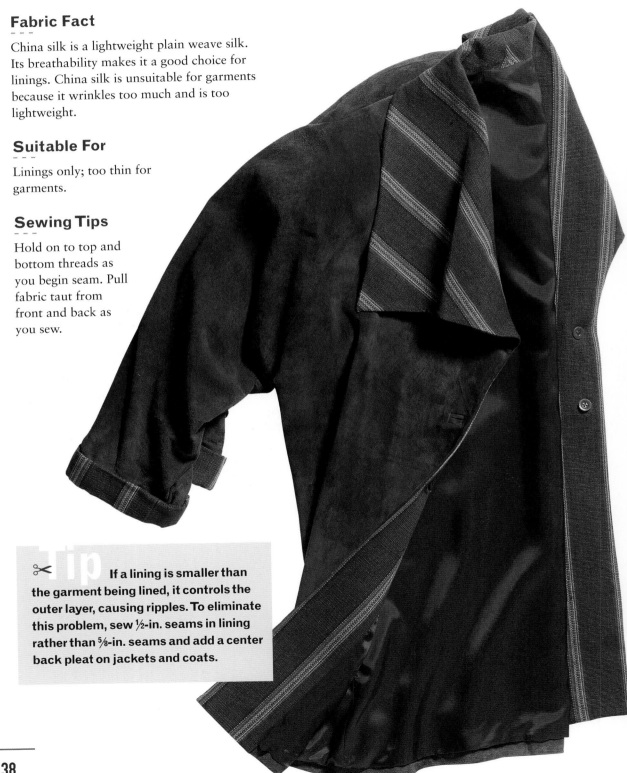

Tip If a lining is smaller than the garment being lined, it controls the outer layer, causing ripples. To eliminate this problem, sew ½-in. seams in lining rather than ⅝-in. seams and add a center back pleat on jackets and coats.

WORKING WITH CHINA SILK

Preshrink

Hand-wash in shampoo, then air-dry. Press while damp.

Layout

"Without nap" layout, double thickness.

Marking

Tracing paper, Pilot Frixion erasable ink pen, Clover white pen for dark colors.

Cutting

Rotary cutter or sharp scissors.

Interfacing

None.

Thread

Fine machine embroidery, such as Seralene, a finer thread, in good-quality cotton, polyester, or silk.

Needle

65/9 HJ or HM, 70/10 HJ or HM.

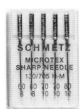
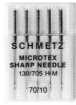

Tip

Wash-away fabric markers may "bleed" into fabric. These are great products, but keep these guidelines in mind:

- **Always test first to see if the marks are easily removed.**
- **Remove marks with clear, cool water first, then wash in detergent.**
- **Do not press over ink, as the heat from the iron may set the marks permanently.**
- **"Green" liquid detergents such as Palmolive® may also set the ink permanently.**

Stitch Length

2.0 mm.

Presser Foot

Straight stitch foot and throat plate. Or use a satin stitch presser foot and throat plate and switch needle to far left position for support on all three sides.

Seam Finish

Pinked. None if lining is fully enclosed. (See #2 on p. 216.)

Pressing

Dry iron on silk setting. Press seams as sewn before pressing open.

Topstitching

None.

Closures

None.

Hem

Double-fold ½-in. hem, then machine-stitch. (See #10 on p. 229.)

Silk Dupioni

Fabric Fact

Silk dupioni, a crisp, natural fabric with irregular slubs in the yarn, is slightly rougher and thicker than Thai silk but not as rough as silk tussah. The irregular slubs in this fabric differentiate it from silk shantung.

Suitable For

Narrow or tailored flat pants, jackets, blouses, fitted dresses, straight skirts, or vests.

Sewing Tips

Hold top and bottom threads when starting seam. Sew tautly, pulling the fabric equally from front and back. Avoid static cling by lining silk garments with Ambiance Bemberg rayon lining or drapery silk.

Tip

Did you know that one section of thread moves back and forth through the needle and fabric 42 times before becoming a stitch? All the more reason to use high-quality thread and to change needles frequently.

WORKING WITH SILK DUPIONI

Preshrink

If you plan to dry-clean the completed garment, hold a steam iron ½ in. above surface. This fabric can be machine-washed on gentle cycle in warm water and machine-dried on the permanent press cycle. Machine washing and drying results in a softer, considerably dulled sheen and a loss of iridescence, if there was any.

Layout

"With nap" layout, double thickness.

Marking

Clover Chaco Liner or Pilot Frixion erasable ink pen.

Cutting

Rotary cutter or scissors.

Interfacing

Since this fabric is prone to wrinkling, I suggest underlining flat-front pants and straight skirts with silk organza. Another option is to underline each garment piece with Sewers' Dream or Fusi-Knit. Fusing flattens the fabric slightly, and the sheen will show up any place where fusing is not complete. I think the 70% reduction in wrinkles that fusing affords is worth the slight change in the fabric. Purists may differ. However, fusing eliminates the fabric's ability to breathe, which can be a problem if you live in a warm climate.

Thread

Good-quality cotton or polyester. If you can't find an exact color match in thread for your fabric, choose a shade darker. Thread always appears lighter after it is sewn.

Needle

70/10 HM or HJ.

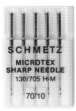

Stitch Length

2.5 mm.

Presser Foot

Standard.

Seam Finish

No seam finish if lined. If not lined, serged or traditional flat fell and pressed open. (See #3 and #9 on p. 216.)

Pressing

Dry iron on silk setting. Steam will cause water spots.

Topstitching

Topstitch close to edge with the help of edge foot or edge-joining foot. (See #3 on p. 222.)

Closures

For buttonholes, use 70/10 HJ needle, fine machine embroidery or silk thread to reduce bulk, and Solvy between presser foot and fabric. Loosen top tension slightly. (See #1 on p. 224.) Frog closures. (See #12 on p. 225.)

Hem

Serge or Hong King finish raw edge. Hand-stitch. (See #13 on p. 230.)

Silk Gazar

Fabric Fact

Silk gazar is perhaps the crispest silk available. Fabric is medium weight with a very refined appearance.

Suitable For

Choose a style with a silhouette that does not rely on fabric drape. Silk gazar is suitable for crisp blouses and loose evening coats. It also makes a good firm interfacing for jackets and stand-up collars.

Sewing Tips

Hold top and bottom threads when you begin seam. Do not backstitch. Sewing tautly prevents puckered seams.

Tip To sew a collar, hand-walk the machine two diagonal stitches at the points of the collar. Reduce the stitch length for ¼ in. before and after the point so that diagonal clipping can be done close to the point.

WORKING WITH SILK GAZAR

Preshrink

Hold steam iron ½ in. above surface. Dry-clean completed garment. Fabric softens considerably if laundered.

Layout

"With nap" layout, double thickness.

Marking

Pilot Frixion erasable ink pen, Clover Chaco Liner, tailor tacks. No waxed chalk as it leaves stains.

Cutting

Rotary cutter or scissors. Substitute second set of fronts for facing to eliminate show-through at edge of facing.

Interfacing

Self-fabric.

Thread

Fine machine-embroidery cotton or silk.

Needle

60/8 or 65/9 HM or HJ.

✂ **Tip** When making a buttonhole, don't help the machine by pulling this way or that. This throws the timing off and causes uneven spacing.

Stitch Length

2.0 mm.

Presser Foot

Use straight stitch foot and single-hole throat plate. Or use satin stitch foot and throat plate and switch needle to far left position for support on three sides.

Seam Finish

Very narrow serger French seam for blouses, flat fell on outerwear. (See #9 on p. 216, #10 on p. 217.)

Pressing

Make sure iron is very clean of residue. Avoid water spots by using a dry iron on silk setting and covering area to be pressed with a press cloth if your iron leaks.

Topstitching

Consider one row of topstitching in shiny rayon very close to fabric edge. Use edge topstitching for accuracy. A topstitching foot helps here. (See #3 on p. 222.)

Closures

For buttonholes, use 70/10 HJ needle and fine machine embroidery thread. Button loops, snaps, and invisible zipper also work. (See #1 on p. 224, #9 and #11 on p. 225, #19 on p. 227.)

Hem

Double-fold hem ¼ in. wide, then machine- or hand-stitch. For ruffles, press ½-in. fold to wrong side. Into the fold slide 20-lb. test, regular fishing line, or 60-lb. test big-game fishing line. Zigzag over fold (0.75 mm wide, 3.0 mm long). Trim raw edge of fold very close to stitching. Satin-stitch edge (1.0 mm wide, 0.5 mm long). (See #10 on p. 229, #19 on p. 231.)

Silk Noil

Fabric Fact

This fabric, sometimes referred to as raw silk, has a dull finish and ravels excessively. It is made from the short waste fibers of silk. It takes dyes beautifully, so the colors are terrific, and it is reasonably priced. Because it is made of waste fibers, the fabric does not look "new" for more than a season.

Suitable For

Full pants, full skirts, big shirts, loose dresses, unstructured loose jackets, and vests if fully interfaced.

Sewing Tips

Easy to sew.

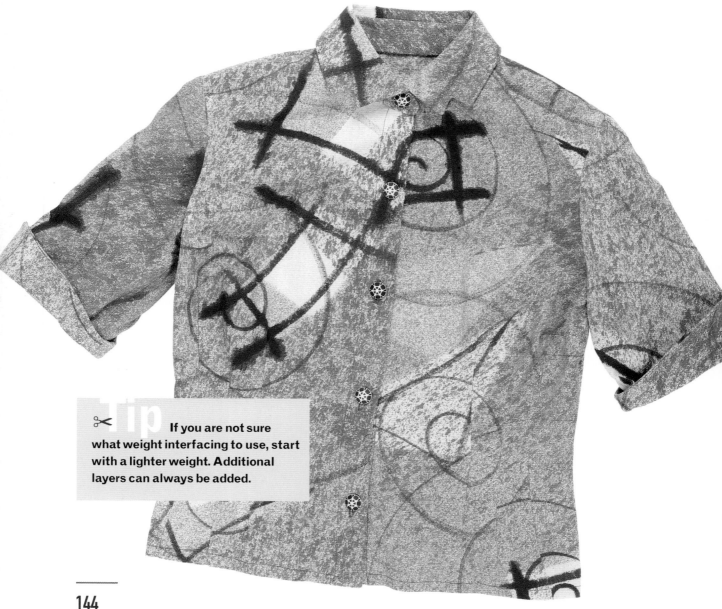

Tip ✂ **If you are not sure what weight interfacing to use, start with a lighter weight. Additional layers can always be added.**

WORKING WITH SILK NOIL

Preshrink

Dark colors fade if washed, but loss of color can be reduced by adding ¼ cup of Epsom salt or Retayne, which sets color, to a small machine load. For light colors, machine-wash in warm water and machine-dry on delicate cycle. Never bleach silk noil, or it will turn yellow.

Layout

"Without nap" layout, double thickness.

Marking

Clover Chaco Liner or Pilot Frixion erasable ink pen.

Cutting

Rotary cutter or scissors.

Interfacing

Sewers' Dream or Fusi-Knit.

Thread

Good-quality cotton or polyester.

Needle

80/12 H.

Stitch Length

2.5 mm straight stitch.

Presser Foot

Standard.

Seam Finish

Flat fell. (See #9 on p. 216.)

Pressing

Medium-high steam iron or dry iron if fabric is not preshrunk. Steam can cause water spots if silk is not prewashed.

Tip

Silk organza makes a great press cloth. You can see through it, it can withstand high heat, and it can be machine-washed and -dried.

Topstitching

Close to edge with help of topstitching foot. (See #3 on p. 222.)

Closures

For buttonholes, use 70/10 HJ needle and fine machine-embroidery thread to reduce bulk. (See #1 on p. 224.) Self-fabric makes attractive button loops. Snaps. (See #9 and #11 on p. 225.)

Hem

Serge raw edge. Coverlock, hand-stitch, or topstitch with double needle. (See #1 and #4 on p. 228.)

Silk Organza

Fabric Fact

Organza is a thin, stiff, and somewhat transparent fabric. While it is available in polyester and rayon, silk organza is far superior because you will not have to deal with puckering seams.

Suitable For

Lightweight silk organza makes the best interfacing and underlining for anything in silk, since it is crisp without being bulky. It has the ability to give support and resists wrinkles. Heavyweight silk organza can work in a blouse. Since this fabric definitely does not drape, choose a style with a pleasing silhouette that doesn't rely on fabric drape. Silk organza makes a great press cloth. It can withstand high heat, you can see through it, and you can throw it in the washing machine and the dryer.

Sewing Tips

Sewing tautly prevents puckered seams. Hold top and bottom threads when you begin seam. Don't backstitch— the doubled-up threads are too visible.

Tip

Invisible thread is terrific for attaching trim and ribbons without visible stitching. Use invisible thread on the top of the machine only with a Metafil® HE needle and regular thread on the bottom. To take out the kinks in this thread, which causes thread breakage, tape a 2-in.-long section of a drinking straw to the top of the machine, and send the thread through the straw as it comes off the spool.

WORKING WITH SILK ORGANZA

Preshrink

Since machine washing and machine drying soften organza slightly, preshrink only if you want to change the hand. Fabric does not shrink, so you can use it as is. Dry-clean finished garment.

Layout

"Without nap" layout, double thickness, using either side of fabric. To be consistent, mark an X on whatever you decide to be the wrong side of fabric.

Marking

Clover Chaco Liner or Pilot Frixion erasable ink pen.

Cutting

Rotary cutter or scissors. Eliminate front facings and substitute second set of fronts to eliminate show-through at edge of facing.

Interfacing

Self-fabric.

Thread

Fine cotton machine embroidery or fine silk machine embroidery.

Needle

60/8 or 65/9 HM or HJ.

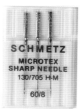

Stitch Length

2.0 mm.

Presser Foot

Straight stitch foot and single-hole throat plate. Or use satin stitch foot with standard plate. Switch needle to the far left position for support on three sides.

Seam Finish

Very narrow traditional French seams without serging. (See #40 on p. 221.)

Pressing

Dry iron on silk setting. Make sure iron is very clean of residue. Avoid water spots.

Topstitching

Consider shiny rayon thread very close to fabric edge. Use topstitching foot for accuracy. (See #3 on p. 222.)

Closures

For buttonholes, use 70/10 HJ needle and fine machine embroidery thread to reduce bulk. Can also use button loops. (See #1 on p. 224, #9 on p. 225.)

Hem

Double-fold hem ¼ in. wide, then machine- or hand-stitch. For ruffles, follow these steps: (1) Press a ½-in. fold. (2) Onto the fold align 20-lb. test regular fishing line or 60-lb. test big-game fishing line. (3) Zigzag over fold with monofilament and 2.5 mm wide, 1.5 mm long stitch. (4) Trim fold very close to stitching. (5) Satin stitch edge with 2.5 mm wide, 0.3 mm long stitch. (See #10 on p. 229, #19 on p. 231.)

Silk, Sandwashed

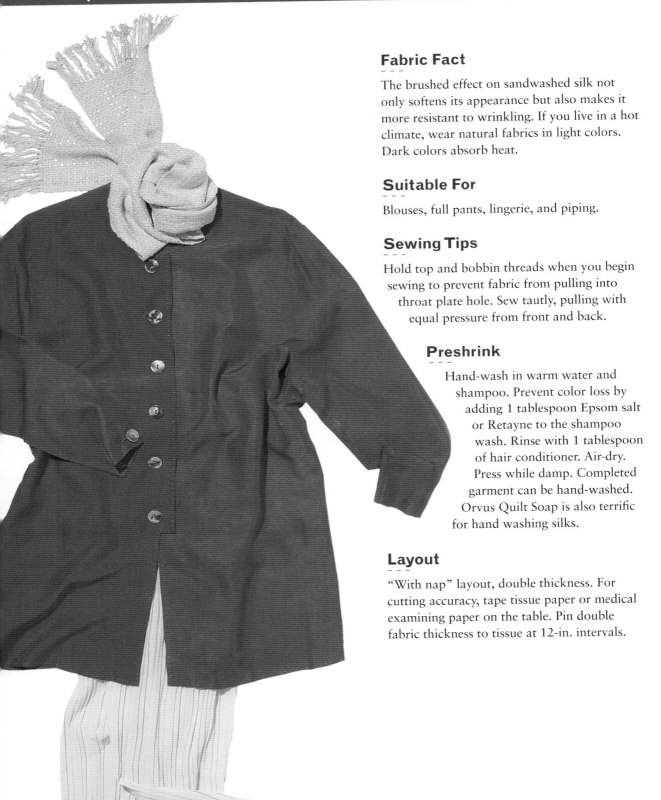

Fabric Fact

The brushed effect on sandwashed silk not only softens its appearance but also makes it more resistant to wrinkling. If you live in a hot climate, wear natural fabrics in light colors. Dark colors absorb heat.

Suitable For

Blouses, full pants, lingerie, and piping.

Sewing Tips

Hold top and bobbin threads when you begin sewing to prevent fabric from pulling into throat plate hole. Sew tautly, pulling with equal pressure from front and back.

Preshrink

Hand-wash in warm water and shampoo. Prevent color loss by adding 1 tablespoon Epsom salt or Retayne to the shampoo wash. Rinse with 1 tablespoon of hair conditioner. Air-dry. Press while damp. Completed garment can be hand-washed. Orvus Quilt Soap is also terrific for hand washing silks.

Layout

"With nap" layout, double thickness. For cutting accuracy, tape tissue paper or medical examining paper on the table. Pin double fabric thickness to tissue at 12-in. intervals.

WORKING WITH SANDWASHED SILK

Marking

Clover Chaco Liner or Pilot Frixion erasable ink pen.

Cutting

Pin pattern through fabric and tissue layers. Keep pins in seam allowances. Cut through all layers.

Interfacing

Silk organza for crispness, silk georgette for drape.

Thread

Good-quality cotton thread gives the best stitch without puckers. Use fine machine embroidery for 2-ply silk and regular-weight thread for 3- or 4-ply silk.

Needle

70/10 HM for 2-ply, 80/12 HJ for 3- or 4-ply. 3- and 4-ply silks are heavier than 2-ply and can be treated less delicately when sewing.

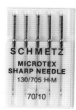 

Stitch Length

2.5 mm straight stitch.

Presser Foot

Straight stitch foot and single-hole throat plate. Or use satin stitch foot and throat plate and switch needle to far left position for support on three sides. Loosen top tension and bobbin tension one-eighth to one-quarter turn.

Seam Finish

Flat fell or French seam. (See #9 on p. 216, #10 on p. 217, #40 on p. 221.)

Pressing

Dry iron on silk setting. Steam can cause water spots.

Topstitching

Topstitch close to sewn edge with fine thread or hand-pick with shiny rayon thread. (See #1 and #3 on p. 222.)

Closures

For buttonholes, use a 70/10 HJ needle with fine machine-embroidery thread to reduce bulk. (See #1 on p. 224.)

✂ **Tip**

When making covered buttons, avoid shiny show-through by interfacing the button fabric before you begin.

Hem

Options: (1) Use the rolled baby hem. Staystitch ½ in. from cut edge. Press ½-in. hem allowance under with staystitching along fold. Trim away fold under hem close to the stitching line. Enclosing the raw edge, roll hem under ⅛ in. to ¼ in. Hand- or machine-stitch into position. (2) Thread bobbin with fusible thread and fine thread on top. With wrong side of fabric against feed dogs, staystitch along hemline. Press to the wrong side to dissolve fusible thread and form sharp crease. Trim hem allowance to ⅛ in. Roll again, enclosing raw edge. Hand- or machine-sew with fine thread. (See #16 and #17 on p. 230.) (3) Serged rolled hem. Run a line of staystitching at ½ in. with finger behind presser foot to prevent fabric from stretching. When serging, remove right needle, and let rolled hem encase staystitching. The differential feed set at 0.7 mm helps here. Use a fine serger thread. (4) Double-fold ¼-in. hem. Hand- or machine-stitch. (See #10 on p. 229.)

Silk Shantung

Fabric Fact

Silk shantung is available in beautiful colors and has a crisp finish with a sheen. It has slubs in the weave like silk dupioni, but it is a bit more refined.

Suitable For

Narrow or tailored pants, jackets, fitted dresses, straight skirts, vests, and special-occasion dresses with full skirts.

Sewing Tips

Hold fabric taut, pulling it equally from front and back.

> ✂ **Tip** Funky buttonholes? Make certain you are using the right presser foot. The buttonhole foot has two long grooves on the bottom, which keeps the rows exactly parallel.

WORKING WITH SILK SHANTUNG

Preshrink

Hold steam iron ½ in. above surface. Dry-clean completed garment when necessary. Fabric will lose luster and body if laundered.

Layout

"With nap" layout, double thickness.

Marking

Pilot Frixion erasable ink pen or Clover white pen for dark colors.

Cutting

Rotary cutter or scissors.

Interfacing

Since this fabric is prone to wrinkling on straight skirts and pants, underline with silk organza. An alternative is to underline each garment piece with Sewers' Dream or Fusi-Knit. Fusing flattens the fabric slightly, and the shine will show up any place where fusing is not complete. An Elnapress® will give the most permanent fuse. I think the 70% reduction of wrinkles that fusing affords is worth the slight change in fabric. Purists may differ. Fusing eliminates the fabric's ability to breathe, however, which can be a problem if you live in a warm climate.

Thread

Good-quality cotton or polyester.

Needle

70/10 HM or 70/10 HJ.

Stitch Length

2.5 mm.

Presser Foot

Standard.

Seam Finish

Flat fell, sewn and serged separately, sewn and bound separately with Hong Kong finish, or pinked. (See #3 and #9 on p. 216, #16 on p. 218.)

Pressing

Dry iron on silk setting. Steam can cause water spots.

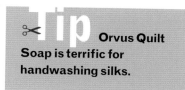

Tip Orvus Quilt Soap is terrific for handwashing silks.

Topstitching

Hand-pick or topstitch ¼ in. from edge using a topstitching foot. (See #1 on p. 222, #10 on p. 223.)

Closures

For buttonholes, use 70/10 HJ needle, fine machine embroidery thread to reduce bulk, and Solvy under presser foot. Loosen top tension slightly. (See #1 on p. 224.) Snaps, invisible zipper. (See #11 on p. 225, #19 on p. 227.)

Hem

Serge or Hong Kong finish. Hand-stitch. (See #4 on p. 228, #13 on p. 230.) Running your thread through beeswax will make a hem stitch too visible. To keep thread from tangling without making it bulky, run your thread through Thread Heaven.

Silk, Thai

Fabric Fact

Thai silk is similar to silk dupion except that it is finer and far less bulky. Interesting sculptural effects are created by shadows when the fabric is folded or crunched. This is especially true of the iridescent colors.

Suitable For

Evening, bridal, and period costumes and wherever a lot of fabric is needed without adding bulk, such as bouffant skirts or sleeves. Makes crisp flat-front pants and tailored blouses. Also makes beautiful home-dec pillows, duvet covers, and window treatments.

Sewing Tips

Taut sewing.

Tip **Do not lift fabric off the table when cutting. Place one hand on the fabric and glide the shears along the cutting surface with the opposite hand.**

WORKING WITH THAI SILK

Preshrink

Hold steam iron ½ in. above surface. Dry-clean completed garment.

Layout

"With nap" layout, slubs going down, double thickness.

Marking

Pilot Frixion erasable ink pen or snips in seam allowances.

Cutting

Rotary cutter or scissors.

Interfacing

Since this fabric is prone to wrinkling, I suggest underlining straight skirts, pants, and straight dresses with silk organza. An alternative is to underline each garment piece with Sewers' Dream or Fusi-Knit. Fusing flattens the fabric slightly, and the shine will show up any place where fusing is not complete. An Elnapress works well here. I think the 70% reduction in wrinkles that fusing affords is worth the slight change in the fabric. Purists may differ. Fusing eliminates the fabric's ability to breathe, however, which can be a problem if you live in a warm climate. Underlining with silk organza allows the fabric to breathe and makes it cooler to wear. For a less crisp underlining, use cotton batiste or lawn.

Thread

Good-quality cotton or polyester.

Needle

70/10 HJ or HM.

Stitch Length

2.5 mm.

Presser Foot

Single-hole foot and throat plate or use standard foot and plate and switch needle to far left position for support on three sides.

Seam Finish

Flat fell, sewn and serged separately, sewn and bound separately with Hong Kong finish, or pinked. (See #2, #3, and #9 on p. 216, #16 on p. 218.)

Pressing

Dry iron on silk setting. Steam can cause water spots.

Topstitching

Topstitch close to edge or ¼ in. from edge. (See #3 on p. 222, #10 on p. 223.) Edge stitching foot helps here.

Closures

For buttonholes, use 70/10 HJ needle, fine machine-embroidery thread to reduce bulk, and Solvy under presser foot. Loosen top tension slightly. (See #1 on p. 224.)

Hem

Serge or Hong Kong finish. Hand-stitch. (See #4 on p. 228, #13 on p. 230.)

Silk Tussah

Fabric Fact

Silk tussah is made from uncultivated silkworms; the filaments are coarse and uneven, resulting in a somewhat rough weave with a nubby appearance. Tussah from India is woven from larger threads and is not nearly as refined or drapey as tussah from China. Tussah is not strong and tends to "pill" in areas of wear.

Suitable For

Narrow or tailored pants, jackets, straight skirts, vests, and structured garments where little or no drape is required.

Sewing Tips

Let fabric feed naturally.

> **Tip**
>
> ✂ **Armo Weft interfacing under wools, cottons, linens, and heavier-weight silks will not need additional stabilizer for embroidery.**

WORKING WITH SILK TUSSAH

Preshrink

Not necessary. Completed garment must be dry-cleaned.

Layout

"With nap" layout, slubs going down, double thickness. Fabric has some drapability if cut on the crossgrain, making it a good choice for skirts or pants.

Marking

Pilot Frixion erasable ink pen or snips in seam allowance.

Cutting

Rotary cutter or scissors.

Interfacing

Use sew-in interfacing if you don't want to flatten the fabric. Suitmaker 601 or Armo Weft, a fusible, flattens the weave very slightly but is still quite attractive and could be used to stabilize the fabric for a jacket or vest.

Thread

Good-quality cotton or polyester.

Needle

70/10 H, 70/10 HJ, or 70/10 HM.

Stitch Length

2.5 mm.

Presser Foot

Standard.

Seam Finish

Flat fell, sewn and serged separately, or sewn and bound separately with Hong Kong finish. (See #3 and #9 on p. 216, #16 on p. 218.)

Pressing

Dry iron on silk setting. Steam can cause water spots.

Topstitching

Close to edge or ¼ in. from edge. (See #3 on p. 222, #10 on p. 223.) Topstitch foot.

Closures

For buttonholes, use 70/10 HJ needle, fine machine embroidery thread to reduce bulk, and Solvy between presser foot and fabric. Loosen top tension slightly. (See #1 on p. 224.) Snaps, invisible zipper. (See #11 on p. 225, #19 on p. 227.)

Hem

Turn up 1½-in. hem. Serge or bind raw edge with Hong Kong finish in lining weight. Hand-stitch. (See #4 on p. 228, #13 on p. 230.)

Silk Tweed

Fabric Fact

If you have time to sew only one jacket, make it a silk tweed. Choose a tweed that coordinates with the dominant colors in your wardrobe, and you'll wear it all the time, with everything.

Suitable For

Jackets and vests. Not suitable for straight skirts or pants because it snags too easily or for full pants because it is too bulky.

WORKING WITH SILK TWEED

Sewing Tips

Silk tweed fabric makes a beautiful warm-weather jacket if the fabric is underlined with Sewers' Dream or Fusi-Knit. Left to its own devices, silk tweed will bag out at the elbows, pockets, and seat. It is also prone to pulled threads, but fused underlining helps that. Let fabric feed naturally.

Preshrink

Hold steam iron ½ in. above surface. Dry-clean completed garment.

Layout

"Without nap" layout, double thickness.

Marking

Safety pins.

Cutting

Rotary cutter or scissors. Handle gently to prevent raveling.

Interfacing

Prevent fabric snags and excess raveling by block-fusing each garment piece with Sewers' Dream or Fusi-Knit before cutting.

Thread

Good-quality cotton or polyester.

Needle

80/12 H.

Stitch Length

2.0 mm straight stitch.

Presser Foot

Standard.

Seam Finish

Serge pieces separately right after fusing. Bind seams with Hong Kong finish or flat-fell seams. (See #9 on p. 216, #16 on p. 218.)

Pressing

Steam iron on a silk setting.

Topstitching

Topstitch close to edge with regular thread or ¼ in. from sewn edge with buttonhole twist or shiny rayon thread using an N needle. Edge foot or edge-joining foot helps here. (See #3 on p. 222, #10 on p. 223.)

Closures

Since machine buttonholes do not wear well in this fabric, consider other options such as bound buttonholes in linen, faced buttonholes, button opening in a seam, or button loops (See #6 on p. 224, #8, #9, and #10 on p. 225.) Snaps aren't suitable; they will work their way out of the loose weave.

Hem

Finish hem edge with Hong Kong finish. Hand-hem. (See #13 on p. 230.)

Tip ✂ **Serger needles do not last forever. Experts suggest changing serger needles after eight hours of serger use to eliminate broken threads, puckered seams, and skipped stitches. For fragile fabrics, use the same needles in your serger as in your conventional machine.**

Slinky Knit

Fabric Fact

This fabric drapes extremely well and never wrinkles, making it great for traveling. There are different grades of slinky knit. The heavier weight, an acetate-Lycra blend, gives the best performance and shrinks the least. The poly-Lycra slinky knit is too thin and wrinkles a lot. This fabric snags easily. Make sure nails and cuticles are smooth and hands are free of lotion, which will transfer as grease spots to the fabric.

Suitable For

Simple styles with few pattern pieces: wrap, A-line, or gored skirts, and full dresses. Fabric has wonderful drape but needs to be at least 4 in. bigger than the body or it looks skimpy and is too figure revealing. Between 4 in. and 10 in. of ease is recommended.

Sewing Tips

Use pins in seam allowances only. To start seam, start sewing for 1 in. on Solvy positioned between feed dog and fabric. Hold onto threads when you begin. As an alternative to facings, trim neckline seam allowance to ⅜ in. Serge ¼-in.-wide clear elastic to the wrong side of neckline raw edge. Turn under ⅜ in. Topstitch with a double-needle ZWI stretch 4.0 mm width from the right side using hand wrapped woolly nylon in bobbin. Prevent shoulder, armhole, crotch, and neckline seams from stretching by sewing through ¼-in.-wide clear elastic. Ease front to back to eliminate dust in bust.

Preshrink

Buy an additional ¼ yd. for every 2 yd. purchased to allow for fabric shrinkage. Black slinky knit can be machine-washed and machine-dried without graying out. Hand-wash or machine-wash in warm water on gentle cycle. Machine-dry on cool setting or dry flat. Fold fabric flat to store; do not hang—the fabric will stretch.

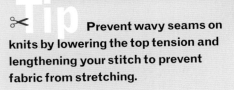

Tip ✂ **Prevent wavy seams on knits by lowering the top tension and lengthening your stitch to prevent fabric from stretching.**

WORKING WITH SLINKY KNIT

Layout

"With nap" layout, double thickness. Either shiny or dull side of fabric can be used as right side. Cover surface with tissue paper unless you are using the rotary cutter. Slinky knit lengthens. Shorten sleeves on pattern 1 in. before cutting. Shorten skirts, pants, and dresses by 2 in. and raise bust darts ¾ in. Support so that fabric does not stretch by hanging off table. Use new pins in seam allowances only or use pattern weights.

Marking

Marking chalk, Pilot Frixion erasable ink pen, tailor tacks. No spoke tracing wheels as they will cause snags and runs.

Cutting

Rotary cutter is the most accurate. For accuracy with scissors, pin double-thickness fabric to tissue paper. Cut fabric and tissue paper as one.

Interfacing

Fusi-Knit. Stabilize shoulder, crotch, neckline, darts, and long vertical seams with ¼-in. clear elastic to prevent seam sag.

Thread

Good-quality polyester.

Needle

75/11 HS.

Stitch Length

Small zigzag (0.5 mm width, 2.5 mm length).

Presser Foot

Walking. Reduce pressure on foot. Loosen top tension slightly.

Seam Finish

Sew seams with 4-thread serger, with woolly nylon on both loopers. Use differential feed if you have it. If garment is close-fitting, sew seam initially with small zigzag, then serge seams together with 3-thread serger right next to it. (See #5 on p. 216, #20 on p. 218.)

Pressing

Medium-temperature iron with lots of steam.

Topstitching

Not successful because of fabric stretch. Consider substituting hand picking close to the edge. (See #1 on p. 222.)

Closures

Invisible zippers work well. Consider buttonhole alternatives such as button loops and snaps. Because this fabric is heavy, stronger elastic is needed for elasticized waists. Ban-Roll® Original elastic works well. Cut 5 in. smaller than waist measurement. (See #9 and #11 on p. 225, #19 on p. 227.)

Hem

Allow finished garment to hang for 24 hours before marking hem since it will lengthen 1 in. to 2 in. Options: (1) Stabilize hem allowance with Lite Steam-A-Seam 2 to prevent stretching. Use Teflon or walking foot for double-needle topstitching. Use double-needle ZWI stretch with hand-wrapped woolly nylon on bobbin. Bypass guide in bobbin case and loosen upper tension slightly. (See #1 and #3 on p. 228.) (2) Hem with a cover hem stitch with differential feed. (See #5 on p. 228.)

Stretch Mesh

Fabric Fact

Stretch mesh is a semi-sheer knit with great recovery. It is available in nylon and polyester in various weights. The heavier mesh is of better quality.

Suitable For

Sheer T-shirts, slips, multilayered skirts, contrast sleeves, binding strips on neck and armholes.

Sewing Tips

Stabilize neck and shoulders with strips from self-fabric, cut to size from the pattern piece. I often make T-shirts with double-stretch mesh fronts and backs for more opaqueness, leaving the sleeves a single layer. If your stretch mesh is a print, make the second layer in a solid to give more clarity to the print.

WORKING WITH STRETCH MESH

Preshrink

Not necessary.

Layout

Since this fabric is very wide, it can be cut single or double, but be sure the greatest stretch is going around the body. Even out crossgrain edges with a T-square.

Marking

Pilot Frixion erasable ink pen or Clover Chaco Liner.

Cutting

Rotary cutter or serrated cutting shears.

Interfacing

None—you can use self-fabric in collar or cuffs.

Thread

Good-quality cotton or polyester.

Needle

75/11 HS.

Stitch Length

Small zigzag (1.0 mm width and 2.5mm length).

Presser Foot

Standard. If fabric is stretching as you sew, switch to a Teflon foot.

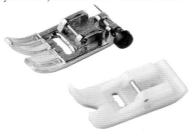

Seam Finish

Small zigzag stitch followed by a 3-thread serger stitch. Bind necklines and armholes with crossgrain strips of self-fabric. (See #20 on p. 218.)

Pressing

No pressing. The mesh will get hard and melt.

Topstitching

Not recommended since it over-stretches the fabric.

Closures

Sew on snaps, button loops, invisible zipper. (See #9 and #11 on p. 225, #19 on p. 227.) Buttonholes are too heavy for this fabric.

Hem

Ready-to-wear often eliminates hems, but over time the raw edge looks rough and unfinished. A hem can be eliminated by cutting the hem crease on the fold so that the garment piece is double. Another option is to double-fold the hem ¼ in. and hand-stitch, stretching the fabric every fourth stitch and making a knot. The last option is to fold up a 1-in. hem. Hold it in place with double-sided tape such as Wonder Tape. Pinch the fabric together at the top of the hem allowance so that the raw edge of the fabric is enclosed. (See #5 on p. 228.) Double needle stitch or coverlock stitch ¼ in. from the fold.

Tip To prevent coverlock stitches from coming out over time, you need to pull the top thread to the bottom and tie the threads in a double knot at the end of the stitching. A dot of glue seals the knot.

Stretch Cotton & Stretch Wovens

Fabric Fact

Lycra, the trade name for spandex, is a man-made elastic fiber combined with wool, linen, denim, microfiber, or silk to produce wovens with a 5% to 10% stretch factor in width and sometimes in length. These Lycra blends look exactly like their 100% natural fiber counterparts except that they have stretch.

Suitable For

Stretch wovens allow close fit without sacrificing comfort. Use any fitted pattern where woven fabric is recommended or slight stretch might add to comfort of garment, such as flat-front pants, straight skirts, and fitted jackets. A pattern for knits is not interchangeable with stretch and requires stretch up and down and around the body.

Sewing Tips

Stabilize neckline and shoulders with ¼-in. fusible stabilizer or narrow selvage. Do not stretch fabric as you sew. On horizontal seams, keep finger behind presser foot as when easing, to prevent seams from stretching. Use triple stretch stitch in areas of stress, such as the crotch. (See #6 on p. 216.) If using a regular pattern for a woven, because the fabric has crosswise stretch, you can sew vertical side seam ½ in. deeper, letting the stretch in the fabric provide the ease. Machine-baste deeper seam first. Let fabric feed naturally.

Preshrink

To preshrink linen/Lycra, cotton/Lycra, and microfiber/Lycra, machine-wash and machine-dry on medium temp. Baste crossgrain edges together to prevent stretching during washing. Never bleach any fabric with Lycra. Bleach will discolor fabric and break down fibers. To preshrink silk/Lycra, hand-wash and air-dry.

> ✂ **Tip** Incorrect threading sequence is the cause of thread breakage and tension problems. Before hauling your serger off to the repair shop, rethread using the following sequence: upper looper, lower looper, right needle, and left needle.

WORKING WITH STRETCH COTTON & STRETCH WOVENS

To preshrink wool/Lycra, hold steam iron ½ in. above fabric surface.

Layout

"Without nap" layout except for Lycra blends with shine where "with nap" layout is recommended. Even crossgrain ends with T-square. Use greatest stretch of the fabric around the body, which may mean cutting on the crosswise grain. Place grainline of pattern piece in the non-stretch direction of fabric. Cut facings in opposite direction to stabilize. On Lycra wovens, ease may be reduced in the fitting stage. Be on the safe side by cutting Lycra woven blends as though there is no stretch in the fabric, but fit as though there is.

Marking

Clover Chaco Liner, Pilot Frixion erasable ink pen, tracing paper.

Cutting

Rotary cutter or scissors.

Interfacing

Suitmaker 601.

Thread

Good-quality polyester thread is ideal because it has stretch. Winding the bobbin too fast will stretch thread, resulting in puckered seams.

Needle

For wool/Lycra, linen/Lycra, and cotton/Lycra, use 80/12 H. For microfiber/Lycra, use 70/10 HM. For silk/Lycra, use 70/10 H.

Stitch Length

Small zigzag (0.75 mm width, 2.5 mm length). Finish seams with 3- or 4-thread overlock with woolly nylon in both loopers.

Presser Foot

Standard.

Seam Finish

A genuine flat fell stretches the fabric, resulting in a bumpy appearance. Fake flat-fell seams work best. Sew seam; press seam open; trim front seam allowance to scant ¼ in. Serge finish back seam allowance. Cover front seam with back seam allowance but do not turn under. From right side, topstitch flat ¼ in. (See #27 on p. 219.)

Pressing

Steam iron at medium setting for most fabrics, but no steam on silk.

Topstitching

Topstitch ¼ in. from finished edge. (See #10 on p. 223.) Use topstitching foot.

Closures

For buttonholes, a strip of preshrunk ribbon between the facing and the fashion fabric, loops, snaps, invisible zippers. Stabilize all zipper seam allowances with ½-in.-wide strips of fusible interfacing cut in the non-stretch direction. (See #1 on p. 224, #9 and #11 on p. 225, #19 on p. 227.)

Hem

Topstitched hems will stretch unless they are faced or interfaced. Cut the facing or interfacing in the non-stretch direction around the hemline. Topstitch with double needle. If you prefer a hand hem, stretch thread every fourth stitch and knot. (See #23 on p. 231, #4 on p. 228.)

Suede

Fabric Fact

Suede can be lamb suede, pig suede, deerskin, or chamois. Check drapability. Pig suede skins are larger and less expensive—great to get your feet wet in suede, but some colors make the pig suede stiff. Fishskin is similar to snakeskin but stronger, more supple and without sheen. The fishy smell is removed during the tanning process. Fishskin can make interesting details such as pocket flaps and appliqués. Suede is sold by the square foot, not the yard. To calculate how much yardage to buy, multiply the yardage needed for 45-in.-wide fabric by 11.25, then multiply again by 1.25. This will give you the amount in square feet. Make sure all hides come from the same dye lot. Don't choose hides with holes and imperfections near the middle of the skin.

Suitable For

If skins are very soft and drapey like lamb suede, use for loose shirts, jackets, semi-fitted pants, or loose pants. Pig suede comes in large skins, which can work in some styles, but it is a lot thicker with less drape, so it needs a more fitted skirt or flat-front pant. Pretest pattern because stitches leave permanent holes. Suede makes a handsome trim on woolen or tapestry fabrics. Petersham ribbon between layers of front and facings gives excellent support for buttons on jackets and coats.

Sewing Tips

Use fabric clips to hold seams together, and cross pin only at seam joints. Do not backstitch, which weakens the fabric. Hold onto top and bobbin threads when you start sewing. Since suede stretches a bit with wear, fit lining looser or lining seams will be stressed. Sew lining seam at ⅜ in.

Preshrink

Not necessary. Store rolled up or perfectly flat. Do not wrap in plastic. To care for suede, spot-clean with cornmeal or suede cleaner. Avoid dry cleaning for as long as possible since dry cleaning dries out the natural tannins. Suede is never as supple after dry cleaning.

WORKING WITH SUEDE

Layout

Suede has a nap. The grainline runs along the backbone of the skin. Mark nap on back of skin. Examine skins for flaws and circle on the wrong side. Place skin wrong side up, single thickness. Make extra pattern pieces so that you have a left and right piece for economical cutting. Use pattern weights. Lay pieces in direction of nap from neck to tail. Parallel to backbone grainline is not necessary.

Marking

Pilot Frixion erasable ink pen or pencils. No waxed-based marking chalk as it leaves stains.

Cutting

Rotary cutter or scissors.

Interfacing

Sewer's Dream or Fusi-Knit.

Thread

Polyester only. Tannins will rot cotton thread.

Needle

70/10 HJ for lightweight skins, 90/14 NTW for pig suede, and glover's needle for hand sewing.

Stitch Length

3.0 mm.

Presser Foot

Teflon or roller.

Seam Finish

Options: (1) Sew plain seam. Seam finish with fake flat fell. Press seam open, then trim one seam allowance. Flip other seam allowance over trimmed one.

Topstitch in place from right side ¼ in. from seam. (See #26 on p. 219.) (2) Finger-press seam open and hold in place with double-sided leather tape. (See #13B on p. 217.)

Pressing

No steam! Use brown bag for a press cloth on the right side. Dry iron at medium setting. Use press-and-lift motion to avoid stretching the skin.

Topstitching

On details, topstitch very close to edge. Topstitch foot helps here. (See #3 on p. 222.)

Closures

Bound buttonholes, snaps, button loops, eyelets, and lacing. (See #8, #9 and #11 on p. 225, #15 on p. 226.) Invisible zipper. (See #19 on p. 227.) Machine buttonholes are possible if you wrap buttonhole area with Solvy so that Solvy is between the presser foot and the skin as well as the skin and the feed dog.

Hem

Double row of topstitching on thin suede. (See #23 on p. 231.) Double-sided leather tape on heavier suede or glue up with Barge rubber cement. (See #7 on p. 229.)

✄ Tip Leather and suede are never the same after dry cleaning because they lose some of their oils and drapability. Tackle dirt and skin oil stains first with a suede and nubuck eraser, found in shoe repair shops.

Fabric Fact

Sunbrella® is a water repellent, sun-resistant, and stain-resistant fabric that feels like a cotton but is actually 100% acrylic. Since it does not retain heat, it is more comfortable than vinyl for outdoor seating and umbrellas. Sunbrella is a workhorse of a fabric that can stand up to sun, wind, salt water, and chlorine. Because it is solution-dyed, it is extremely fade resistant.

Suitable For

Outdoor furniture covers on cushions, pillows, tables, umbrellas, and awnings. Since this fabric feels like cotton, it is also a great choice for indoor furniture or window coverings in rooms that get bright sun.

Sewing Tips

Let fabric feed naturally.

WORKING WITH SUNBRELLA

Preshrink

Not necessary.

Layout

"Without nap" layout, double thickness.

Marking

Pencil or Pilot Frixion erasable ink pen.

Cutting

Rotary cutter or sharp scissors.

Interfacing

Not necessary. Fabric has enough body without it to support zippers and button closings.

Thread

Nylon upholstery thread.

Needle

90/14 HJ.

Stitch Length

2.5 mm.

Presser Foot

Standard.

Seam Finish

On enclosed pieces such as cushion covers, sew plain seams and press open. (See #1 on p. 216) On exposed seams, such as for table or umbrella covers, use flat-fell seams. (See #9 on p. 216.)

Tip Scissor care: Never strain scissors by cutting too many layers at once. Wipe blades after using and occasionally apply a drop of sewing machine oil near the screw that holds the blades together.

Tip If you're feeling optimistic and hate to machine-baste, sew side seams with a slightly lighter or darker thread in the bobbin. If you have to rip out stitches, the slight color variance makes the thread easier to see and you may be able to get away without resewing.

Pressing

Steam iron on cotton setting. Press on wrong side of fabric.

Topstitching

Helps flatten edges; close to seam. (See #3 on p. 222.)

Closures

Zippers, grommets, and snaps (See #11 on p. 225, #18 and #19 on p. 227.) Put ribbon between layers to secure permanently.

Hem

Machine-topstitched hem, double-turned ¼ in. (See #10 on p. 229.)

Sweatshirting

Fabric Fact

Good-quality sweatshirt fabric has a fuzzy fleece side and a knitted flat side. Some grades of sweatshirt fabric are thicker and more colorfast than others. Buy ¼ yd., run it through the laundry, then decide whether it is worth your time to construct a garment from it.

Suitable For

Sweatshirts, pull-on pants, and jogging suits.

Sewing Tips

Stabilize neck, shoulder, and waistline seams with ¼-in. clear elastic.

Preshrink

Buy an additional ¼ yd. for every 2 yd. purchased to allow for fabric shrinkage. Sew crosswise ends together to prevent stretching during washing. Fabric has progressive shrinkage, which means it must be machine-washed in warm water and machine-dried at regular temperature two times before cutting out. Wash separately—this fabric produces a lot of lint.

Tip

Prevent buttonholes on knits, loose wovens, or jackets from stretching by cording the buttonhole or stabilizing with clear elastic on the wrong side of the buttonholes.

WORKING WITH SWEATSHIRTING

Layout

Straighten crosswise ends with a T-square. "Without nap" layout, double thickness. Use pattern weights—pins tear tissue. If crosswise ends won't lie flat, apply spray starch and iron to flatten.

Marking

Snips at notches, Clover Chaco Liner, Pilot Frixion erasable ink pen.

Cutting

Rotary cutter or scissors.

Interfacing

French Fuse or Fusi-Knit.

Thread

Polyester is the best choice since it has some stretch. Wind bobbin slowly.

Needle

75/11 HS.

Stitch Length

Tiny zigzag (0.5 mm width, 2.5 mm length).

Presser Foot

Teflon or walking.

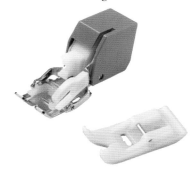

Seam Finish

Sew seams first with a lightening stitch. Reduce pressure on presser foot or keep finger pushing fabric behind presser foot to prevent stretching. Use triple stitch on areas of stress, such as crotch and underarm seams (See #6 on p. 216, #12 on p. 217.) Finish seams with a 3-thread overlock with woolly nylon on loopers. (See #20 on p. 218.) Use differential feed or your finger behind presser foot to prevent stretching as you serge. If you don't own a serger, use the overcasting foot to finish edges that do not curl.

Pressing

Steam iron on cotton setting.

Topstitching

Topstitch ¼ in. from finished edge using edge foot or edge-joining foot as a guide and lengthening stitch to 4.0 mm. (See #10 on p. 223.)

Closures

Stabilize buttonhole area with lengthwise grain interfacing parallel to buttonhole. For buttonholes, use 70/10 HJ needle and Solvy between the presser foot and sweatshirt fabric. Cord buttonholes to prevent stretching. Stabilize zipper and snap seam allowances with ½-in. strips of fusible interfacing. (See #3 and #5 on p. 224, #11 on p. 225, #19 on p. 227.)

Hem

Ribbing, or serge raw edge. Topstitch with double-needle ZWI stretch using woolly nylon in bobbin. Loosen top tension to flatten ridge between rows of stitches. (See #1 on p. 228, #23 on p. 231.) Another option is the serger coverstitch. (See #5 on p. 228.)

Taffeta

Fabric Fact

Taffeta is a noisy fabric that rustles when you walk. Taffeta also creases easily, a tendency that can be reduced by underlining in organza or net.

Suitable For

Full skirts and party dresses. Fabric does not ease well, so choose a style without princess seams if possible. Silk taffeta can make a great A-line skirt if underlined in silk organza.

Sewing Tips

Experiment with tension on scrap fabric. Puckers become permanent. Sew tautly, pulling with equal pressure from front and back. Don't over-fit garment since seams will weaken and shred.

Tip On any fabric that must be matched, like a print or plaid, the top fabric can shift while sewing despite your best efforts at matching the pattern. Narrow double-sided adhesive zipper tape eliminates the problem completely.

WORKING WITH TAFFETA

Preshrink

Not necessary. Dry-clean completed garment. Machine washing and machine drying create an interesting, pebbly appearance that can hide puckered seams, but most of the sheen disappears.

Layout

"With nap" layout, double thickness.

Marking

Clips in seam allowance or Pilot Frixion erasable ink pen. No waxed chalk as it leaves spots.

Cutting

Rotary cutter or scissors.

Interfacing

Sew-In Durapress or silk organza. Consider lining with netting to hold out skirt.

Thread

Good-quality cotton.

Needle

70/10 HJ or 70/10 HM.

Stitch Length

2.5 mm straight stitch.

Presser Foot

Straight stitch foot and single-hole throat plate.

Seam Finish

Since taffeta is so prone to wrinkling, underline in silk organza. Hand-baste edges together. Then serge all edges before seaming since fabric ravels excessively. Seam and press open. (See #3 on p. 216.)

Pressing

Steam iron on medium setting. Always use an organza press cloth to prevent water spots. If taffeta has been washed for a pebbly texture, water spotting is not a problem. Press over a rounded seam stick or use brown bag strips under seam allowances to prevent seam show-through.

Glitter taffeta has beads glued to the surface. This fabric must be pressed with a dry iron on a medium setting, using a press cloth. Do not leave the iron in one place too long or the beads will melt.

Topstitching

Rarely appropriate.

Closures

For buttonholes, use 70/10 HJ needle and fine machine-embroidery thread. (See #1 on p. 224.) Button loops work well for this fabric. (See # 9 on p. 225.)

Hem

For blouse, ¼-in. double-fold machine hem. (See #10 on p. 229.) For full skirt, use rolled hem on the serger with right needle on serger removed so that the stitch takes a bigger bite out of the fabric and will not pull off. (See #17 on p. 230.)

Tencel

Fabric Fact

Tencel® is produced by treating wood pulp with a recyclable nontoxic dissolving agent. Tencel is soft and drapey and is often combined with other fibers in both knits and wovens. It is comfortable to wear because it breathes. It behaves very much like cotton without as much wrinkling. It does wrinkle, however, and does not make a great travel garment. Tencel blends wrinkle less easily. Colors are vivid and do not fade. Black Tencel is a winner because it stays black without fading after washing.

Suitable For

Styles that need to be soft and drapey such as full pants, fullish skirts, big shirts, and pajamas. Garments should be loose with blousy waists, tucks, soft pleating, and deeper armholes to take advantage of the drape.

Sewing Tips

Let fabric feed naturally.

> ✂ **Tip** **Instead of pinning on trim, machine-baste into place with fusible thread on the bobbin. Press trim into position. You are now ready to machine- or hand-sew the trim in place.**

WORKING WITH TENCEL

Preshrink

Machine-wash on regular cycle in warm water. Machine-dry on permanent press. Remove fabric promptly from dryer to prevent wrinkles from setting. Completed garment can be washed or dry-cleaned.

Layout

"Without nap" layout, double thickness.

Marking

Pilot Frixion erasable ink pen, tracing wheel, Clover white marking pen for dark colors.

Cutting

Rotary cutter or scissors.

Interfacing

Sewers' Dream for medium weights, So-Sheer for lighter weights.

Thread

Cotton gives best results.

Needle

70/10 HM, 70/10 HJ, 70/10 H.

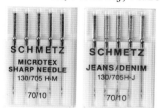

Stitch Length

2.5 mm straight stitch for horizontal seams; narrow zigzag (0.5 mm width, 2.5 mm length) for vertical seams.

Presser Foot

Standard.

Seam Finish

Since fabric does ravel, use flat-fell seams or press open and serge separately. (See #3 and #9 on p. 216)

Pressing

Steam iron at medium setting. Press on the wrong side.

Topstitching

Topstitching helps flatten seams. Topstitch close to the finished edge, with the help of topstitching foot, or ¼ in. away from finished edge. Lengthen stitch to 3.5 mm. (See #3 on p. 222, #10 on p. 223.)

Closures

For buttonholes, use 70/10 HJ needle. (See #1 on p. 224.) Also use zippers. (See #19 on p. 227.)

Hem

Serge raw edge, fold up hem, and topstitch with double needle. For short skirts, full skirts, and pants hems, use a double-fold ¼-in. hem. (See #1 on p. 228, #10 on p. 229.)

Terrycloth

Fabric Fact

Terrycloth is 100% cotton, absorbent, and comfortable to wear. French terry has a knit side and a fluffy side. It is very soft to the touch and a big favorite. Terrycloth feels like a towel. Stretch terry is softer and more pliable. It is knit on one side and terry on the other.

Suitable For

Beach jackets, hoodies, sportswear, and robes.

Sewing Tips

Stabilize neck, shoulders, and waistline seams with ¼-in. clear elastic. Eliminate facings whenever possible. Options: (1) Add ribbing. (2) Bind edges with cotton knit strips cut on the crossgrain.

Tip ✂ **Accessorize with smooth jewelry only when wearing terrycloth, or it will get caught in the loops of the fabric.**

WORKING WITH TERRYCLOTH

Preshrink

Buy an additional ¼ yd. for every 2 yd. purchased to allow for fabric shrinkage. Fabric has progressive shrinkage, which means it must be machine-washed in warm water and machine-dried at regular temperature twice before cutting out.

Layout

"Without nap" layout, double thickness. Use pattern weights—pins will tear the tissue.

Marking

Clover Chaco Liner or safety pins.

Cutting

Rotary cutter or scissors. Serge all edges immediately to prevent raveling. A 4-thread serger stitch adheres to fabric more securely than a 3-thread serger and will not pull off.

Interfacing

None. Fabric has enough body on its own.

Thread

Good-quality cotton or polyester.

Needle

80/12 H or 90/12 H.

Stitch Length

3.0 mm.

Presser Foot

Walking or roller.

Seam Finish

Mesh layers together as you sew. Sew seam with a 4-thread serge. (See #5 on p. 216.)

Pressing

Steam iron on cotton setting.

Topstitching

Coverstitch or double needle. (See #6 on p. 223.)

Closures

Stabilize buttonhole area with lengthwise grain of interfacing parallel to buttonhole. For buttonholes, use 70/10 HJ needle and Solvy between the presser foot and the terrycloth. Cord buttonhole to prevent stretching. (See #5 on p. 224.) Fabric is too thick for zippers. Snaps can be used if they have extra-long prongs (available from www.snapsource.com).

Hem

Flatlock or serge raw edge. Turn up 1¼ in. Topstitch with double needle, lengthening stitch to 4.0 mm. (See #2 on p. 228.) Coverstitch on the serger also works well with this fabric. (See #5 on p. 228.)

Tulle & Net

Fabric Fact

Tulle is softer to the touch than net and has smaller holes. Tulle is used for soft support while net is used for a stiffer look. Neither has stretch. Since so few people sew bridal or dressy dresses, color selection in tulle and net is extremely limited. Consider purchasing white and dying it to the color you want.

Suitable For

Interfacing behind lace, bridal veils, underskirts with multiple layers, sleeve heads, underlining in satins and taffetas, and slightly transparent portions of a bodice. Tulle also works as an overskirt.

Sewing Tips

Place small square of Solvy between the presser foot and the fabric at the beginning of seams and beginnings and ends of darts to keep the fabric from pulling down into the machine. Hold on to the top and bottom threads at beginning of all machine sewing. Let fabric feed naturally. Store petticoats inside out, with netting layers facing upward to retain fullness.

Tip While both tulle and net are 100% nylon, net has larger holes and is stiffer, making it suitable for petticoats. Tulle has smaller holes and is softer to the touch, making it suitable for bridal veils.

WORKING WITH TULLE & NET

Preshrink

Not necessary.

Layout

"Without nap" layout, double thickness.

Marking

Safety pins or tailor tacks made with yarn. If tailor tacks are the only markings visible on your fabric, use different-color threads for different markings. For example, use one color for notches, another color for darts, and another color for buttonholes.

Cutting

Rotary cutter or sharp scissors.

Interfacing

Self-fabric. Stabilize neck and shoulders with selvage cut from chiffon, georgette, or silk organza.

Thread

Good-quality polyester or cotton.

Needle

70/10 H.

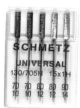

Stitch Length

1.5 mm straight stitch.

Presser Foot

Straight stitch for seaming, standard or grooved for hemming.

Seam Finish

Netting and tulle do not fray so serging is not necessary. Plain seams are the least visible. (See #1 on p. 216.)

Pressing

Low-temperature dry iron. Use silk organza press cloth.

Topstitching

Not necessary.

Closures

Buttonholes are not recommended because they will pull out of the fabric. Substitute button loops or very small snaps. (See #9 and #11 on p. 225.) For petticoats, use exposed zipper with stitching close to teeth. (See #19 on p. 227.)

Hem

Options: (1) Not necessary since fabric doesn't ravel. (2) Use rayon embroidery thread to zigzag over rattail cord ½ in. from edge. Trim off excess after sewing. (3) Use grooved presser foot to zigzag over topstitching machine thread. Pull slightly on fabric behind the foot. (4) Serge or zigzag over 25-lb. fishing line for a flounced effect. (See #19 and #21 on p. 231.)

Tip Glitter tulle has beads glued to the surface. This fabric must be pressed with dry iron on a medium setting, using press cloth. Do not leave iron in one place too long or the beads will melt unless they are glass.

Upholstery

Fabric Fact

Quite a few fabrics from the home-dec department can be used in structured styling. Tapestries, brocades, and damasks work for clothing since they are not too stiff.

Suitable For

Vests and jackets as well as home-dec projects. Upholstery does not drape, so structured styling is a must. A style that is too full will make you look "big." Fitted styles with set-in sleeves and high armholes are more flattering and less bulky than boxy styles in this fabric. Upholstery fabric has no give on crossgrain, so consider cutting jacket back one size larger so that it is more comfortable to drive in.

Sewing Tips

Because of upholstery's tendency to ravel, serge all edges immediately after cutting with a 4-thread serger. On a conventional machine, sew tautly, pulling with equal pressure from front and back as you sew.

Preshrink

Fabric is too stiff to use "as is" for garments. Fabric shrinks in length and width, so buy an extra ⅓ yard. Overlock crossgrain ends to prevent raveling.

Tip Since upholstery fabrics have no give, cut garments one size larger from top to the bottom of the armhole on back. Cut entire sleeve one size larger and run ease line all around the cap.

WORKING WITH UPHOLSTERY FABRICS

Machine-wash in cold water on gentle cycle. Machine-dry on permanent-press cycle. Some upholstery fabrics appear more muted after machine washing. Dry-clean finished garment since fabric is too weak for continued machine washings.

Layout

"Without nap" layout, double thickness. Use pattern weights. Eliminate as many seams as possible to take advantage of fabric design. For garments with set in sleeves, cut jacket back one size larger or split back pattern from shoulder to hem and add ½ in. vertically to provide give. Ease back to front at shoulders.

Marking

Clover Chaco Liner or Clover white marking pen for dark colors.

Cutting

Sharp scissors or rotary cutter. Serge-finish all pieces immediately after cutting. Round corners on jacket fronts and collars so that they can be turned right side out smoothly. Cut upper collars, cuffs, and front facing above roll line with an extra ¼ in. on outside edges. Cut undercollars and undercuffs from lighter-weight coordinating fabric to eliminate bulk.

Interfacing

Armo Weft. Block-fuse since loose weave will close up, making the fused piece smaller.

Thread

Good-quality cotton or polyester for apparel. Nylon upholstery thread for home-dec projects.

Needle

90/14 HJ or 100/16 HJ.

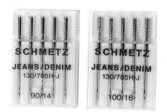

Stitch Length

3.0 mm straight stitch.

Presser Foot

Walking or Teflon foot works best for high-texture upholstery or if pattern matching is necessary.

Seam Finish

Press seams open. Bind with double-fold bias or Hong Kong finish. (See #16 and #19 on p. 218.)

Pressing

Steam iron on cotton setting. Pound seams flat with a tailor's clapper.

Topstitching

Topstitch ¼ in. from edge and lengthen stitch to 4.0 mm. Use topstitching thread and N needle. (See #10 on p. 223.)

Closures

Since this fabric ravels so easily, consider alternatives to buttonholes, such as button loops, frogs, faced openings, or button openings in a seam. (See #6 on p. 224, #9, #10, and #12 on p. 225.)

Hem

Finish raw edge with double-fold bias or Hong Kong finish. Hand-hem. (See #13 and #14 on p. 230.) If garment is unlined, consider using faux stretch leather strips to bind all edges, eliminating hems altogether.

Velour

Fabric Fact

Grades of velour vary. Look for the thicker variety, which keeps its shape and has more depth of color. Velour feels a lot like velvet but has stretch and is machine washable, keeps its shape, drapes nicely, and is comfortable to wear. Velour is a workhorse while velvet is the racehorse and needs lots of care.

Suitable For

Robes, tops, overshirts, caftans, pull-on pants, and tablecloths that need no ironing. Because stretch velour can be machine-washed and -dried without affecting the nap adversely, it is an easy-care choice for children's dress-up clothes and for casual styles for adults.

Sewing Tips

Do not stretch fabric as you sew. It is easy to sew. Push into presser foot. If you do not have a walking foot, reduce pressure on presser foot or keep finger pushing fabric behind presser foot to prevent stretching, whether sewing on a conventional machine or a serger.

> ✂ **Tip** **Fusible interfacing causes facings in knits to get smaller. Block-fuse fabric first or cut ends of facings ½ in. longer than the pattern. Fuse. Check the size of fused piece against the pattern piece.**

WORKING WITH VELOUR

Preshrink

Buy an additional ¼ yd. for every 2 yd. purchased to allow for fabric shrinkage. Fabric has progressive shrinkage, which means it must be machine-washed in warm water and machine-dried at regular temperature two times before cutting out. Always hang velour fabric over a shower rod for 24 hours after drying. A heavy velour can stretch 6 in. in length, reducing the circumference around the body and resulting in overfitting.

Layout

"With nap" layout, double thickness wrong sides in; single thickness if fabric is heavy. Use pattern weights.

Marking

Clover Chaco Liner, Pilot Frixion erasable ink pen, Clover white marking pen for dark colors.

Cutting

Rotary cutter or scissors. Cut wider seam allowances to overcome curling edges. Excess can be trimmed off as you serge.

Interfacing

Fusi-Knit.

Thread

Good-quality cotton or polyester.

Needle

75/11 HS.

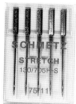

Stitch Length

Small zigzag (1.0 mm width, 2.5 mm length).

Presser Foot

Walking.

Seam Finish

First sew seams with a tiny zigzag. Then serge seams together. (See #20 on p. 218.)

Pressing

Steam iron on a cotton setting. Place right side of fabric against needle board or fluffy towel. Press on wrong side only.

Topstitching

Topstitch ¼ in. from the edge with the help of topstitching foot. Lengthen stitch to 3.5 mm. (See #10 on p. 223.)

Closures

Stabilize buttonhole area with lengthwise grain of interfacing parallel to buttonhole and clear elastic behind buttonhole. Use 70/10 HJ needle, fine thread, and Solvy between the presser foot and the velour and velour and feed dog. Sew a corded buttonhole to prevent stretching. Stabilize zipper seam allowances with 1-in. strips of fusible interfacing. Invisible zippers preferred. (See #3 and #5 on p. 224, #19 on p. 227.)

Hem

Options: (1) Fuse with ½-in. strip of Lite Steam-A-Seam 2. Then sew with double-needle ZWI. (2) Sew a stretch blindstitch, using woolly nylon hand-wrapped on the bobbin and regular thread on top. (3) Flatlock. (4) Ribbing. (5) Coverstitch on serger. (See #1, #2, #3, and #5 on p. 228, #31 on p. 233.)

Velvet

Fabric Fact

The drapiest velvet is a rayon and silk blend. Microfiber velvet does not seat out and can be machine-washed and -dried, but it does not drape, ease, or press well. Microfiber velvet seams pucker slightly, preventing a good press.

Working on velvet is time-consuming since the silky nap makes it difficult to control.

Suitable For

Full pants, skirts, vests, capes, dresses, gored skirts, and loose, boxy, or semifitted jackets. Let the fabric do the talking. Eliminate fussy details. Avoid curved princess seams because they do not press well.

Sewing Tips

Pretest pattern. Needle holes do not come out. Use double-sided narrow adhesive tape in the seam allowance to hold velvet pieces together for sewing. Sew next to tape, not over it. Mush layers together to marry naps in front of presser foot as you sew. Sew in direction of pile whenever possible, lifting presser foot every 4 in. to allow fabric to relax as you sew. Lifting both layers of velvet in front of the presser foot helps it to feed evenly. When joining velvet to other fabrics, sew with velvet on the bottom.

Preshrink

If completed garment will be dry-cleaned, hold steam iron ½ in. above wrong side of fabric surface before cutting. Rayon-blend velvet can be machine-washed on the gentle cycle in cool water and machine-dried. This changes the nap and gives it a more vintage look. Try a sample swatch. Microfiber velvet changes little in this process.

WORKING WITH VELVET

Layout

Cover cutting surface with tissue paper, then overlay velvet, single thickness with nap down. Make duplicate of any pattern piece labeled "cut on fold." Tape new piece to original along foldline so that entire pattern can be cut through a single thickness. Use pattern weights.

Marking

Tailor tacks, Clover Chaco Liner, Pilot Frixion erasable ink pen. No tracing wheels.

Cutting

Micro-serrated shears eliminate slippage. You can also cut out with pinking shears, eliminating a seam finish. Cut facings, undercollars, and undercuffs from a lighter-weight fabric such as silk charmeuse. Cutting wider seam allowances makes fabric easier to sew. Cut in direction of pile for smoother cuts.

Interfacing

No fusibles; silk organza is your best choice. For ease in sewing and to give more body, underline jackets or bodices with cotton batiste, lawn, or prewashed silk organza. Underlining prevents dart and seam imprints from showing on right side. China silk makes the best lining for this fabric.

Thread

Good-quality cotton, polyester, or silk.

Needle

70/10 HJ or HM for wovens, 75/11 HS for stretch velvets.

Stitch Length

Small zigzag (1.0 mm width, 2.5 mm length) on long vertical seams to prevent them from drawing up when fabric relaxes. Straight stitch 3.0 mm on horizontal seams.

Presser Foot

Walking or Velva "V." If possible, reduce presser foot pressure.

Seam Finish

Press open, then pink or serge singly. (See #2 and #3 on p. 216.)

Pressing

Never touch the fabric with the iron. Steam iron on medium setting (no hotter or you will melt the rayon). Place right side of velvet against needle board. Hold iron ½ in. above velvet and steam. Lightly finger-press seams open.

Topstitching

Never topstitch. Hand picking can help flatten edges. (See #1 on p. 222.)

Closures

Consider alternative to machine buttonholes. Try fabric loops, frogs, bound buttonholes in fabric contrast, or button openings in a seam. Hand-picked zippers only. Place hanging loops inside waistband to avoid crushing pile with pinchers on hangers. (See #8, #9, #10, and #12 on p. 225, #19 on p. 227.)

Hem

Serge, pink, or use Hong Kong finish. Hand-hem twice to distribute the weight and make the hem less visible, once halfway up hem and the second at the top of the hem. (See #32 on p. 233.)

Velveteen

Fabric Fact

Velveteen is a cotton or cotton-blend fabric with short, dense pile. Velveteen lacks the sheen and drape of velvet, but it is a lot easier to sew. In addition, it is a strong fabric that holds its shape.

Suitable For

Vests, straight skirts, jeans, structured jackets, evening coats, and children's clothes. Velveteen is a great home-dec fabric for draperies, pillows, upholstery, and floor cushions.

Sewing Tips

Let fabric feed naturally.

Preshrink

If you plan to dry-clean completed garment, hold steam iron ½ in. above surface. If not, turn fabric right side in and stitch ends closed. Machine-wash and machine-dry on delicate cycle. For home-dec projects, no preshrinking is necessary. Garment care: Turn inside out, machine-wash and machine-dry on delicate cycle. Dry cleaning keeps the garment looking new longer. Restore flattened pile by tumble drying with damp towel for 10 minutes. Remove immediately and hang up. Avoid lint transfer by drying dark velveteen with a dark towel and light velveteen with a light-colored towel.

WORKING WITH VELVETEEN

Layout

"With nap" layout, double thickness. Place fabric wrong sides together for accuracy while cutting. Pile wears better if pieces are cut with pile going down. For richer colors, let pile run up.

Marking

Clover Chaco Liner, Pilot Frixion erasable ink pen, white pencils, tailor tacks.

Cutting

Rotary cutter or scissors. Use smooth cotton for facings to eliminate bulk.

Interfacing

Sewers' Dream or Fusi-Knit.

Thread

Good-quality cotton or polyester.

Needle

80/12 H.

Stitch Length

2.5 mm.

Presser Foot

Walking or roller. Loosen top tension slightly.

Seam Finish

Serge pieces separately or use flat-fell seam. (See #3 and #9 on p. 216.)

Pressing

Steam iron on cotton setting. Cover pressing surface with fluffy towel, self-fabric, Velvaboard, or needle board. Press lightly with point of iron in seam allowance. Avoid pressing on right side of fabric.

Topstitching

Close to edge of details using a topstitching foot.

Closures

For buttonholes, use 70/10 HJ needle and fine machine-embroidery thread to reduce bulk. Lengthen and widen stitch slightly. Wrap buttonhole area with Solvy to prevent the stitches from sinking into the fabric. Place hanging loops inside of waistband to avoid crushing pile with pinchers on hangers. Snaps are good looking on sportswear and children's clothes. (See # 4 on p. 224, #11 on p. 225.)

Hem

Finish raw hem edge with a Hong Kong finish or with a serger. Hand-hem adult clothes; machine hemming is acceptable on children's clothes. (See #4 and #6 on p. 228, #13 on p. 230.)

> **Tip** Creating a beautiful garment is only the first step. Take time to put it together with the right shoes and accessories.

Vinyl & Oilcloth

Fabric Fact

Vinyl and oilcloth are similar and most often used for home-dec projects such as tablecloths and seat covers.

Suitable For

Upholstery projects, handbags, tablecloths, cushions. Avoid curved seams because vinyl sticks to itself, making it difficult to sew two reverse curves together.

Sewing Tips

Cut a 1-in. square out of Teflon press sheet for feed dogs. Tape to bed of machine with hole cut out over feed dogs. Fabric will now slide easily without sticking to the bed of the machine. Needle holes are permanent. Hold layers together with fabric clips.

Tip Revive finishes on vinyl and patent leather with **Pledge**® furniture polish. Buff off residue.

WORKING WITH VINYL & OILCLOTH

Preshrink

Not necessary.

Layout

Single thickness. Grainline is not important—pattern pieces may be positioned in any direction for fabric economy. Use pattern weights. Needle holes are permanent.

Marking

Pilot Frixion erasable ink pen or pencil. No spoked tracing wheel as it leaves holes.

Cutting

Heavy-duty shears or large rotary cutter for thick vinyl.

Interfacing

None.

Thread

Good-quality polyester.

Needle

70/10 HJ or 70/10 H for thin weights, 140/16 HJ for thicker weights.

Stitch Length

Use a long stitch (3.5 mm); smaller stitches will weaken fabric.

Presser Foot

Teflon or roller. Loosen top tension slightly.

Seam Finish

No overlocking, as it stretches seam. Finger-press open and glue, or use double-sided leather tape. (See #13B on p. 217.)

Pressing

Test scrap. Some vinyl melts even under a very low-temperature iron and must be finger-pressed only. Others tolerate low-temperature iron on the wrong side, using a press cloth.

Topstitching

For lightweight vinyl, topstitching is not recommended. It devalues the finished garment. On heavier-weight vinyl, topstitching can be quite attractive ¼ in. from finished edge and is needed to flatten edges. Use N needle, 4.0 mm length stitch, and topstitching thread. (See #10 on p. 223.)

Closures

Snaps require interfacing between layers. (See #11 on p. 225.)

Hem

Glue up hem with fabric glue or double-sided leather tape followed by optional topstitching. (See #7 on p. 229.)

Viyella

Fabric Fact

Viyella® is a 50% wool, 50% cotton year-round fabric that breathes, drapes slightly, and gets better with age.

Suitable For

Men's and women's shirts, bathrobes, and tailored dresses.

Sewing Tips

Let fabric feed naturally.

Tip For identical pieces cut in plaid, never cut through both fabric layers at the same time. Cut the first piece through one fabric thickness from the pattern. With right sides of the plaid together, use the cutout first piece to cut the second piece, laying it on the fabric so that the plaids match exactly.

WORKING WITH VIYELLA

Preshrink

Hand-wash in warm water and shampoo. Spin in no-heat dryer or air-dry.

Layout

"Without nap" layout, double thickness.

Marking

Tracing wheel, Clover Chaco Liner, Pilot Frixion erasable ink pen.

Cutting

Scissors or rotary cutter.

Interfacing

ShirtMaker's Choice for crisp details or Fusi-Knit for softer support.

Thread

Good-quality polyester or cotton.

Needle

80/12 H.

Stitch Length

2.5 mm straight stitch.

Presser Foot

Standard.

Seam Finish

Flat fell. (See #9 on p. 216.)

Pressing

Steam iron on wool setting.

Topstitching

Topstitch close to the finished edge with topstitching foot ¼ in. in from finished edge. (See #3 on p. 222, #10 on p. 223.)

 Tip When decorative stitching, use presser foot with wide grooves in the bottom, allowing the foot to ride over decorative work.

Closures

70/10 HJ needle for buttonholes. Decorative snaps. (See #1 on p. 224, #11 on p. 225.)

Hem

For shirts and robes, turn under ¾ in. twice and topstitch. For skirts and dresses, serge or Hong Kong finish raw edge; turn up 1½ in. for skirts and dresses. (See #10 on p. 229, #13 on p. 230.)

Water & Wind Resistant

Fabric Fact

Sold under the names Commander, Touchdown, Tactel, and Chicago, these tightly woven fabrics of cotton/polyester and cotton/nylon resist wind and water by their tight weave. Chicago, a cotton/nylon blend, has a durable water-repellent finish that makes it particularly resistant to water.

Suitable For

Windbreakers, ski wear, parka shells, trench coats.

Sewing Tips

Because they are not slippery, these fabrics are easy to sew. Don't rush, though. The material is dense, and if you hurry, you will break a needle. Let fabric feed naturally into the machine.

✂ **Tip** **Difficulty holding tough fabric layers together? Forget pins. Hold them together with fabric clips.**

WORKING WITH WATER- & WIND-RESISTANT FABRICS

Preshrink

Machine-wash in cool water and machine-dry on low temperature.

Layout

"Without nap" layout, double thickness. Use pattern weights; pinholes are permanent.

Marking

Smooth tracing wheel, Pilot Frixion erasable ink pen, Clover white marking pen for dark colors.

Cutting

Rotary cutter or scissors.

Interfacing

Sew-in interfacings on all, fusibles on some. Try a sample to make sure bond is secure.

Thread

Good-quality polyester.

Tip Skipped stitches when crossing seams can be eliminated by pounding the seams flat with a hammer before sewing over them.

Needle

80/12 HM or 70/10 HM.

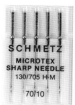

Stitch Length

3.0 mm.

Presser Foot

Standard or Teflon.

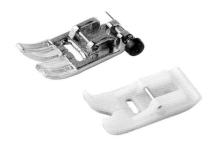

Seam Finish

These fabrics fray. Sew with a 4-thread serger. (See #5 on p. 216.)

Pressing

Warm, dry iron. These fabrics do not press well. Use press cloth and press on wrong side of vinyl-coated fabric.

Topstitching

Since these fabrics do not press well, topstitching close to the edge of details helps flatten. (See #3 on p. 222.) A topstitching foot helps here.

Closures

YKK plastic zippers or snaps. For snaps, add interfacing or ribbon directly behind snap, or snap will tear from fabric. (See #11 on p. 225, #19 on p. 227.)

Hem

Double needle topstitching looks the most professional. Ribbing is a popular alternative. (See #1 on p. 228, #31 on p. 233.)

Waterproof Breathables

Fabric Fact

These slippery nylon fabrics are sold under the trade names of Ultrex®, Dermoflex, Hydroflex®, and Gore-Tex®. A microporous coating on the underside allows the water vapor caused by body heat to escape while keeping you dry from external elements such as rain and snow. Since there are so many outerwear fabrics on the market, buy from someone who is knowledgeable about the properties of each. Mail-order sources are great for product information. Explain how garment will be used, and you will be directed to the fabric that best suits your needs.

Suitable For

Rainwear, ski wear, and golf suits. Select styles with limited seams since each seam must be sealed.

Sewing Tips

These slippery fabrics require skillful handling. Don't try to sew fast, or you will lose control of fabric. Sew tautly, pulling with equal pressure from front and back. Since every seam produces lots of needle holes, each seam should be sealed with seam-sealant tape or seam-sealant glue to protect the waterproof coating on the wrong side of the fabric. Line garment with a moisture-wicking lining such as Hydrofil® or fleece.

✂ **Tip** **Reduce stitch length when applying front zippers to outerwear to give them more durability.**

WORKING WITH WATERPROOF BREATHABLES

Preshrink

Not necessary. Machine-wash completed garment in powdered detergent. Double-rinse to get out all detergent. Machine-dry in hot dryer to reactivate water repellency.

Layout

Some of these fabrics have a slight nap; others do not. Check in natural light and lay out accordingly. Double thickness.

Marking

Smooth tracing wheel, Pilot Frixion erasable ink pen, Clover white marking pen for dark colors.

Cutting

Rotary cutter or scissors.

Interfacing

Self-fabric. Coating on wrong side of fabric prevents fusibles from long-term adhesion. Line with a "wicking lining" that will keep you dry by transferring moisture to the outside.

Thread

Good-quality polyester or nylon.

Needle

80/12 HM or 70/10 HM. Change needles often.

Stitch Length

3.0 mm to minimize number of holes.

Presser Foot

Teflon or walking.

Seam Finish

Sew seams with straight stitch, press open, and apply seam-sealant tape. No seam finish is necessary because fabric frays little. If you prefer the look of topstitched seams, sew fake flat fell, then apply seam sealant. To apply, set iron on nylon setting. Place shiny glue side of tape down. Adhere tape with point of iron. Cover area with press cloth. Tape will turn clear when fully applied. If you see white spots on tape, press again. (See #32 on p. 220, #38 on p. 221.)

Pressing

Dry, low-temperature iron. Test scrap first. You may need a press cloth to prevent shine.

Topstitching

Topstitch ¼ in. from edge. (See #10 on p. 223.) Seam sealant not necessary on details such as outside edges of collar and pocket flaps.

Closures

YKK plastic zippers, snaps, Velcro. (See #11 on p. 225, #16 on p. 226, and #19 on p. 227.) Zippers must be covered by double flaps to prevent moisture leakage. Don't forget to seal all seams. High-end ski wear is often embellished with embroidery at center back. Don't forget to seal needle holes.

Hem

Ribbing not recommended since it traps water. Since the fabric is rather stiff, use narrow plain hems, casings with elastic or shock cord drawstrings in.

Fabric Fact

These non-slippery fabrics are sold under the names Glacier, Oxford, Cordura®, Spotlight, Linebacker, and Quarterback. Fabric surface is coated on the outside with a polyurethane or polyvinyl chloride (PVC) coating, making it impervious to water. These fabrics, while they are truly waterproof, do not breathe. Because of this, they cost considerably less than waterproof breathables.

Suitable For

Soft luggage and bags, ponchos, ski jackets, rain suits. Avoid patch pockets, which trap water.

Sewing Tips

Install eyelets in underarm area to allow for air circulation. Use absorbent lining such as Hydrofil or Coolmax® to reduce the clammy feeling when wet.

Tip Before tossing out those old scissors, try wiping the blades clean with rubbing alcohol.

WORKING WITH WATERPROOF NON-BREATHABLES

Preshrink

Not necessary. For completed garments, machine-wash in cold water. Rinse two times to prevent the soap from clogging fabric pores. Machine-dry on low heat.

Layout

"Without nap" layout, double thickness. Since fabrics are coated and therefore stabilized, they can be cut lengthwise or crosswise.

Marking

Clover Chaco Liner, Pilot Frixion erasable ink pen, smooth tracing wheel.

Cutting

Rotary cutter or scissors.

Interfacing

Self-fabric or silk organza.

Thread

Good-quality polyester for lightweight fabrics, nylon for heavier weight in areas of high stress.

Needle

70/10 HM or 70/10 H for lighter weight; 80/12 H, 80/12 HM, 90/14 HM, 90/14 H for heavier weights.

Stitch Length

2.5 mm straight stitch.

Presser Foot

Teflon or walking.

Seam Finish

On coated fabrics, press seams open or to one side. For a fake flat-fell, trim one seam allowance, flip the other one over it, and topstitch ¼ in. from seamline on right side. Seal all seams with seam-sealant tape or seam-sealant glue unless you don't plan to wear garment in extreme weather conditions. (See #33 on p. 220.)

Pressing

Dry, low-temperature iron. Press lightly. Experiment on a scrap to see if fabric melts or sticks to the iron. If not, go ahead and press.

Topstitching

Topstitch ¼ in. away from finished edge. (See #10 on p. 223.) A topstitching foot helps here.

Closure

YKK plastic zippers, snaps, Velcro, or the softer hook-and-loop closures called Fixvelour. (See #11 on p. 225, #16 on p. 226, and #19 on p. 227.)

Hem

Ribbing is not recommended since it traps water. Since the fabric is rather stiff, use narrow (¾-in.) plain hems, casings with elastic or shock cord drawstrings.

Wetsuit

Fabric Fact

Sold under the names Neoprene and Polartec Thermal Stretch, wetsuit fabrics are designed to keep you warm, even when wet. Neoprene has a foam layer between Lycra layers. Polartec Thermal Stretch has a polyester fleece layer between Lycra layers.

Suitable For

Wetsuits and any water sportswear.

Sewing Tips

Let fabric feed into machine naturally. A roller foot is the answer to sewing on foam-backed fabrics.

Tip **For easier needle threading either by hand or at the machine, always cut the thread at an angle.**

WORKING WITH WETSUIT

Preshrink

Not necessary. Machine-wash completed garments in warm water. Air-dry or machine-dry on low temperature.

Layout

"Without nap" layout, single thickness.

Marking

Clover Chaco Liner or snips in the seam allowance.

Cutting

Large rotary cutter or scissors.

Interfacing

Not necessary.

Thread

Nylon.

Tip If you don't own a serger, use the overcasting foot to prevent edges from curling.

Needle

75/11 HS.

Stitch Length

Tiny zigzag (0.5 mm width, 2.5 mm length).

Presser Foot

Roller.

Seam Finish

Serging the seams with a flatlock stitch is your best choice since bulk is eliminated on the inside. Second choice would be to sew with a small zigzag (0.75 mm width, 2.5 mm length) and serge seams closed with a 4-thread serger using woolly nylon on both loopers. (See #20 on p. 218, #41 on p. 221.)

Pressing

None.

Topstitching

Flatlock ¼ in. from edge. (See #41 on p. 221.)

Closures

YKK plastic zippers. (See #19 on p. 227.)

Hem

Turn up ¾-in. hem. Machine-stitch with triple zigzag for the most stretch. Flatlock on the serger is also suitable. (See #2 on p. 228, #26 on p. 232.)

Windbloc

Fabric Fact

Windbloc® is a two-color, double-sided breathable fleece that is windproof on one side and water resistant on the other. The fabric has the same insulation as wool, with half its weight.

Suitable For

It makes up well in jackets, pullovers, skiwear, and rain suits, but Windbloc is not as flexible or drapey as fleece.

Sewing Tips

Staystitching stretches this fabric. Stabilize necklines with ¼-in. Stay Tape cut to size from pattern tissue and hand-basted on seamline before construction.

Tip If you find yourself getting frustrated with a project, set it aside. The solution will often come after a good night's sleep.

WORKING WITH WINDBLOC

Preshrinking

Not necessary. To clean completed garment, turn inside out, machine-wash separately in cool water, and machine-dry on low setting to prevent excess pilling.

Layout

"With nap" layout, double thickness. Use pattern weights.

Marking

Clover Chaco Liner, smooth tracing wheel, safety pins.

Cutting

Scissors or large rotary cutter.

Interfacing

Nonfusible interfacing, such as silk organza, behind zipper on facings. Use ribbon between garment and facing when using snap components so that they will not tear out of the fabric.

Thread

Polyester.

Needle

80/12 HM.

Stitch Length

3.0 mm.

Presser Foot

Satin stitch or embroidery to eliminate wavy seams.

Seam Finish

Finger-press seam allowances open. Topstitch with double-needle ZWI stretch 4.0 mm, straddling seam allowance on right side of fabric. Trim seam allowances close to stitching. (See #13 on p. 217.)

Pressing

No pressing.

Topstitching

Not recommended on edges, since they will stretch.

Closures

YKK plastic zippers. Snaps must be reinforced between layers to prevent pulling out of fabric. (See #11 on p. 225, #19 on p. 227.) Machine buttonholes stretch out of shape unless you first baste a strip of clear elastic to the wrong side of the fabric in the buttonhole location. Make the buttonhole through the clear elastic. (See #3 on p. 224.)

Hem

Flatlock, topstitch with double needle, or bind in faux leather or knit cut on crossgrain. (See #1 and #2 on p. 228.)

Wool Bouclé

Fabric Fact

Bouclé is a loosely woven or knitted fabric with small curls or loops that provide a nubby surface.

Suitable For

Sweater looks, vests, and unstructured, unlined coats.

Sewing Tips

Push fabric into the presser foot.

WORKING WITH WOOL BOUCLÉ

Preshrink

Hold steam iron ½ in. above fabric surface.

Layout

"With nap" layout, single thickness. Use pattern weights.

Marking

Tailor tacks or safety pins.

Cutting

Rotary cutter or sharp scissors.

Interfacing

Sew-in interfacing to avoid flattening texture.

Thread

Good-quality silk, polyester, or cotton.

Tip Hand-baste the outside edges of a jacket or blouse before you press. You will get a much sharper crease. Don't forget to use silk thread for the basting. Other threads can leave a memory.

Needle

80/12 H.

Stitch Length

3.0 mm straight stitch.

Presser Foot

Walking or roller.

Seam Finish

Straight seam. Serge seams together and press to one side. (See #4 on p. 216.)

Pressing

Steam iron on wool setting. Cover pressing surface with a fluffy towel. Press only on wrong side with a light touch or you will flatten the texture. Do not use a clapper. Flatten finished edges with hand-picking since overpressing will flatten surface.

Topstitching

Hand picking ⅛ in. from finished edge. (See #1 on p. 222.)

Closures

Faced buttonhole or snaps. (See #6 on p. 224, #11 on p. 225.)

Hem

Serge raw edge. Hand-hem. Stretch hem every 4 in. and knot thread. (See #4 on p. 228.) You can also finish edges with ribbing or crossgrain knit strips.

Wool Challis

Fabric Fact

Wool challis is a lightweight plain-weave wool. It is one of those fabrics that makes up well in almost anything. It breathes, is comfortable to wear, and wrinkles little.

Suitable For

Shirts, dresses, A-line or full skirts, luxurious bathrobes.

Sewing Tips

Easy to sew.

> ✂ **Tip** If you love glossy, thick, decorative machine threads but can't get them to work on your machine, hand-wind them onto your bobbin. Skip the bobbin tension. Put regular thread on the top. Work facedown with the right side against the feed dogs. Thread problems are eliminated, and you are able to add decorative stitching with the thread you want.

WORKING WITH WOOL CHALLIS

Preshrink

Hold steam iron ½ in. above fabric or hand-wash in cool water and Ivory liquid. Air-dry.

Layout

"Without nap" layout, double thickness.

Marking

Clover Chaco Liner, Pilot Frixion erasable ink pen, Clover white marking pen for dark colors.

Cutting

Scissors or rotary cutter.

Interfacing

Fusi-Knit or So-Sheer for soft support.

Thread

Good-quality cotton, silk, or polyester.

Needle

80/12 H.

Stitch Length

2.5 mm straight stitch.

Presser Foot

Standard.

Seam Finish

Flat fell or pressed open and serged separately. (See #3 and #9 on p. 216.)

Pressing

Steam iron on wool setting. Allow fabric to dry and cool completely before moving. Handle carefully to avoid distortion.

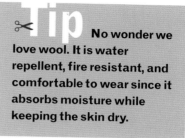

✂ **Tip** No wonder we love wool. It is water repellent, fire resistant, and comfortable to wear since it absorbs moisture while keeping the skin dry.

Topstitching

Topstitch ¼ in. from finished edge. Use a 70/10 HJ needle; topstitching foot helps here. (See #10 on p. 223.)

Closures

For corded buttonholes, use 70/10 HJ needle and fine machine-embroidery thread on bobbin. (See #5 on p. 224.)

Hem

Serge or Hong Kong finish. Turn up 2 in. and hand-hem. (See #4 on p. 228, #13 on p. 230.)

Wool Crepe

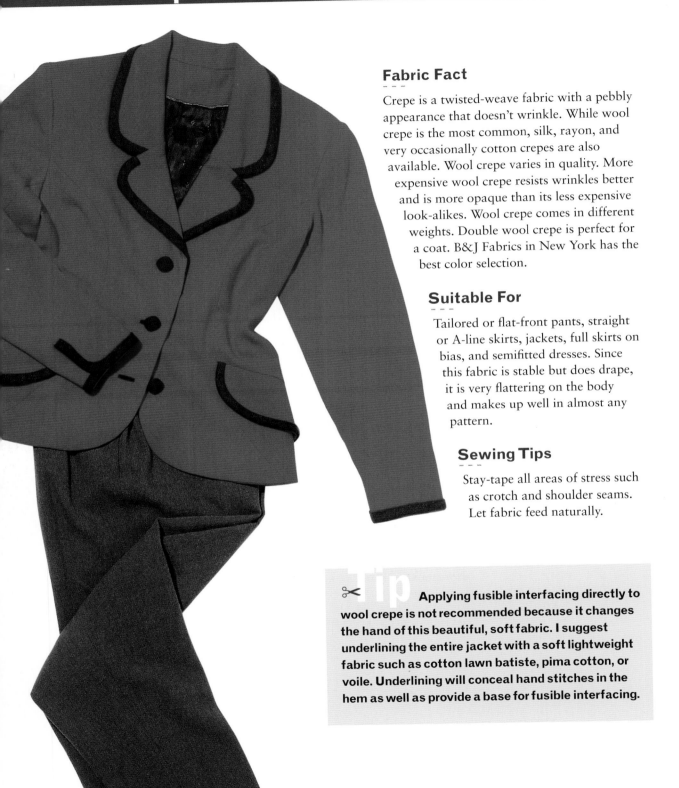

Fabric Fact

Crepe is a twisted-weave fabric with a pebbly appearance that doesn't wrinkle. While wool crepe is the most common, silk, rayon, and very occasionally cotton crepes are also available. Wool crepe varies in quality. More expensive wool crepe resists wrinkles better and is more opaque than its less expensive look-alikes. Wool crepe comes in different weights. Double wool crepe is perfect for a coat. B&J Fabrics in New York has the best color selection.

Suitable For

Tailored or flat-front pants, straight or A-line skirts, jackets, full skirts on bias, and semifitted dresses. Since this fabric is stable but does drape, it is very flattering on the body and makes up well in almost any pattern.

Sewing Tips

Stay-tape all areas of stress such as crotch and shoulder seams. Let fabric feed naturally.

Tip Applying fusible interfacing directly to wool crepe is not recommended because it changes the hand of this beautiful, soft fabric. I suggest underlining the entire jacket with a soft lightweight fabric such as cotton lawn batiste, pima cotton, or voile. Underlining will conceal hand stitches in the hem as well as provide a base for fusible interfacing.

WORKING WITH WOOL CREPE

Preshrink

Must be preshrunk at dry cleaner or the garment will shrink a whole size the first time it is dry-cleaned. I know from experience! Another option is to machine-wash with Eucalan Delicate Wash in cool water on gentle cycle. Machine-dry on low-heat setting.

Layout

"Without nap" layout, double thickness.

Marking

Clover Chaco Liner, Pilot Frixion erasable ink pen, tailor tacks.

Cutting

Rotary cutter or scissors. Cutting seam allowance ¼ in. wider will enable seams to press flatter.

Interfacing

Apply Textured Weft or Armo Weft to underlining. Underline jackets with cotton lawn, which comes in colors. Cotton lawn gives support behind pockets without stiffness, prevents a board-like appearance on styling details, and makes the color more opaque.

Thread

Good-quality cotton, polyester, or silk.

Needle

80/12 H.

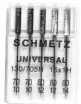

Stitch Length

2.5 mm.

Presser Foot

Standard.

Seam Finish

Press seam open and overlock seam allowances separately with woolly nylon on the lower looper. If lined, no seam finish is necessary. (See #3 on p. 216.)

Pressing

Steam iron on the wool setting. Press as you stitch. Press seams open over a seam stick or half-round to prevent seam shadows. On the right side, use a self-fabric press cloth and press again. Let fabric dry before moving off the pressing surface.

Topstitching

Topstitch ¼ in. from finished edge using a topstitching foot, or hand-pick with shiny rayon or pearl cotton thread. (See #1 on p. 222, #10 on p. 223.)

Closures

Use cord to prevent machine buttonholes from stretching, or use bound buttonholes. (See #5 on p. 224, #8 on p. 225.)

Hem

Serge or Hong Kong finish. Turn up 1½ in. and hand-hem. (See #4 on p. 228, #13 on p. 230.)

Wool Double Cloth

Fabric Fact

Wool double cloth is actually two different fabrics joined with threads in between that are invisible from either side of the fabric. Wool double cloth is terrific for reversible garments since it has two different sides that can be sewn as one piece. Double cloth tends to be softer and more flexible than wool melton.

Suitable For

Coats and vests. Because this fabric is bulky, choose a shape that does not rely on drape. A large coat in double cloth can make you look big if you lean in that direction. A shorter coat will be more flattering.

Sewing Tips

Let fabric feed naturally.

Tip A pure wool garment can be made new again by brushing with a soft brush and hanging in the fresh air for a few hours.

WORKING WITH WOOL DOUBLE CLOTH

Preshrink

Hold steam iron ½ in. above surface.

Layout

"With nap" layout, single thickness. Use pattern weights.

Marking

Tailor tacks or safety pins.

Cutting

Scissors or rotary cutter. If you are going to butt edges and featherstitch as well as finish outside edges with trim, cut all seam allowances off.

Interfacing

None; fabric has enough body on its own.

Thread

Good-quality polyester, wool, or silk thread.

Needle

90/14 H.

Stitch Length

3.0 mm to 3.5 mm.

Presser Foot

Teflon.

Seam Finish

Cut off seam allowances. Butt edges together over 1½-in.-wide wool jersey strip. Machine-sew a featherstitch to join edges to each other and the strip. Trim off one side of the wool strip. Fold over the other side, concealing the stitches, and hand-stitch. Sew darts in the same manner. This method is my favorite because it eliminates bulk. (See #14 on p. 217.) A second option is much more time-consuming and results in bulky seams. Do not cut seam allowances off to make seam construction invisible, pull apart wool layers for 1¼ in. in seam area. Sew a ⅝-in. seam in outer layer. Press open. On inner layers, trim seam allowances to ⅜ in. Fold in each edge ¼ in. until folds meet. Press. Slipstitch inner seam allowances together. (See #29 on p. 220.)

Pressing

Steam iron on wool setting. Use piece of wool as a press cloth when pressing on right side. Don't remove from pressing surface until wool dries.

Topstitching

Hand picking ⅜ in. from edge, if desired. (See #1 on p. 222.)

Closures

Corded buttonholes. (See #5 on p. 224.) Also consider button loops or faced buttonholes. (See #6 on p. 224, #9 on p. 225.)

Hem

Bind edge with crossgrain wool jersey or faux leather. Another option, although more bulky, is to separate layers 1¼ in. Miter corners separately on both layers. Turn in edges ⅝ in. and trim underlayer seam allowance to ⅜ in. Slipstitch layers together. (See #25 on p. 232.)

Note: The edge finish on the jacket shown on the facing page was achieved by threading the loopers on the serger with two different color threads so that the navy thread showed on the green side and the green thread showed on the navy side.

Wool Gauze

Fabric Fact

Wool gauze is the least stable fabric in the wool family. It is quite sheer. Since this fabric is weak and filmy, it needs at least 4 in. of ease at bust and hip. Double layers are used for less transparency.

Suitable For

Loose tops, dresses, or full skirts with slip dress or beautiful slip underneath. Undergarment outline will show.

> **Tip** For barely visible seams in tailored wool garments, machine-sew with silk thread.

WORKING WITH WOOL GAUZE

Sewing Tips

Staystitching can stretch this fabric. Stabilize neck with fusible or sew in ¼-in. Stay Tape or fusible stabilizer, cut to size from the pattern piece. Do not stretch fabric as you sew. Push into the presser foot.

Preshrink

Hold steam iron ½ in. above fabric. Dry-clean completed garment when needed.

Layout

"Without nap" layout, double thickness.

Marking

Clover Chaco Liner or Pilot Frixion erasable ink pen.

Cutting

Rotary cutter or scissors.

Interfacing

Silk organza to maintain transparency.

Thread

Good-quality cotton or polyester.

Needle

70/10H.

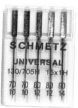

Stitch Length

2.0 mm.

Presser Foot

Standard.

Seam Finish

Serged French seams. (See #10 on p. 217.)

Pressing

Steam iron on wool setting. Don't move off pressing surface before dry, or a puffy appearance will result. Avoid overpressing on wools by using a press cloth made from self-fabric. You can also use an iron shoe.

Topstitching

Not recommended.

Closures

For buttonholes, use 70/10 HJ needle and fine machine-embroidery thread to reduce bulk. (See #1 on p. 224.)

Hem

Serged rolled hem. Remove right needle in serger so that it takes a bigger bite and will not pull off fabric. Use differential feed or keep finger behind presser foot to prevent stretching. (See #17 on p. 230.)

Wool Jersey

✂ **Tip** Silk thread is the number one choice for hand basting wherever you press since it leaves no imprint after pressing.

Fabric Fact

Coco Chanel launched her career with wool jersey, formerly used for men's underwear. This is one of those fabrics that falls into the "fabric friend" category. Wool jersey makes up well in styles where drape is needed. This fabric drapes beautifully, it is flattering on the body, and comfortable to wear, and it resists wrinkles. It is not suitable for skinny pull-on pants because the fabric is not strong enough to recover from prolonged stretch at the knees and seat.

Suitable For

Wrap tops, semi-fitted or full dresses, full pants, full tops, full or gored skirts.

Sewing Tips

Let fabric feed naturally.

Preshrink

Since wool jersey shrinks in both length and width, it must be preshrunk. To do this at home, lay out fabric on a long table or on the floor. Hold iron ½ in. above fabric surface, letting the steam flow into the fabric. You need an iron that puts out plenty of steam. Let fabric dry completely before moving.

Layout

"Without nap" layout, double thickness.

Marking

Clover Chaco Liner or Pilot Frixion erasable ink pen.

Cutting

Rotary cutter or scissors.

WORKING WITH WOOL JERSEY

Interfacing

Fusi-Knit.

Thread

Good-quality silk, cotton, or polyester.

Needle

75/11 HS.

Stitch Length

Tiny zigzag (0.5 mm width, 2.5 mm length) or lightning stitch on long vertical seams to allow seams to relax with the fabric. Use straight stitch on horizontal seams and styling details.

Presser Foot

Standard.

Seam Finish

Options: (1) Sew seams with small zigzag to allow seams to relax as the fabric relaxes. Finish seams with a 3-thread serger. (See #20 on p. 218.) (2) Sew seam with lightning stitch, then press open. (3) Fake flat-fell seam using small zigzag. (See #12 on p. 217, #26 on p. 219.)

Pressing

Steam iron on wool setting. Press on right side using press cloth or iron shoe. Let fabric dry and cool before moving to avoid stretching.

Topstitching

Topstitch close to the edge with the topstitching foot. (See #3 on p. 222.)

Closures

Stabilize buttonhole area with lengthwise-grain interfacing parallel to buttonhole and Solvy above and below fabric. Cord buttonholes in jackets to prevent stretching. Stabilize zipper seam allowances with ½-in. strips of fusible interfacing. Hand-picked zipper is the most attractive. (See #3 and #5 on p. 224, #19 on p. 227.)

Hem

Coverlock hem, or pink or serge raw hem edge. Turn up 1½-in. hem. Topstitch using double-needle ZWI stretch with woolly nylon hand-wrapped on bobbin and Teflon foot. On right side, sew ¼ in. from hem crease. Skip 1 in. and sew another row of double-needle stitching parallel to the first. Loosen top tension. (See #22 on p. 231.)

Wool Melton

Fabric Fact

Wool melton is a heavily felted, full wool with a smooth, napped surface. It is very warm to wear but also thick and bulky if sewn with traditional methods.

Suitable For

Simply styled coats, vests, and jackets. A lower armhole, as in a raglan or dolman sleeve, is more comfortable. Avoid gathers or pleats. Use in-seam or welt pockets. Reduce bulk whenever possible—eliminate facings, hems, and linings. For a warm coat that is not bulky, consider an unstructured, unlined coat trimmed with wool jersey or faux leather.

Sewing Tips

If the melton is not too thick, conventional tailoring methods can be used. Substitute other fabric for pocket welts or bound buttonhole strips. If melton is heavy, eliminate the seam allowances and butt edges together. To use this method of construction, cut off seam allowances wherever you plan to use the butt-and-sew method. (See #14 on p. 217.)

✂ **Tip** **Moth problems? Even a cedar chest won't guarantee complete protection from moths. For extra protection, clean an old cedar chest with rubbing alcohol. Then add a natural herbal repellent like Moth-Away® to any spot where wool is stored. (See Sources for information on Gardens Alive®.)**

WORKING WITH WOOL MELTON

Preshrink

Hold steam iron ½ in. above fabric surface or toss into dryer and run at permanent press setting with a wrung-out wet towel.

Layout

"With nap" layout—not always necessary but a safe bet. Single thickness. Use pattern weights because pins tear tissue.

Marking

Tailor tacks, safety pins, Clover Chaco Liner.

Cutting

Rotary cutter or sharp scissors.

Interfacing

None; fabric has enough body without it. Stabilize neck and shoulder with Stay Tape.

Thread

Silk thread is the best choice because it marries with the fabric, making the seams almost invisible. Good-quality cotton or polyester is also suitable.

Needle

90/14 H.

Stitch Length

3.0 mm to 3.5 mm.

Presser Foot

Teflon.

Seam Finish

For less bulky seams, trim off the seam allowance. Butt edges together over 1½-in.-wide wool jersey strip. Machine-sew a featherstitch to join the edges to the strip and each other. Trim off one side of the wool jersey strip. Fold the other over the stitching and hand-stitch. Sew darts in the same manner. (See #14 on p. 217.) For a lighter-weight melton, simply sew traditional seams, press open, and bind with Hong Kong finish. (See #16 on p. 218.)

Pressing

Steam iron on wool setting. Use a piece of wool as press cloth when pressing on the right side.

Topstitching

Options: (1) Unnecessary when using binding. (2) Hand-pick. (See #1 on p. 222.) (3) Topstitch ⅜ in. from edge using an N needle and topstitching thread, lengthening stitch to 4.0 mm. (See #10 on p. 223.)

Closures

Too thick for machine or bound buttonhole. Consider alternative closures: faced buttonhole, button in a seam, button loops, and zippers. (See #6 on p. 224, #9 and #10 on p. 225, #19 on p. 227.)

Hem

On heavier meltons, trim off hem allowance, and bind cut edge with wool jersey or faux leather. (See #9 on p. 229.) For lighter-weight meltons, turn up a 2½-in. hem with Hong Kong finish. Hem halfway up hem allowance and hem again at top of hem to distribute weight. (See #32 on p. 233; see also Hong Kong finish #13 on p. 230.)

Woolens & Worsteds

Fabric Fact

Woolens are softer, are fuzzier, have more nap and more stretch, and appear spongier than worsteds. Worsteds are harder, smoother, stronger, and more lustrous. They also hold a crease and drape better and are often used in men's suits.

Suitable For

Fabric weight determines suitable garment. Heavier woolens make great coats. Heavier worsteds make good jackets. Lighter-weight woolens and worsteds can be used for unstructured jackets; draped, shaped, or slightly gathered dresses; wrap skirts; slightly gathered or A-line skirts; bias-cut skirts or dresses; or soft tailored pants. Dresses, pants, and skirts must be lined or they will seat out. Men's pants are lined to just below the knee.

Sewing Tips

Let fabric feed naturally into machine. To eliminate bulk in darts, cut dart open to 1 in. from dart point. Press dart open. Overcast sides of dart to fabric only if dart will not stay open when pressed.

Tip **Better woolens are made with long rather than short fibers, enabling them to return to their original shape after a rest, removing most of the wrinkles.**

WORKING WITH WOOLENS & WORSTEDS

Preshrink

Hold steam iron ½ in. above surface, preshrink at the dry cleaner, or toss into a dryer with a wrung-out wet towel, and run at permanent press setting.

Layout

"Without nap" layout, double thickness.

Marking

Tailor tacks or Clover Chaco Liner.

Cutting

Rotary cutter or scissors. Cutting seams ¼ in. wider than ⅝ in. enables seams to be pressed flatter.

Interfacing

Armo Weft or Suitmaker 602.

Thread

Silk thread is preferable because it marries with the fabric, making the seams almost invisible. Good-quality polyester or cotton also is suitable but does not press as flat.

Needle

80/12 H.

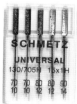

Stitch Length

2.5 mm.

Presser Foot

Standard.

Seam Finish

Press open and pink seams or serge seam allowances separately using woolly nylon on the lower looper or apply a Hong Kong finish. Use a flat fell on lightweight sporty styles. (See #2, #3, and #9 on p. 216, #16 on p. 218.)

Pressing

Steam iron on wool setting. Press as you sew. With seam positioned over a seam roll, seam stick, or half-round to prevent seam allowance show-through on right side, dribble a bead of water in the valley of the seam. Press with steam iron on the wool setting.

On right side of fabric, once again position seam over half-round. Cover with self-fabric press cloth. Press again with steam. Let fabric cool and dry before moving from the pressing surface or fabric will have a puffy appearance. To set crease lines, spray fabric with solution of 3 tablespoons white vinegar to 1 cup water. Cover with a press cloth and iron using plenty of steam and a clapper.

Topstitching

Options: (1) Use buttonhole twist thread, an N needle, 4.0 mm stitch length, and edge foot or edge-joining foot. Topstitch close to the edge or ¼ in. from the edge using a topstitching foot. (2) Hand-pick ¼ in. from edge with stitches ¼ in. apart using buttonhole twist or shiny rayon thread. (See #1 and #3 on p. 222, #10 on p. 223.)

Closures

For machine buttonholes, use a 70/10 HJ needle. Cord buttonholes to prevent stretching. Hand or bound buttonholes are also an option for coats and jackets. (See #5 on p. 224, #8 on p. 225.)

Hem

Hong Kong finish, or serge raw edge. Turn up a 2-in. hem. Press and hand-hem. (See #4 on p. 228, #13 on p. 230.)

Seams

Since I have used all of the fabrics in this book to make garments or home-dec projects, I suggest seams and seam finishes that, from my experience, are the most compatible and attractive for each fabric.

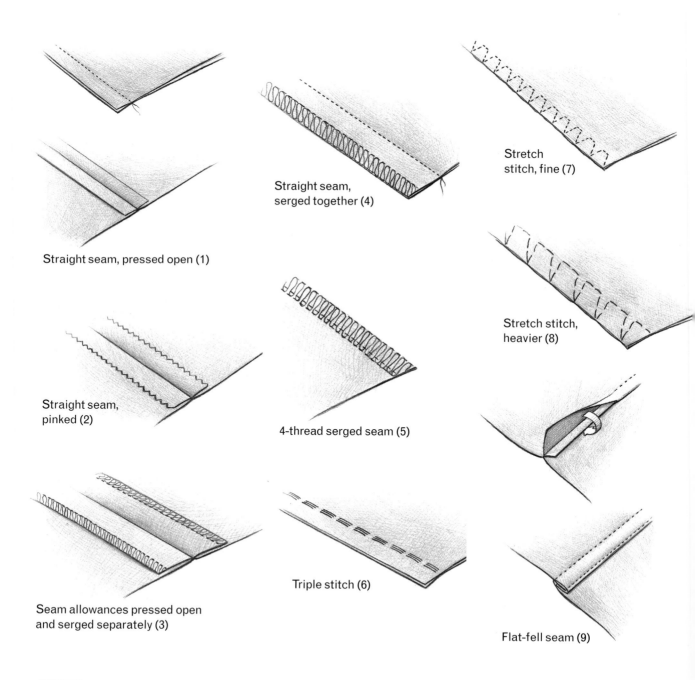

Straight seam, pressed open (1)

Straight seam, pinked (2)

Seam allowances pressed open and serged separately (3)

Straight seam, serged together (4)

4-thread serged seam (5)

Triple stitch (6)

Stretch stitch, fine (7)

Stretch stitch, heavier (8)

Flat-fell seam (9)

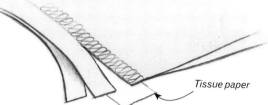

Tissue paper

Narrow rolled hem serger stitch, right sides out, cuts 1/4 in. off with serger blade.

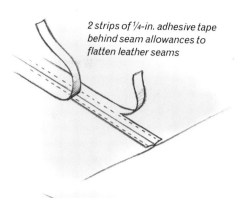

2 strips of 1/4-in. adhesive tape behind seam allowances to flatten leather seams

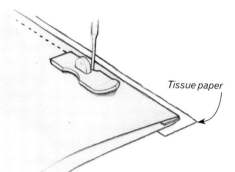

Tissue paper

Wrong sides out, sew close to enclosed serging with zipper foot through tissue paper.

Serger French Seam (10, 11); see also French Seam #40 on p. 221

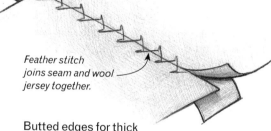

Seams held open with leather tape. Pat seams flat. (13B)

Feather stitch joins seam and wool jersey together.

Butted edges for thick nonraveling fabrics (14)

Lightning stitch (12)

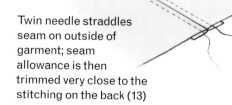

Twin needle straddles seam on outside of garment; seam allowance is then trimmed very close to the stitching on the back (13)

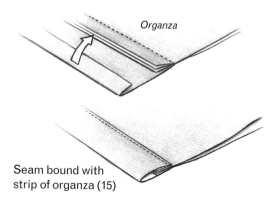

Organza

Seam bound with strip of organza (15)

Seams

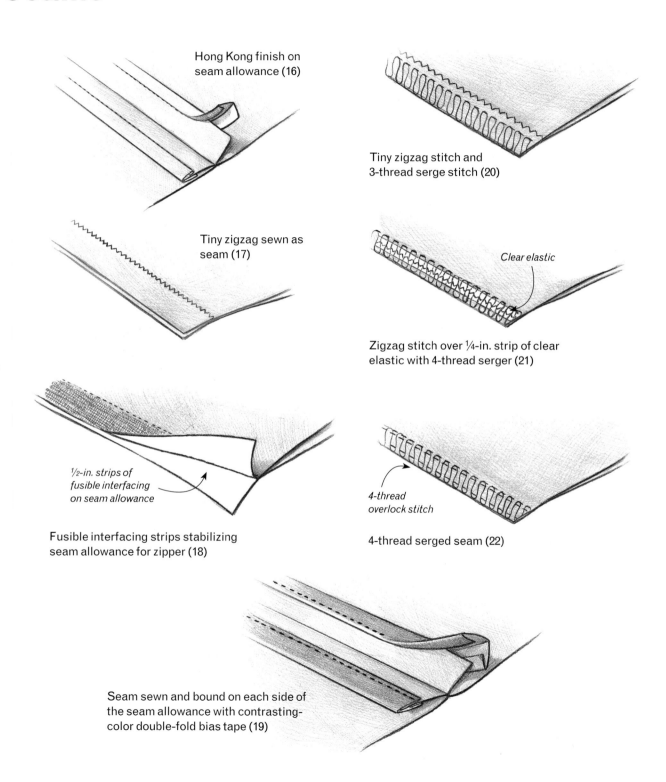

Hong Kong finish on
seam allowance (16)

Tiny zigzag stitch and
3-thread serge stitch (20)

Tiny zigzag sewn as
seam (17)

Clear elastic

Zigzag stitch over ¼-in. strip of clear
elastic with 4-thread serger (21)

*½-in. strips of
fusible interfacing
on seam allowance*

*4-thread
overlock stitch*

Fusible interfacing strips stabilizing
seam allowance for zipper (18)

4-thread serged seam (22)

Seam sewn and bound on each side of
the seam allowance with contrasting-
color double-fold bias tape (19)

Sew seams wrong side together, then flatten together toward front. Cover seam allowances with trim or braid and topstitch on both sides of trim.

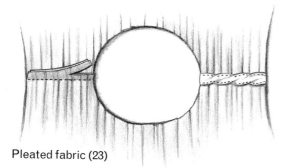

Pleated fabric (23)

Trim seam allowance, then overlap trimmed seam allowance.

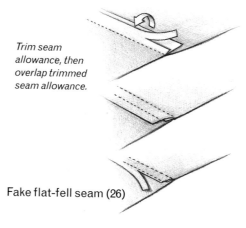

Fake flat-fell seam (26)

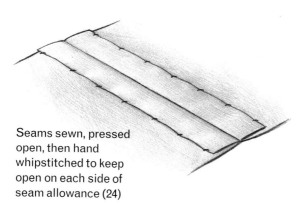

Seams sewn, pressed open, then hand whipstitched to keep open on each side of seam allowance (24)

1. Sew seam.

2. Trim one side of seam allowance to a scant ¼ in. Serge the other side along edge at ⅝ in.

3. Overlap serged seam and topstitch over trimmed seam.

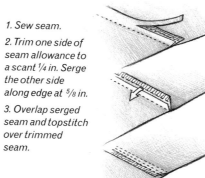

Serged fake flat-fell seam (27)

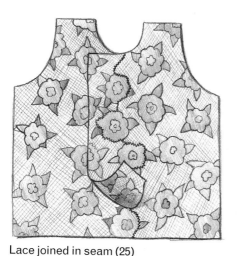

Lace joined in seam (25)

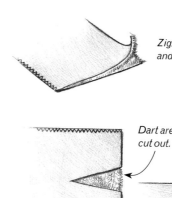

Zigzag runs on and off raw edge.

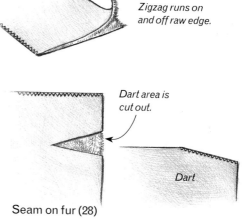

Dart area is cut out.

Dart

Seam on fur (28)

Seams

Seam for double-sided wool (29)

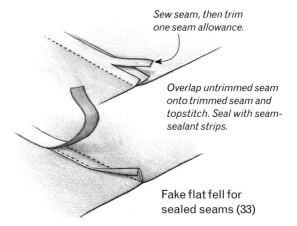

Sew seam, then trim one seam allowance.

Overlap untrimmed seam onto trimmed seam and topstitch. Seal with seam-sealant strips.

Fake flat fell for sealed seams (33)

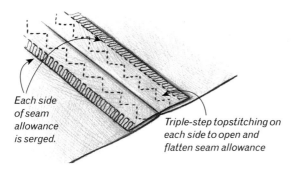

Each side of seam allowance is serged.

Triple-step topstitching on each side to open and flatten seam allowance

Seam on terrycloth (30)

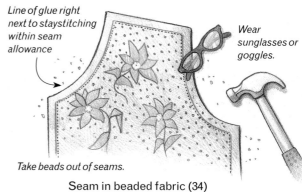

Line of glue right next to staystitching within seam allowance

Wear sunglasses or goggles.

Take beads out of seams.

Seam in beaded fabric (34)

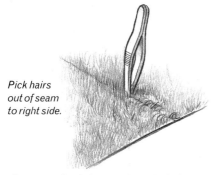

Pick hairs out of seam to right side.

Seam on fur fabric, right side (31)

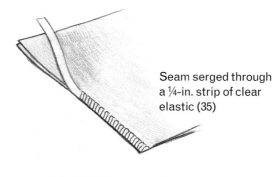

Seam serged through a ¼-in. strip of clear elastic (35)

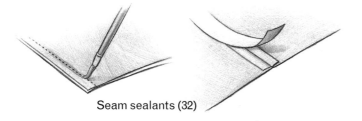

Seam sealants (32)

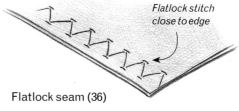

Flatlock stitch close to edge

Flatlock seam (36)

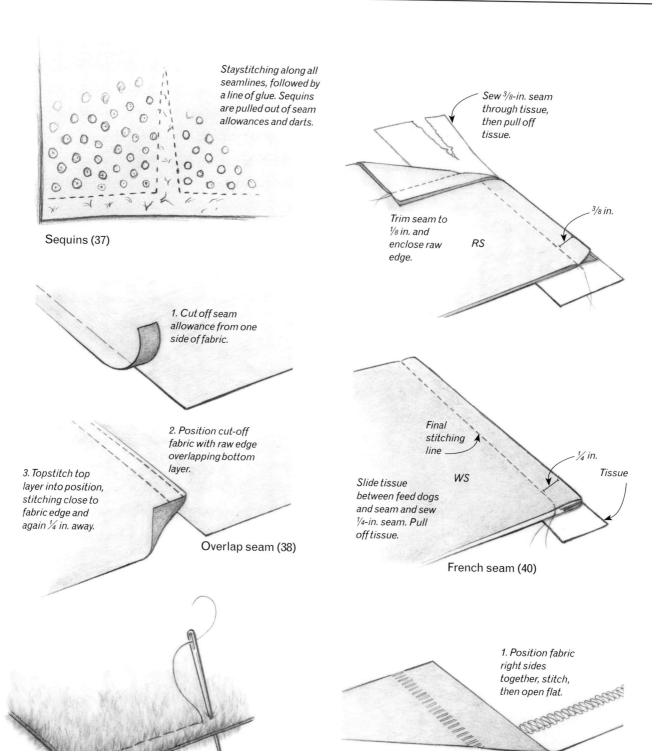

Staystitching along all seamlines, followed by a line of glue. Sequins are pulled out of seam allowances and darts.

Sequins (37)

Sew ³/₈-in. seam through tissue, then pull off tissue.

Trim seam to ⅛ in. and enclose raw edge.

RS

³/₈ in.

1. Cut off seam allowance from one side of fabric.

2. Position cut-off fabric with raw edge overlapping bottom layer.

3. Topstitch top layer into position, stitching close to fabric edge and again ¼ in. away.

Overlap seam (38)

Final stitching line

WS

¼ in.

Tissue

Slide tissue between feed dogs and seam and sew ¼-in. seam. Pull off tissue.

French seam (40)

Stab stitch (39)

1. Position fabric right sides together, stitch, then open flat.

2. Stitch on the fold, right side up, then open flat.

Flatlocking (41)

Details

Certain fabrics lend themselves to machine topstitching, others to serger finishes, and others to hand stitches. In the fabric descriptions, I suggest treatments that I find the most attractive. Much of this is personal taste. You, of course, can decide what you like.

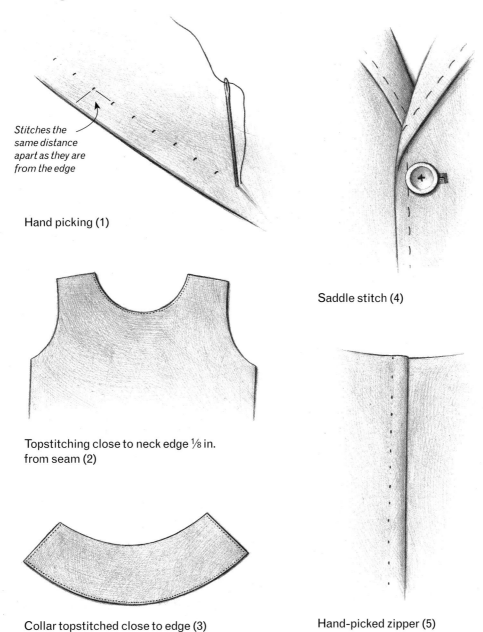

Stitches the same distance apart as they are from the edge

Hand picking (1)

Saddle stitch (4)

Topstitching close to neck edge ⅛ in. from seam (2)

Collar topstitched close to edge (3)

Hand-picked zipper (5)

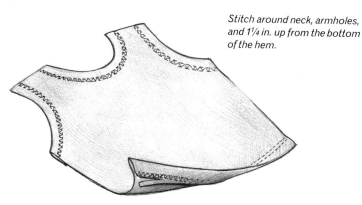

Stitch around neck, armholes, and 1¼ in. up from the bottom of the hem.

Fold the hem to the wrong side and sew it down from the right side with a coverstitch or twin needle. Trim excess fabric close to the seam on the wrong side.

Cover stitch (6); see also Flatlocking #41 on p. 221

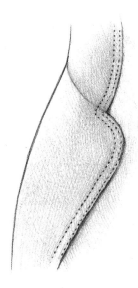

Double topstitching once close to seam or edge and again ¼ in. in from first line of stitching (9)

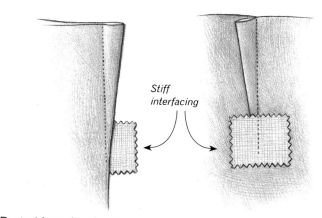

Stiff interfacing

Dart without dimple (7)

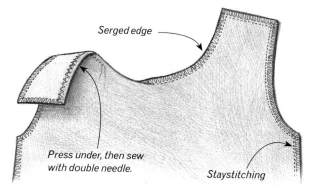

Serged edge

Press under, then sew with double needle.

Staystitching

Topstitching with double needle (8)

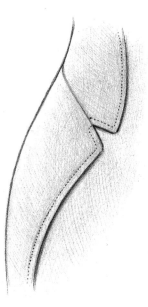

Topstitching on lapel ¼ in. or ⅜ in. from edge (10)

Closures

Within the text, you will find closure suggestions for each fabric. I base these suggestions on two things: what is used most often in ready-to-wear and what I have found from my personal experience to be the most compatible for the fabrics.

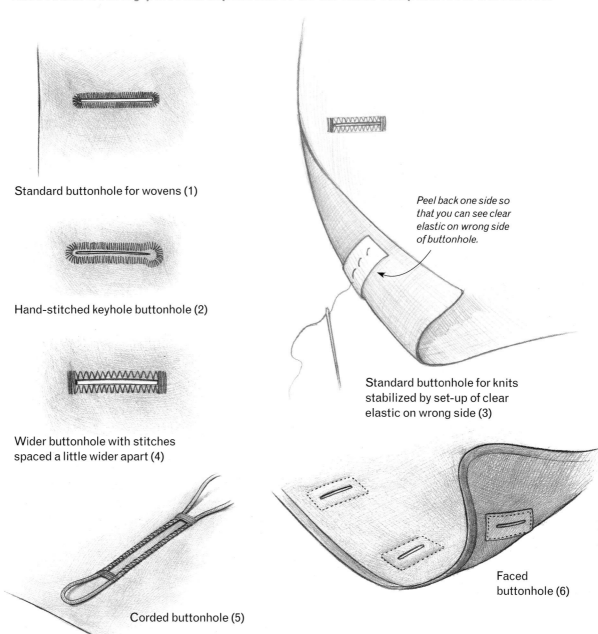

Standard buttonhole for wovens (1)

Hand-stitched keyhole buttonhole (2)

Wider buttonhole with stitches spaced a little wider apart (4)

Peel back one side so that you can see clear elastic on wrong side of buttonhole.

Standard buttonhole for knits stabilized by set-up of clear elastic on wrong side (3)

Corded buttonhole (5)

Faced buttonhole (6)

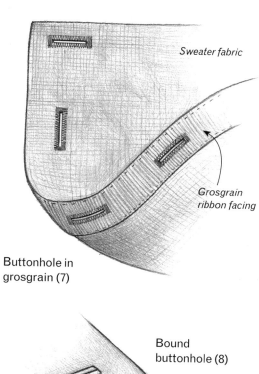

Sweater fabric

*Grosgrain
ribbon facing*

Buttonhole in
grosgrain (7)

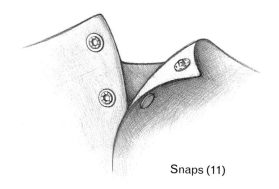

Snaps (11)

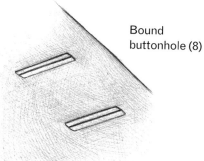

Bound
buttonhole (8)

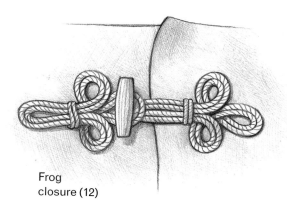

Frog
closure (12)

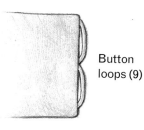

Button
loops (9)

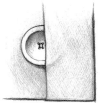

Buttonhole
in seam (10)

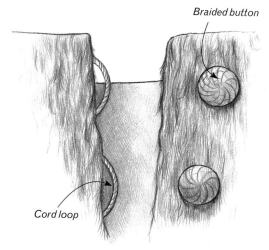

Braided button

Cord loop

Button loops made in cord
with braided buttons (13)

Closures

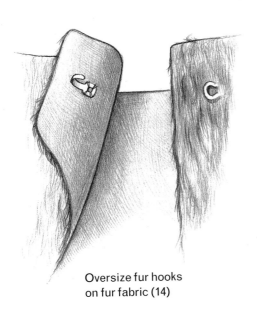

Oversize fur hooks
on fur fabric (14)

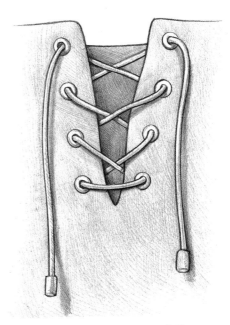

Eyelets and lacing (15)

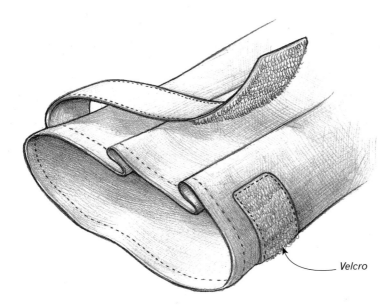

Velcro

Cuff with Velcro strap closure (16)

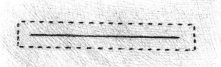

Topstitch ¼-in. rectangle, then cut opening for buttonhole.

Cut-open buttonhole
on leather (17)

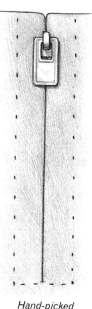

Hand-picked

Fly front

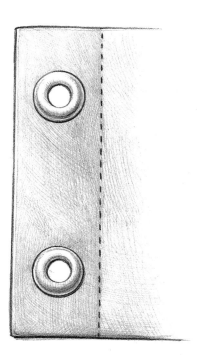

Oversized grommets
on canvas (18)

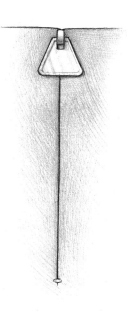

Invisible

Exposed

Zippers (19)

Hems

In this book, you will find hem suggestions determined by my experience with the fabric. My goals in hemming are to eliminate bulk, prevent stretching, and render the hem either as invisible as possible or as an attractive machine detail.

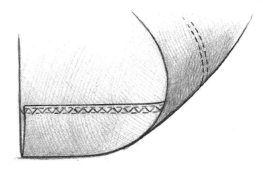

Hand hemstitch, folded or serged edge (4)

Double-needle hemstitch (1)

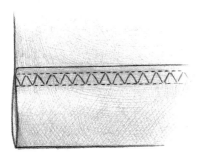

Flatlock hemstitch (2)

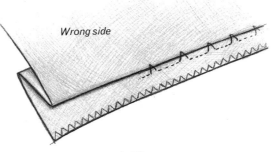

Cover hem topstitch (5)

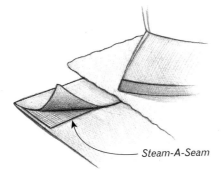

Hem with Lite Steam-A-Seam 2 inside (3)

Steam-A-Seam

Machine hemstitch (6)

Wrong side

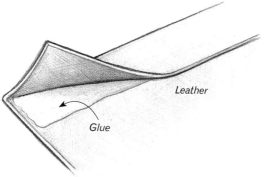

Glue or leather tape within hem (7)

Raw edge with binding (9)

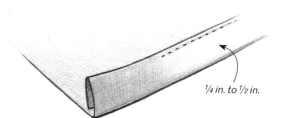

Double-fold machine hem (10)

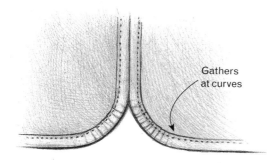

Easestitch to gather up curves slightly (8)

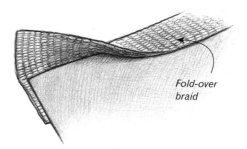

Bind edges (11)

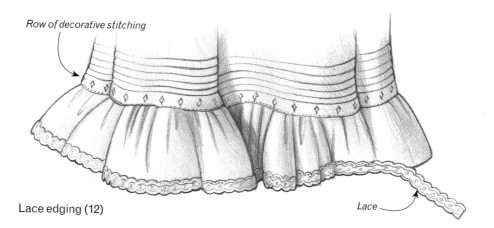

Lace edging (12)

Hems

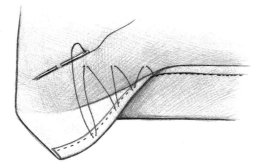

Hong Kong finish on raw edge
with hand stitching (13)

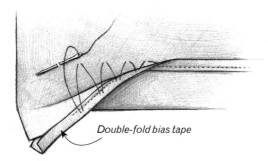

Double-fold bias tape

Raw edge covered with
double-fold bias tape (14)

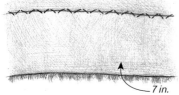

Low-loft fur

2 in.

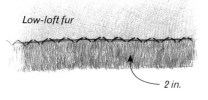

High-loft fur (faced with satin bias)

7 in.

Hems on fur (15)

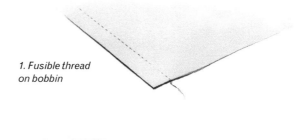

*1. Fusible thread
on bobbin*

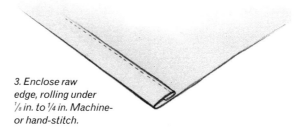

*2. Press down on
hem crease to melt
fusible thread and make a
sharp crease. Trim very
close to stitching.*

*3. Enclose raw
edge, rolling under
⅛ in. to ¼ in. Machine-
or hand-stitch.*

Three steps to a rolled hem (16)

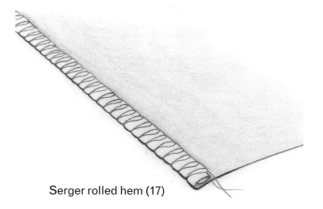

Serger rolled hem (17)

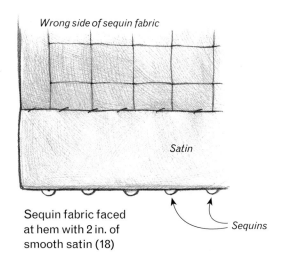

Wrong side of sequin fabric

Satin

Sequins

Sequin fabric faced at hem with 2 in. of smooth satin (18)

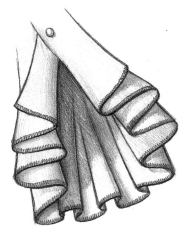

Ruffles created by serging over fishing line (19)

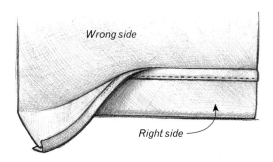

Wrong side

Right side

Raw edge covered with double-fold bias tape, then machine-stitched (20)

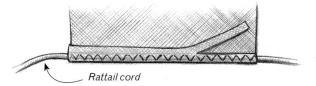

Rattail cord

Zigzag sewn over rattail cord on bridal net (21)

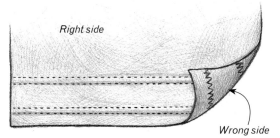

Right side

Wrong side

Two rows of double-needle stitching 1 in. apart (22)

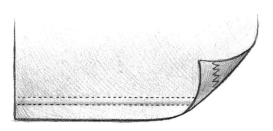

Double row of topstitching done with twin needle (23)

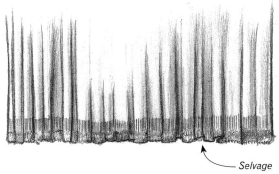

Selvage

Pleated fabric with selvage as hem (24)

Hems

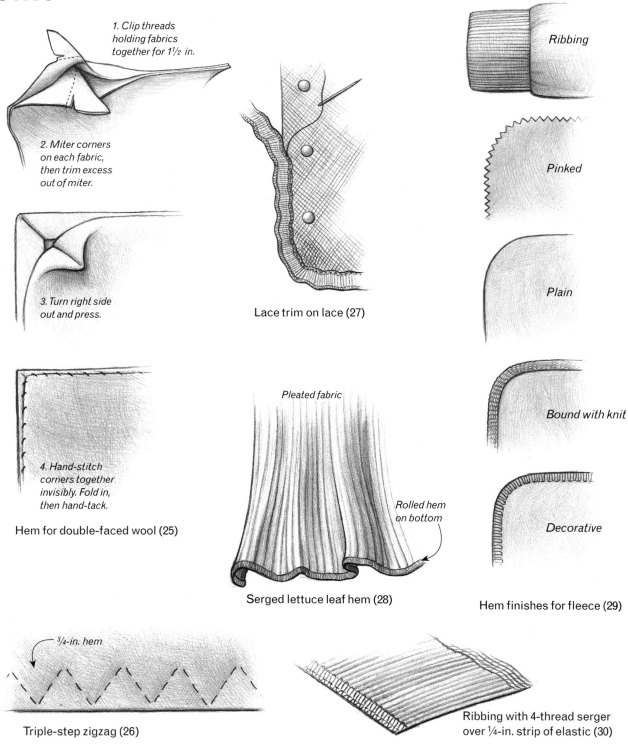

1. Clip threads holding fabrics together for 1½ in.

2. Miter corners on each fabric, then trim excess out of miter.

3. Turn right side out and press.

4. Hand-stitch corners together invisibly. Fold in, then hand-tack.

Hem for double-faced wool (25)

Lace trim on lace (27)

Pleated fabric

Rolled hem on bottom

Serged lettuce leaf hem (28)

Ribbing

Pinked

Plain

Bound with knit

Decorative

Hem finishes for fleece (29)

¾-in. hem

Triple-step zigzag (26)

Ribbing with 4-thread serger over ¼-in. strip of elastic (30)

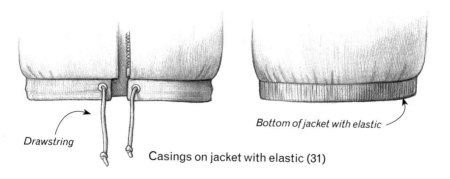

Drawstring

Bottom of jacket with elastic

Casings on jacket with elastic (31)

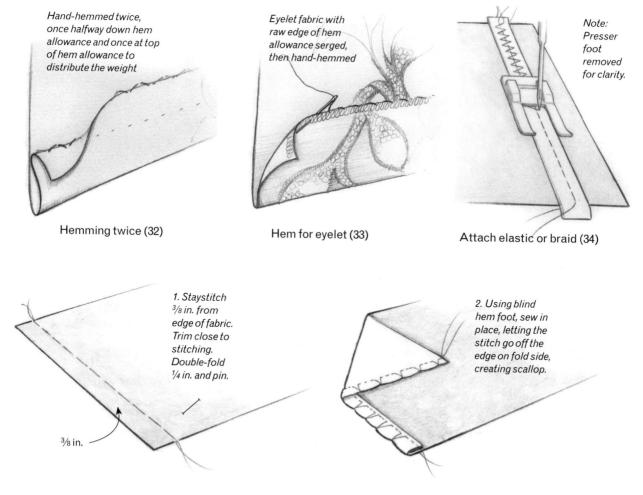

Hand-hemmed twice,
once halfway down hem
allowance and once at top
of hem allowance to
distribute the weight

Hemming twice (32)

Eyelet fabric with
raw edge of hem
allowance serged,
then hand-hemmed

Hem for eyelet (33)

Note:
Presser
foot
removed
for clarity.

Attach elastic or braid (34)

1. Staystitch
³⁄₈ in. from
edge of fabric.
Trim close to
stitching.
Double-fold
¹⁄₄ in. and pin.

³⁄₈ in.

2. Using blind
hem foot, sew in
place, letting the
stitch go off the
edge on fold side,
creating scallop.

Blind-hem stitch for lingerie (35)

Hand Picking

Hand picking gives a couture touch to plain colored fabric and is typically done to highlight the shape of lapels, collars, pocket flaps, and zippers. It can also highlight seams in a multi-seam jacket.

Hand picking is done with thicker thread than sewing thread, such as buttonhole twist or pearl cotton, in a shade slightly darker than or in high contrast to the garment fabric, such as white on black. You will need a hand needle with an eye large enough to accommodate one thread without shredding as you stitch.

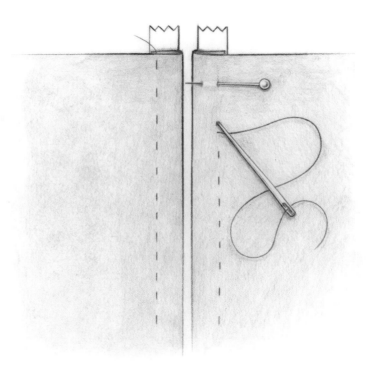

To hand-pick, knot the single thread and hide the knot between layers, bringing the needle out on the right side of the fabric. Insert the needle back into the fabric a scant ¼ in. behind where the thread came out, making a backstitch. Be sure you take a stitch through all layers. Don't pull the thread too tightly—you want it to "float" on the surface so that it can be seen. Continue taking stitches ¼ in. apart and ¼ in. or ⅜ in. from the seam edge until you've completed the area to be stitched.

Neckline Finish for Knits

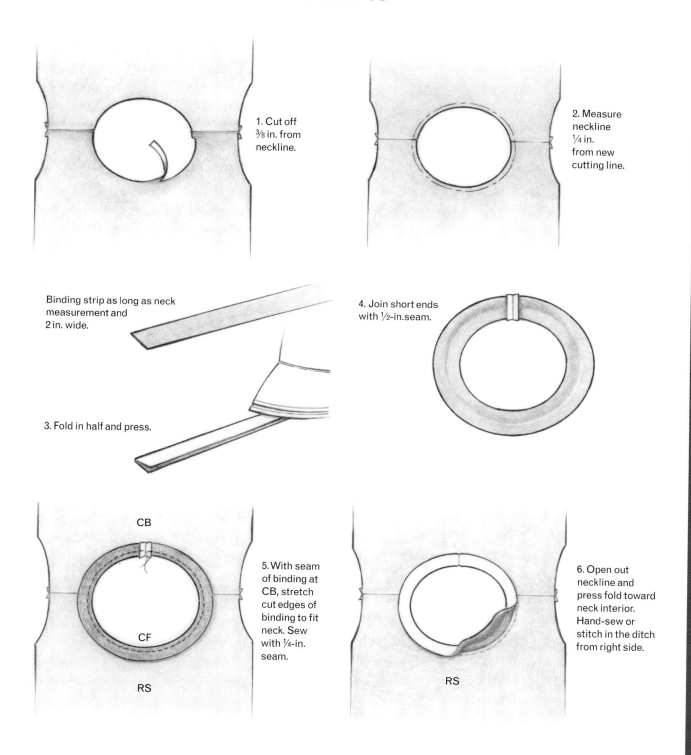

1. Cut off ⅜ in. from neckline.

2. Measure neckline ¼ in. from new cutting line.

Binding strip as long as neck measurement and 2 in. wide.

3. Fold in half and press.

4. Join short ends with ½-in. seam.

CB

CF

RS

5. With seam of binding at CB, stretch cut edges of binding to fit neck. Sew with ¼-in. seam.

RS

6. Open out neckline and press fold toward neck interior. Hand-sew or stitch in the ditch from right side.

What Is Interfacing?

Interfacing is an added layer of fabric that gives crispness and support to garment details such as collars, neckbands, lapels, plackets, pocket welts, and waistbands. Interfacing also must be used behind all closures, such as button and pocket openings and zippers. In these instances, the interfacing not only stabilizes but also eliminates rippling on the face of the fabric. Interfacing should not be visible. Without interfacing, garment details lack the crispness needed to make them look professional.

Interfacings come in knits, wovens, and spun (that is, Pellon) and can be fused or sewn in. A fusible, while fast and easy to apply, can sometimes cause puckering and stiffness. Silk organza is a sew-in interfacing that is a great alternative to a fusible. In fact, it is my favorite interfacing for silks. Beware: Don't use polyester organza, which causes puckering in the seams. And never use it as a press cloth because it melts!

The factor that determines whether or not you can use a fusible is how the glue affects your fashion fabric. Experiment on a scrap of fashion fabric. The interfaced fabric should be compatible with the fabric that is not fused—crisp but not stiff, and invisible. Start with lightweight fusible interfacing; if the results aren't what you need, add another layer. I never use a fusible on a lightweight silk because I have yet to find one that works as well as silk organza, which is a sew-in.

MY FAVORITE INTERFACINGS

ARMO WEFT
A fusible woven interfacing and a favorite for tailoring. This product and Stylemaker 602 give similar results.

FUSI-KNIT
A longtime favorite. This knit interfacing is very compatible with knits, but it is also great with wovens if you want light- to medium-weight body.

PALMER /PLETSCH PERFECTFUSE™
Makes four weights of interfacing: sheer, light, medium, and tailor. These interfacings are very popular in the Northwest, where Patti Palmer has good distributors.

PELLON
Comes in different weights and as fusible and nonfusible. It is suitable for craft projects or to stabilize the back of a pattern you want to preserve. It is often used in ready-to-wear, especially children's clothes. The industry uses it because it can be cut on any grain and is inexpensive. I stabilize patterns with it.

SEWERS' DREAM
Similar to Fusi-Knit but results in a more flexible hand. Canadian designer Ron Collins fuses Sewers' Dream onto the wrong side of all of his linen jackets to prevent excess wrinkling.

SILK ORGANZA
My favorite interfacing for all lightweight silks and to underline if I want to add crispness and body to the whole garment. Do not preshrink silk organza unless you are using it in something that will be machine-washed and -dried.

SO-SHEER

A very lightweight fusible woven, giving minimum support. Because it is a knitted interfacing, it works really well on knits or wovens when you want medium body.

STYLEMAKER 601

This woven fusible is preshrunk and a perfect weight for unstructured jackets and details in medium-weight fabrics.

STYLEMAKER 602

This woven fusible is preshrunk. It is the perfect weight for tailored coats and jackets.

VERISHAPE

A stiff nonfusible interfacing that works well on stand-up coat collars as well as cummerbunds and clutch purses. Use in any area where you need stiff support.

Tips for Fusing Interfacing

- **Don't buy the cheap interfacing. Using cheap interfacing on expensive fabric will decrease the value of your fashion fabric. Thanks, Ron Collins!**

- **Interfacing must be preshrunk to prevent bubbling. Fold the piece loosely and immerse in hot tap water. Let sit for 15 to 20 minutes, or until the water cools. Do not agitate the piece, as the resins may loosen. Drain water and remove excess water by squeezing, not wringing. Lay flat or hang over shower rod to dry.**

- **Remember that a fusible, once fused to a fabric, will feel slightly crisper and firmer. Experiment with a sample on a scrap of your fabric.**

- **An Elnapress produces the longest-lasting fuse because it gives 100 lb. of pressure per square inch as it fuses.**

- **If you don't have an Elnapress, use an ironing board cover that can breathe—so don't use an ironing board cover that is reflective or uses a Teflon finish, which will reflect the heat, causing damage to both fabric and interfacing if too hot.**

- **Press your fabric before applying interfacing. Fabric that is smooth, wrinkle-free, and warm will be more receptive to the fusible resins.**

- **Use the cotton setting on your iron. If your iron doesn't produce a lot of steam, mist the fabric or dampen the press cloth (silk organza). You can also mist the interfacing lightly with water to help the fuse be more successful.**

- **Press firmly, with steam, for 8 to 10 seconds. The heavier the fabric, the more time it takes, so adjust your time accordingly. Do not glide the iron back and forth; use a lift-and-press motion. Be sure to fuse each area of larger garment sections by slightly overlapping iron positions. Lower the ironing board to enhance your pressure on the iron.**

Presser Feet Parade

Different types of sewing require different presser feet on the machine to ensure sewing success. It takes just a few minutes to swap out a standard foot for one of the different feet. Here's a snapshot of presser feet you should get to know.

All purpose/
standard/universal

Buttonhole

Cording

Edge

Embroidery

Flat fell

Invisible zipper

Narrow hem

¼ in.

Quilting/straight stitch

Roller

Satin stitch

Single hole

Single-hole throat plate

Standard zipper

Teflon roller

Teflon square with hole
cut for feed dogs

Topstitching

Velva "V"

Walking/even feed

Zipper

Recommended Tools and Notions

A Tool box

B Stay Tape

C Measuring tape

D Kai shears, scissors

E Kai 5-in. trimmers

F Threaders for lower loopers

G ¼-in. and ½-in. Steam-A-Seam

H Seam ripper

I Curve Runner™ measuring wheel

J Clear elastic

K FrayBlock

L Point turner

M E6000® glue

N Rub 'n Buff®

O Buttonhole chisel

P Pilot Frixion erasable ink pen

Q Sewers Aid

R Grandma's Secret Spot Remover™

S Clover Chaco Liner

T Magnetic pin cushion

U Elnapress

V Good-quality iron (shown Reliable Velocity 200IR)

Knit Know-How

As an instructor, I see my students experience the most difficulty and disappointment from choosing the wrong knit for their pattern. Just because a pattern says "for knits only" does not mean that any knit will work.

TESTING KNIT FABRIC

Good marriages between pattern styles and knits can be observed by shopping ready-to-wear. Feel and notice the weight and drape of knits used for narrow pants, shift dresses, full pants, wrap dresses, unstructured coats, fitted T-shirts, and fullish T-shirts. Make a few notes.

While you are in the store, check the fiber contents of the ready-to-wear garments. You may not be able to find exact fiber percentages because the fabric may be custom milled for the designer, but at least you will know what fiber contents to look for.

Back at home, look in your fabric stash and find a knit that will work with the pattern you have in mind based on the content information you gathered at the store. Once you have chosen both the knit and the pattern, find another knit in your stash or at a discount store with similar stretch and drape to the good one. This will be used as a test fabric, so it can be ugly. From the test fabric, make a sample of the pattern, following these guidelines:

- **Side seams:** Add 1 in. fit insurance to the side seams to account for differences in stretch. This way, when you baste together the garment sides, you have room to let out—or take in—the seams for better fit.

- **Neckline:** Finish the neckline called for in the pattern so you can determine if another neckline would be more flattering or should be finished differently than originally planned.

- **Skipped stitches:** To eliminate skipped stitches, review your options. (1) Check your needle to be sure you're using a 75/11 stretch needle. (2) Preshrink the fabric. (3) Change your presser foot to a roller foot if fabric is stretchy.

- **Fabric stretch while sewing:** If your test knit is stretching as you sew, position strips of Sulky Totally Stable® Stabilizer under the stitching lines.

FIBER CONTENT

Fiber content—and thus a garment's wearability—is what will determine how often you wear the garment.

- **Acetate knits** are commonly known as slinky knits. Garments made from these knits travel well since they never wrinkle. They also do not breathe. They make great pants, skirts, and loose dresses. See Slinky Knit (p. 158) for information on how to sew them.

- **Bamboo knits,** while beautiful on the bolt, wrinkle a lot after laundering, grow in length and width, and simply lose their shape. The fiber content for most bamboo knit is 95% bamboo and 5% spandex. I did find one bamboo knit that was 67% bamboo, 30% cotton, and 3% spandex, which was more stable. I don't recommend sewing with these knits.

- **Barcelona** is one of the ITY polyester knits with great drape and recovery. It's good for tops, dresses, and full pants but too thin for close fitting skirts and pants.

- **Cashmere knits** are difficult to find and very expensive. The only places I know that carry them are B&J Fabrics in New York and Banksville Designer Fabrics in Norwalk, Conn. They make beautiful garments, however, so consider cashmere knits when making a special top.

- **Cotton knits** breathe the best but need to be combined with other fibers, especially Lycra, to keep their shape. Check for recovery (see the facing page). Not all cotton knits are created equal.

- **Cotton ponte** fades and does not have enough recovery unless it has at least 6% spandex.

- **ITY knits** are made from twisted polyester yarn similar to that found in Diane von Furstenberg wrap dresses. These knits have a smooth, silky hand and terrific drape, perfect for wrap dresses, tops, or very full pants. Open necks are advised since ITY is still polyester. These 6% spandex yarns have a 50% crossgrain stretch and great recovery.

- **Linen knits** are super comfortable to wear but do not have great recovery, so choose a style accordingly, such as a loose top or cardigan. These knits also can be a bit see-through, so consider double layers; I made a double-layered linen knit skirt, and the layers stuck together, when they should have been drapey.

- **Microfiber knits** have the very best drape, but they are polyester (see below).

- **Nylon knits** were originally known as knit tricot and used for slips and nightwear. Nylon knits in a different form are known as stretch mesh. There are different grades of stretch mesh. Look for the slightly heavier ones with good recovery. Stretch mesh makes great sleeves, T-shirts, and slips under lace dresses.

- **Polyester knits** seem to come in the best prints, are rather shiny in appearance, and do not breathe. That does not mean they should be avoided completely, however. They are fine in open necks, wrap tops, sleeveless tops and dresses, and loose pants where air can reach. Double knits with a high polyester content tend to pill.

- **Ponte** is a type of double knit that looks the same on both sides. It comes in different weights and different fiber contents. The heavyweight works well for pants, jackets, shifts, and straight skirts. The mid-weight works well for tops, wraps, and dresses, and the lightweight works very well for lightweight T-shirts. My favorite ponte has a high rayon fiber content.

- **Rayon knits** are best when combined with a fair amount of Lycra. Rayon knits are super comfortable to wear but do wrinkle a bit.

- **Rayon ponte** is used in Eileen Fisher clothes. The fiber content is 65% rayon, 15% nylon, and 20% Lycra. The rayon makes garments breathable and comfortable to wear; the nylon makes the fabric more stable, and the Lycra gives both the stretch and recovery.

- **Silk knits** are wonderful to wear from a comfort standpoint, but tend to run or snag easily. Be careful in the layout process—make sure your cuticles and nails are smooth. Plain colors are usually too thin to wear as outer garments.

- **Sofia** is the most readily available ponte, with a fiber content of 67% polyester, 30% rayon, and 15% spandex. While the heavier weight makes wonderful pants, such a high polyester content means the fabric will pill over time.

- **Viscose knit** is a higher-quality rayon. While more expensive than regular rayon, it has better drape, a more weighty hand, and better recovery.

- **Wool jersey** is a knit often found in better ready-to-wear. It makes beautiful tops, skirts, and pants. It is wonderful to wear but must be dry-cleaned.

SINGLE AND DOUBLE KNIT COMPATIBILITY

In fabric stores, you will find single and double knits. Single knits, often called jerseys, have only one fabric layer with a knit stitch on one side and a purl stitch on the other. Single knits are thinner, are less stable, and have a better drape than double knits, making them good candidates for T-shirts, full dresses, and full skirts. Double knits have two knitted layers, making them thicker and stronger than single knits. They have good recovery, making them the perfect choice for pants, straight skirts, shift dresses, and jackets. An interlock is a smooth double-knit jersey.

WHAT IS RECOVERY?

Recovery is how fast a knit bounces back to the original crossgrain after it has been pulled on the crossgrain. Check recovery by pulling the fabric on the crossgrain. If the fabric does not return to its original form, then it does not have good recovery. This may not be so important on a single knit that is used for a drapey top or wrap dress. However, recovery is important for a fitted T-shirt, which you do not want to stretch out of shape. Recovery is most important in a double knit, which will be used for pants, straight skirts, or shift dresses. Bad recovery will cause the seat and the knees to bag out of shape.

The addition of Lycra, the trade name for Spandex, is what gives a fabric stretch and allows it to recover. Spandex/Lycra is added to many different fibers and in different amounts. Knits can have one- or two-way stretch. The greatest stretch of the knit is usually on the crossgrain and should always go around the body. If you are making exercise wear or a pair of very close-fitting pants, you may want a fabric with two-way stretch that will not only go around the body, but also up and down to allow the garment to stretch in both directions as the body moves. In this case, you want a knit that stretches crosswise and lengthwise.

Determining Fabric Content

Determining the fiber content is not an exact science since more and more fabrics are a combination of fibers. If a fabric is pure, fiber content can usually be determined by what is often referred to as the "burn test." Snip off a small piece of fabric. Holding fabric with tweezers (not between your fingers), subject the fabric to a flame from a burning match. Watch fabric closely.

ACETATE	Melts under the flame and leaves a brittle black bead. Smells like vinegar.
ACRYLIC	Melts under the flame and keeps burning after flame is removed. Leaves a brittle black bead. Has no smell.
COTTON	Burns quickly with a yellow flame and continues burning after flame is removed. Leaves soft gray ash. Smells like burning paper.
LINEN	Burns quickly with a yellow flame and continues burning after flame is removed. Leaves soft gray ash. Smells like burning paper.
NYLON	Melts and burns slowly. Leaves a hard gray bead. Smells like celery.
POLYESTER	Burns slowly, trailing black smoke. Leaves a hard black bead. Has no smell.
RAYON	Burns quickly with a yellow flame and continues burning after flame is removed. Leaves soft gray ash. Smells like burning paper.
SILK	Sizzles in the flame and burns slowly. Leaves crushable black ash. Smells like burning hair or feathers.
WOOL	Sizzles in the flame and burns slowly. Leaves crushable black ash. Smells like burning hair or feathers.

Linings

If you are willing to take the extra time to line either a garment or a window treatment, it is helpful to know not only what products are available but the properties of each. This knowledge will help ensure an intelligent decision when purchasing lining fabric.

APPAREL PROJECTS

ACETATE

100% acetate ravels excessively, does not breathe, wrinkles, and retains perspiration stains. So why would anyone use it? Acetate is good for men's wear since it comes in prints and pinstripes.

AMBIANCE BY BEMBERG

100% rayon lining that breathes and can be machine-washed and machine-dried. Eliminates static cling on silk garments. Because it resists wrinkles, it makes a great lining in pants and skirts. Better-quality men's suits are lined in Bemberg because it wears better than silk.

BATISTE, LAWN, PIMA COTTON, AND ORGANZA

None of the above works as a lining since they do not drape and they stick to other garments, but all are suitable as underlinings.

CHINA SILK

100% silk. Very lightweight and breathes, but wrinkles and is too fragile for machine wash and dry. A challenge to iron. Because this lining is so lightweight to be almost nonexistent, it is very comfortable to wear. A designer favorite inside of jackets, among them Coco Chanel.

FLANNEL

100% cotton. Adds warmth and resists wrinkles. Works well in a vest or body of an outerwear garment but should never be used in sleeves, skirts, or pants. since flannel does not slide over the body. Flannel can be used as an underlining in a silk jacket. Jacket is then lined with something slippery.

HANG LOOSE

100% polyester lining that does not breathe or wrinkle; can be machine-washed and machine-dried but not a good choice if you get hot easily.

HYDROFIL

Has a smooth taffeta-like surface. Makes a terrific lining for outerwear since it breathes and wicks moisture to the outside, keeping you dry and comfortable. Machine washable.

KASHA

52% acetate, 48% cotton. Very popular in Canada to line winter coats. Kasha is shiny on one side with a cotton flannel backing. Must be dry-cleaned.

NYLON TRICOT

Slips are usually made in this fabric. Also makes an excellent lining for knits or bathing suits.

SILK CREPE DE CHINE

If price is no object, silk crepe de Chine makes a beautiful lining, luxurious and drapey.

SILK GEORGETTE

Makes an excellent lining for burnout velvet and chiffon.

HOME-DEC PROJECTS

BLACKOUT

Cotton/poly blend available in white and cream. Used in draperies to block out all light. Good for people with varied sleep schedules.

RAIN-NO-STAIN®

Cotton/poly blend. Available in white and cream, a lightweight lining for draperies, upholstery, and pillows to prevent show-through. Works well as a lining for heavier fabrics such as velveteen to prevent the draperies from becoming so heavy they pull the brackets off the wall.

SPECIAL SUEDE

Cotton/poly blend. Feels a bit rubbery, available in white and cream. Can be used in the same way as Rain-No-Stain. A favorite among interior designers, but not to be used with very heavy fabrics because of its weight.

SELF-FABRIC

Sheer drapes are often backed with another layer of the same fabric to give more depth to the window treatment while still letting in maximum light.

Stain Removal Guide

Repeated treatment or, in some cases, soaking overnight is often necessary. It is best to use a weak solution initially, repeating several times. Rinse out cleaning solution between treatments. Test chemical solutions, bleach, or solvent on a seam allowance before applying to the spot. Do not mix chemicals. Chlorine and ammonia form toxic gases when mixed. Apply remover from the underside of a garment, working the stain out through the direction it came. Home dry-cleaning products work for normal soil, but spots don't come out at home. Dry-cleaners know a trick or two.

How to make an enzyme paste: Combine Biz®, Wisk®, or Axion® plus enough water to make a paste. Rub into stain.

ALCOHOLIC BEVERAGES

Washable fabrics: Soak first in cold water and then sudsy water. If stain persists on washable fabrics, combine 2 Tbsp. of hydrogen peroxide to 1 gal. of water. Soak for ½ hour and rinse well.
Dry-cleanable fabrics: Rub with water and cornstarch.

BARBEQUE SAUCE

Pat glycerin on spot. Let set for 5 minutes. Rinse with cool water. Combine 1 part glycerin and 1 part Shout®. Mix. Apply to spot and let sit 15 minutes. Rinse with cool water.

BALLPOINT PEN

Spray polyester fabric with hairspray. Marks will often disappear. If this fails and for other fabrics, rub stain with rubbing alcohol, then saturate with soap and wash.

BEETS

Soak bread in cold water. Place over stain. Let bread absorb stain.

BERRY STAINS

Apply white vinegar and rinse well.

BIRD DROPPINGS

Add ¼ tsp. of ammonia to 2 Tbsp. dishwashing detergent. Rub in. Rinse off with water.

BLOOD

For a small amount, such as a pinprick: Wet with your own saliva. Blot. Repeat. Blot. For larger stains in washable garment, flush with cool tap water. Soak in solution of 3 Tbsp. ammonia to 1 gal. cool water for about an hour. Rinse. If stain remains, try enzyme paste, soak, and rinse. For dry-cleanable garments, mix cornstarch and water into thick paste. Spread on blood. Brush off when dry. Repeat.

BUTTER

Saturate with enzyme paste and wash in plenty of water.

CANDLE WAX

Remove waxed surface with a dull knife. Place the stain between two white paper towels or napkins. Press with a warm iron. If color traces remain, wash using soap (not detergent) and 1 cup baking soda in hottest water safe for fabric.

CAT URINE

Deep-clean area with a carpet shampoo. Rinse with cool water and no chemicals. Spread 2 cups of pet odor neutralizing powder, such as Nature's Miracle®, on area. Use lots! Let sit for 8 hours. Vacuum. Repeat with cool water shampoo and another treatment of powder if odor remains.

CHEWING GUM

Put the garment in freezer or apply ice. Pry gum from surface with a knife. Soak gummed area in cleaning fluid.

CHOCOLATE

Washable fabrics: Soak in 4 Tbsp. of borax and 2½ cups warm water.
Dry-cleanable fabrics: Pat mixture onto chocolate and blot. Rinse and blot. If stain remains, spread on a paste of borax and water. Let set for 1 hour. Rinse.

COFFEE

Stretch fabric over bowl. Pour boiling water through the stain from a 3-foot height. If coffee was mixed with milk, spray with Biz first.

COSMETICS, GENERAL

Apply prewash soil remover and wash using regular detergent. Rinse thoroughly and air-dry. Repeat if necessary.

CRAYONS

Remove waxed surface with a dull knife. Place the stain between two white paper towels or napkins. Press with a warm iron. If color traces remain, wash using soap (not detergent) and 1 cup baking soda in hottest water safe for fabric.

DYE

Sometimes colors are released from one fabric to another in the washing machine. A product called Runaway® by Dylon removes unwanted color.

FINGERPRINTS AND SCUFFS ON CLOTH PURSES AND SHOES

Mix solution of 1 part Dove or Ivory and 1 part water. Rub in. Rinse with cool water. Heavy stains may require dry cleaning.

FRUIT STAINS

Apply white vinegar and rinse well.

FUR

Work cornmeal into spot with toothbrush. Let stand overnight. Brush well.

GLUE

Soak glue stain in non-acetate nail polish remover. Rub with Wisk and water mixed in equal amounts. Let sit in warm place for 30 minutes. Rinse with clear water.

GRASS

Try rubbing with detergent first. If stain remains, rub with 1 part alcohol and 2 parts water. Let sit for 15 minutes. If stain persists, use chlorine or peroxide bleach. Rinse well.

GREASE

Murphy's Oil Soap® works wonders on greasy stains. If stain remains, try pouring cleaning fluid through the stain. For dry-clean-only fabrics, try soaking in trichloroethylene, available in drugstores.

ICE CREAM

Washable fabrics: Make solution of 1 Tbsp. Wisk and 2 cups of water. Rub into spot and let sit 10 minutes. Saturate with prewashable soil remover. Let stand for $\frac{1}{2}$ hour. Wash. Rinse with a solution of $\frac{1}{4}$ cup vinegar to 1 gal. water.
Dry-cleanable fabrics: Apply rubbing alcohol and let sit 10 minutes. Rinse spotted area with mild detergent such as Woolite® mixed with a little water. Rinse away residue with cool water.

JELLY

Make a paste of borax and water. Rub in with toothbrush. Let set 1 hour. Rinse.

KETCHUP

Soak in cool water for $\frac{1}{2}$ hour. Apply prewash soil remover. Rinse. Apply enzyme paste. Rinse. Add clear vinegar to last rinse.

LINT

Toss item in dryer with a pair of old nylons.

LIPSTICK

Rub with white vinegar and rinse off. If lipstick is stubborn, apply prewash soil remover and wash using regular detergent. Rinse thoroughly and air-dry. Repeat if necessary.

LIQUID MAKEUP

Apply enzyme paste and wash in sudsy water.

MASCARA

Apply enzyme paste and wash in sudsy water.

MILDEW

Treat as soon as possible with alternating applications of detergent and rubbing alcohol. Expose to sunlight.

MILK

Apply enzyme paste and soak for 30 minutes. Rinse. Saturate with prewashable soil remover. Let stand for $\frac{1}{2}$ hour. Wash. Rinse with a solution of $\frac{1}{4}$ cup vinegar to 1 gal. water.

MUD

Let mud dry and brush off.
Washable fabrics: Mix solution of gentle detergent such as Woolite and water. Rub in. Rinse. Rub a solution of 1 part white vinegar and 1 part water into any remaining stain. Let sit 30 minutes. Rinse.
Dry-cleanable fabrics: Dab on a solution of 1 part Ivory liquid and 1 cup water. Rinse by dabbing plain cool water on spot.

MUSTARD

Rub in enzyme paste and let sit for 3 hours. Machine-wash in Clorox 2®.

NAIL POLISH

Work in acetone from the underside, blotting with a white paper towel from right side. Be sure to test for fabric safeness on a seam allowance first, since some fabrics will dissolve.

OLD AGE

Restore antique linens and laces to like-new appearance. Fill a 5-qt. pot three-quarters full of water. Bring to a boil. Throw in 20 tablets of denture cleaner and stir until dissolved. Add antique fabric. Reduce to a low boil and cook for 20 minutes. Rinse with clear water. Air-dry. Works wonders!

PAINT, OIL-BASED

Try to keep paint from drying by wrapping the item in plastic. Sponge with cleaning fluid, paint thinner, or turpentine. Work in detergent. Rinse. Soak in hot detergent solution overnight. Wash. Air-dry.

PAINT, WATER-BASED

Spot-wash with cool water and detergent. Work in prewash soil remover. Rinse. Apply cleaning fluid on remaining stain. Soak spot in rubbing alcohol. Cover with plastic for 1 hour. Scrub off. Repeat if necessary.

PENCIL

Marks may sometimes be removed with an eraser or by alternating treatments of ammonia and detergent.

PERFUME

Rub area with glycerin and clean per usual.

PERSPIRATION

Soak in salt water for 1 hour. Then sponge spots with 50:50 solution of white vinegar and water. Rinse well. Sponge a fresh stain with ammonia.

PILLING

Try a product called Grip-It. Roll onto affected areas and pull off pills.

RUST

A product called Rustiban® removes rust from most fabrics. Use with rubber gloves. For set-in stains, try a solution of distilled water, lemon juice, cream of tartar, and salt.

SALAD OIL

For fresh stains, sprinkle cornstarch on spot and brush off. If stain remains, rub in glycerin and let sit for 1 hour. Rinse with detergent and water.

SCORCH MARKS

Alternate applications of ammonia, detergent, and water. Rinse area well before re-pressing. If this treatment fails, mix a few drops of ammonia with 1 Tbsp. of peroxide. Rub mixture into the stain. Rinse well. For wools, it may be necessary to sand the scorched area with very fine sandpaper.

SHOE POLISH

Remove waxed surface with a dull knife. Place the stain between two white paper towels or napkins. Press with a warm iron. If color traces remain, wash using soap (not detergent) and 1 cup baking soda in hottest water safe for fabric.

SHINE FROM IRONING

Make a solution of hot vinegar and water or ammonia and water. Rub into fabric. Rinse well. If the fabric is a synthetic, shine is permanent since the fibers have melted.

TAR

Rub soiled area with Goop®, a waterless soap found in hardware stores. Rinse with cool water.

TEA

Stretch fabric over bowl. Pour boiling water through the stain from a 3-ft. height.

TOMATO SAUCE

Soak in cool water for ½ hour. Apply prewash soil remover. Rinse. Apply enzyme paste. Rinse. Add clear vinegar to last rinse.

URINE

Soak area with solution of 1 part ammonia and 1 part water. Let sit 15 minutes. Rinse.

VOMIT

Apply a few drops of ammonia to liquid detergent. Work solution into stain and let sit for 30 minutes. Rinse with water. Sponge with a solution of ¼ cup salt to 2 qt. water. Let sit 15 minutes. Rinse again with water.

WINE

White and red: Soak area with sparkling water as soon as possible. Cover stain with salt. Stretch fabric over a bowl. From a height of 1 ft., pour boiling water through stain. If stain remains, rub area with glycerin. Rinse.
For dry-cleanable fabrics: Blot area with Woolite. Feather outside edge with Shout. Mix 1 part white vinegar to 2 parts water. Let stain soak in solution for 5 minutes. Rinse with cold water.

CARING FOR LEATHER AND SUEDE

LEATHER

The main drawback in owning real suede or leather garments is having to dry-clean them. If a leather garment is really quite soiled, professional dry cleaning may be necessary. However, many stains can be removed at home. For protection against water and stains, spray your new leather garment with All Protector, which keeps spots from setting in. High-gloss leather is more difficult to keep looking new than a natural finish and may show spots and streaks if worn in rain or snow. If you get caught in the rain while wearing a smooth leather garment, the leather will probably stiffen up a bit after it dries. To return the garment to its original supple condition, rub Cadillac Leather Lotion into it. These products are available in good-quality leather clothing shops. If you get a grease spot on smooth leather, here's what you can do: Purchase a paste of mink oil from a shoemaker. Apply a small amount to a soft cloth such as an old T-shirt. Rub the cloth over the bristles of a soft brush, distributing the mink oil evenly. Brush over the entire garment, blending the mink oil into the grease mark. This drastic measure works, although it deepens the color.

SUEDE

If you spill wine on suede, clean the spot with a water-soaked cloth using a blot-and-lift motion. To remove a food spot from suede, rub in cornmeal and let dry overnight, or sand lightly with a very fine grade of sandpaper. If you notice a grease mark, apply cornmeal or baking powder to absorb the grease. Brush carefully with a medium-bristle brush. Chandler's Shoe Stores carries a product called Dry-Clean®, which takes out ballpoint pen marks. To remove body oils from suede at the neck, cuff, and elbow areas, try a product called NuBuck Leather Conditioner.

For more information, check out *The Super Stain Remover Book* by Jack Cassimatis. This is a handy reference for removing stains on furniture, carpets, handbags, shoes, jewelry, and others.

Glossary

ACETATE
A filament fiber made from acetate with a crisp hand and high luster. Drapes well. Acetate woven fabric is often used for linings, but it shows perspiration stains. (Sew as crepe de Chine; see p. 40.)

ACRYLIC
A synthetic fiber that has a soft hand and good wrinkle resistance. It is often used in blankets and socks. (Sew as wool flannel; see p. 62.)

ADMIRALTY CLOTH
Melton cloth often used in military uniforms and pea coats. (Sew as wool melton; see p. 212.)

AIDA CANVAS
Stiff, coarse fabric used for needlework. (Sew as canvas; see p. 24.)

ALBERT CLOTH
A reversible wool double cloth with different colors on front and back. Used for coats. (Sew as wool double cloth; see p. 206.)

ALENÇON LACE
A needlepoint lace with fine net background with cord outlining design. (Sew as lace; see p. 90.)

BARK CLOTH
Rugged looking 100% cotton, formerly used to make draperies but now used for unlined jackets and straight or A-line skirts. (Sew as damask; see p. 44.)

BEMBERG
This rayon lining material has a soft, silk-like quality and comes in several weights. (Sew lightweight Bemberg as China silk; see p. 138. Sew heavyweight Bemberg as silk noil; see p. 144.)

BENGALINE
A lustrous, durable, warp-faced fabric with corded appearance most often used in millinery, ribbons, and suits. (Sew as gabardine; see p. 68.)

BOTANY WOOL
Originally referred to Australian wool of fine quality but now refers to fine wool from all over the world. (Sew as worsted wool; see p. 214.)

BOYNGE
Thermal underwear fabric. (Sew as lightweight knit; see p. 80.)

BROADCLOTH
A fine, closely woven, lustrous cotton or poly-cotton blend with an unbalanced weave that creates a fine rib. An excellent shirting material. (Sew as shirting; see p. 136.)

BUCKRAM
A coarse, stiff, plain open-weave fabric used as a stiffener. (Sew as canvas; see p. 24.)

BURLAP
Very rough, inexpensive, open-weave fabric. Can be used as window coverings but tends to fade and stretch over time.

CABRETTA
A fine lightweight goatskin. Excellent choice for garment sewing, especially pants. (Sew as leather; see p. 96.)

CALICO
A plain cotton weave with a typically busy, small floral pattern. (Sew as shirting; see p. 136.)

CAMBRIC
A soft plain-weave cloth or linen with a slight luster used for handkerchiefs, aprons, and underwear. (Sew as cotton batiste; see p. 10.)

CAVALRY TWILL
A popular fabric for military uniforms. Its distinct twill weave makes it an excellent choice for a jacket or coat. Wrinkle resistant. (Sew as wool flannel; see p. 62.)

CHAMBRAY
Has the appearance of very fine denim, with a plain weave using colored warp and white weft. Makes great shirts and pajamas. (Sew as cotton shirting; see p. 136.)

CHAMOIS
Lightweight leather from sheepskin. Used for buffing cars and American Indian–inspired garments. (Sew as suede; see p. 164.)

CHARMELAINE
A wool twill dress fabric with a ribbed face and smooth back. (Sew as wool gabardine; see p. 68.)

CHINTZ
Plain-weave cotton fabric with a glazed finish often used for slipcovers and curtains. (Sew as cotton piqué; see p. 114.)

CHINO
A durable twill-cotton fabric with a slight sheen that makes excellent work clothes or casual pants. (Sew as cotton piqué; see p. 114.)

COOL WOOL
A trade name used to denote a lightweight "tropical" wool. Armani suits are often made in this fabric. (Sew as wool crepe; see p. 204.)

COVERT
A durable twill-weave fabric made from tightly twisted yarns. Wool covert makes an excellent topcoat that can be waterproofed. Cotton covert makes good work clothes or sportswear. (Sew as wool gabardine; see p. 68.)

CREPE-BACKED SATIN
A reversible satin weave with one side dull and crepe-looking, the other shiny and smooth. Crepe-backed satin is often used in bridesmaids' dresses and is flattering when cut on the bias. (Sew as satin; see p. 128.)

DACRON®
A trademark of Du Pont, this polyester is an old favorite for housedresses. (Sew as polyester silky but cut on lengthwise grain; see p. 116.)

DEERSKIN
Soft, supple leather skin from deer hide. Makes first-quality garments, especially soft shirts, loose pants, and skirts. (Sew as leather; see p. 96.)

DONEGAL TWEED
A rather coarse, wrinkle-resistant multicolored wool most often used in men's sports jackets. (Sew as worsted wool; see p. 214.)

DOTTED SWISS
A sheer cotton or nylon fabric patterned with small dots that are woven in or glued on. Makes good summer blouses and curtains. (Sew as cotton batiste; see p. 10.)

DRILL
A strong, dense, medium- to heavy-weight cotton of twill weave. Used for uniforms, lining shoes, work clothes, and mattress ticking. (Sew as denim; see p. 46.)

DUCHESSE SATIN
A highly lustrous, smooth, very finely woven silk fabric. Used in bridal or evening wear where volume without bulk is desired. (Sew as satin; see p. 128.)

DUCK
A durable, plain-weave cotton that is flexible. Used for sails, tents, and awnings. (Sew as canvas; see p. 24.)

EGYPTIAN COTTON
A high-quality long-staple cotton used in the finest sheets. (Sew as cotton shirting; see p. 136.)

ENGLISH NET
A cotton netting with a hexagonal weave that dyes well. Used in evening wear for sheer sections and as underlining in bodices. (Sew as tulle and net; see p. 176.)

FACILE
A trademark of Skinner Co., this faux suede is lightweight and drapes better than Ultrasuede. (Sew as faux suede; see p. 58.)

FAILLE
A flat, ribbed fabric with a light luster. Fabric has body but drapes and tailors well. Makes beautiful spring suits and coats. (Sew as satin; see p. 128.)

FLAX
Used to make linen. (Sew as linen; see p. 98.)

FUJI SILK
A lightweight, plain-weave silk used in blouses. (Sew as silk shantung; see p. 150.)

FUKUSA
A silk square used in Japan to wrap gifts. Can be combined in garments for beautiful effects. (Sew as rayon crepe; see p. 40.)

GAUZE
A fine, transparent, plain-weave fabric with open texture. (Sew as unstable knit; see p. 88.)

GINGHAM
A lightweight plain-weave fabric often woven in checks. Great for pattern pretests. (Sew as cotton shirting; see p. 136.)

GORE-TEX
A trademark of WL Gore and Assoc. Inc., this porous fabric repels water but allows body moisture to escape, making it comfortable for active outerwear. (Sew as waterproof breathables; see p. 192.)

GROSGRAIN
A closely woven ribbed ribbon made with a rayon warp. Must be preshrunk.

HABUTAI
A soft, lightweight plain-weave silk usually referred to as China silk. (Sew as China silk; see p. 138.)

HANDKERCHIEF LINEN
A plain weave of the lightest-weight linen. Used for handkerchiefs, blouses, and bias binding. (Sew as cotton batiste; see p. 10.)

HARRIS TWEED
A woolen fabric hand-woven on the islands off the coast of Scotland. It is wrinkle-resistant and often used in men's sport jackets. (Sew as worsted wool; see p. 214.)

HOPSACKING
A coarse, loosely woven fabric woven in hopsack or basket weave. Burlap is a rough hopsack. Cotton or linen hopsacking is more pliable and can be used in lightweight, loose coats. (Sew as linen; see p. 98.)

JACONET
A fine, sheer plain-weave cotton fabric used in children's summer clothing. (Sew as cotton batiste; see p. 10.)

JACQUARD
A weaving system that can produce large woven designs.

LAWN
A finely woven, semi-crisp fabric woven in cotton or linen. It is primarily used in heirloom dresses, blouses, collars, and cuffs. Also makes great underlining. (Sew as cotton batiste; see p. 10.)

LEATHERETTE
A coated fabric that simulates leather. Used in upholstery. (Sew as vinyl; see p. 186.)

LIBERTY
A trademark of Liberty Ltd. England for hand-blocked floral prints in silk, rayon, cotton, and wool challis.

LODEN CLOTH
A thick, soft, oily green wool fabric that repels water and is typically seen in coatings. (Sew as wool melton; see p. 212.)

MADRAS
A fine cotton, hand-loomed in the Madras region of India, dyed with natural dyes. (Sew as cotton shirting; see p. 136.)

MATELASSE
A fabric with crepe and ordinary yarn interfaced in the warp. When the crepe yarn shrinks, it causes the ordinary yarn to pucker, creating raised patterns. Can be made in cotton, silk, or wool. (Sew as prepleated fabric; see p. 118.)

MERINO WOOL
A very fine, dense wool from the merino sheep. Takes dye well. (Sew as wool flannel; see p. 62.)

MESH
Woven, knitted, crocheted, or knotted with open spaces between yarns. Supple and elastic. Used in men's sport shirts. Lightweight mesh is used in evening wear. (Sew as tulle and net; see p. 176.)

MOIRÉ
A wavy, waterlike pattern produced onto a fabric surface by engraved rollers during the finishing process.

MOMME
A Japanese unit of weight for silk fabrics.

MONK'S CLOTH

A heavy, coarse cotton fabric with a loose basket weave. Used in draperies, slipcovers, and upholstery. (Sew as canvas; see p. 24.)

MUSLIN

A firm plain-weave cotton found in many weights. Great for pattern pretests. (Sew as cotton shirting; see p. 136.)

NAPA

A soft, thin, very drapey leather skin used for quality garments. (Sew as leather; see p. 96.)

OILCLOTH

(1) An oil-coated fabric with a waterproof surface. Clean with water. Used for table or shelf covers. (Sew as vinyl; see p. 186.) (2) A lightweight silk that has been lightly coated with oil, making the fabric waterproof. (Sew as sandwashed silk; see p. 148.)

ORGANDY

A very fine, sheer cotton with a crisp hand. (Sew as organza; see p. 146.)

OXFORD CLOTH

A plain weave with twice as many threads in the warp as in the weft, resulting in a basket weave. (Sew as cotton shirting; see p. 136.)

PANNÉ SATIN

A high-gloss satin fabric. (Sew as satin; see p. 128.)

PANNÉ VELVET

Often with a knitted base, pile on this velvet is pressed down in one direction, resulting in a shiny appearance. (Cut as velvet; see p. 182. Sew as stable knit; see p. 80.)

PATENT LEATHER

Shiny, hard, smooth leather created by applying a solution that hardens to the surface of the leather. (Sew as vinyl but use a leather NTW needle; see p. 186.)

PEAU DE SOIE

A heavy, soft silk with a satin finish. (Sew as satin; see p. 128.)

PERCALE

A lightweight, firm cotton with a balanced weave that can be piece-dyed or printed. (Sew as cotton shirting; see p. 136.)

PETERSHAM

A flexible, moldable ribbed rayon/cotton ribbon used in hat bands or as waistline facings. Must be preshrunk. (Sew as cotton piqué; see p. 114.)

PIGSKIN

A sueded leather skin that can be drapey or firm depending on the dye lot. Works well in jackets, slim pants, and straight skirts. (Sew as suede; see p. 164.)

PIMA COTTON

A very fine American Egyptian cotton that is great for underlining. (Sew as cotton batiste; see p. 10.)

PLISSÉ

A puckered or crinkled cotton. (Sew as crinkle cotton; see p. 42.)

POINT D'ESPRIT

A netting with a rectangular dot in a regular, allover pattern. (Sew as tulle and net; see p. 176.)

PONGEE

A plain-weave, medium-weight silk with a finer warp than weft; feels like a starched China silk. (Sew as silk tussah; see p. 154.)

POPLIN

Fabric with a similar weave to broadcloth but the rib is larger and the fabric heavier. (Sew as cotton damask; see p. 44.)

POWERNET

A four-way stretch fabric often used for girdles. (Sew as stable knit; see p. 80.)

RASCHEL KNIT

A warp-knitted fabric that comes in a variety of patterns. (Sew as stable knit; see p. 80.)

SATEEN

Fabric made of long staple cotton or filament yarns to produce a strong, lustrous surface. (Sew as cotton damask; see p. 44.)

SEA ISLAND COTTON

The finest grade of cotton. (Sew as cotton batiste; see p. 10.)

SEERSUCKER

A permanently crinkled cotton stripe. Crinkle is produced in the weave and is not destroyed by heat. (See p. 130.)

SHARKSKIN

A worsted wool with a mottled effect often found in men's suitings. A lighter weight in cotton is used in sportswear and uniforms. (Sew as worsted wool; see p. 214.)

SHEEPSKIN

Suede produced from a breed of sheep that grows hair rather than wool. (Sew as faux fur but use a leather NTW needle; see p. 54.)

SILK BROADCLOTH

A fine, closely woven silk with a fine rib. (Sew as sandwashed silk; see p. 148.)

SPANDEX

A manufactured fiber of at least 85% polyurethane with excellent recovery and flexibility. (Sew as Lycra; see p. 82.)

SURAH

A soft, lightweight, lustrous silk characterized by fine twill lines. Because it isn't durable, it's best used in ties and vest fronts. (Sew as silk crepe de Chine; see p. 40.)

SWISS COTTON

A fine, sheer, crisp cotton. (Sew as cotton shirting; see p. 136.)

THERMOLITE®

A Du Pont–trademarked fabric made from inter-locked polyester that is coated to be slippery and durable. (Sew as water and wind resistant; see p. 190.)

THERMOLOFT®

A Du Pont–trademarked insulation fabric. (Sew as insulation; see p. 12.)

THINSULATE™

A thermal insulation that can't be dry-cleaned. It provides twice the insulation of similar thicknesses of polyester, down, or wool. (Sew as insulation; see p. 12.)

TICKING

A durable plain-, twill-, or satin-weave cotton fabric most often used as covering for mattresses and pillows and sometimes for upholstery. (Sew as denim; see p. 46.)

TRIACETATE

A modified acetate fiber that is stronger than acetate when wet, with greater resistance to heat, shrinking, wrinkling, and fading.

TRICOT

A warp knit fabric with a horizontal rib often used in women's lingerie. Makes a great lining for knitted pants. Fusible tricot makes an excellent lightweight interfacing. (Sew as unstable knit; see p. 88.)

TROPICAL WORSTEDS

Lightweight suiting made of highly twisted yarns that permit air circulation. One yard weighs 7½ oz. to 10 oz. (Sew as worsted wool; see p. 214.)

VICUNA

The finest wool woven from a small South American relative of the camel. Very soft to touch and very warm to wear. (Sew as cashmere; see p. 26.)

WHIPCORD

A strong worsted fabric with an upright twill weave. Very resistant to wrinkling or stretching out of shape. Used in riding habits, uniforms, sportswear, and coatings. (Sew as denim; see p. 46.)

Sources

B&J FABRICS
525 7th Ave. #2
New York, NY 10018
(212) 354-8150
www.bandjfabrics.com

BANKSVILLE DESIGNER FABRICS
115 New Canaan Ave.
Norwalk, CT 06850
(203) 846-1333
**www.banksville
designerfabrics.com**

BRITEX FABRICS
146 Geary St.
San Francisco, CA 94108
(415) 392-2910
www.britexfabrics.com

CALICO CORNERS
203 Gale Lane
Kennett Square, PA 19348
(800) 213-6366
www.calicocorners.com

CAROL'S ZOO
Carol Cruise
992 Coral Ridge Cir.
Rodeo, CA 94572
(510) 245-2020
www.carolszoo.com

CHRISTINE JONSON
86 E. Ten Mile
Hazel Park, MI 48030
(248) 547-1080
www.cjpatterns.com

FABRIC DEPOT
700 SE 122nd Ave.
Portland, OR 97233
(503) 252-9530
www.fabricdepot.com

HABERMAN FABRICS
905 Main St.
Royal Oak, MI 48067
(248) 541-0010
www.habermanfabrics.com

JOSEPHINE'S DRY GOODS
3050 SE Division St. #165
Portland, OR 97202
(503) 224-4202
www.josephinesdrygoods.com

KAREN'S KREATIONS
Karen Rudman
6542 125th Ave. SE
Bellevue, WA 98006
(425) 643-9809

LINDA KUBIK
310 E. 8th Ave.
Ritzville, WA 99169
(509) 659-0209
www.lindakubik.com

LINDA MACPHEE
Box 10 Site 16 R.R. 8
Edmonton, AB T5L 4H8
Canada
(888) 622-7433
www.macpheeworkshop.com

MENDEL'S FAR OUT FABRICS
1556 Haight St.
San Francisco, CA 94117
(415) 621-1287
www.mendels.com

MOOD FABRICS
225 W. 37th St.
New York, NY 10018
(212) 730-5003
www.moodfabrics.com

MOOD FABRICS
645 S. La Brea Ave.
Los Angeles, CA 90036
(323) 653-6663
www.moodfabrics.com

MULBERRY SILKS
200 N. Greensboro St.
Carrboro, NC 27510
(919) 942-7455
www.mulberrysilks.net

NANCY'S NOTIONS
333 Beichl Ave.
Beaver Dam, WI 53916
(800) 833-0690, (920) 887-0391
www.nancysnotions.com

OUT OF HAND
12-6449 Crowchild Trail SW
Calgary, AB T3E 5R7
Canada
(800) 263-3353
www.out-of-hand.com

PANDA THREAD
247 W. 38th St.
New York, NY 10018
(800) 878-6336, (212) 302-9434
www.activetrimming.com

PERFECT LEATHER GOODS
555 King St. W.
Toronto, ON M5V 1M1
Canada
(416) 205-9775
www.perfectleathergoods.com

PIEDMONT FABRIC
4009 Piedmont Ave.
Oakland, CA 94611
(510) 655-1213
www.piedmontfabrics.com

POWER SEWING
5 Upper Ter.
San Francisco, CA 94117
(415) 876-2434
www.powersewing.com

RICHLAND SILK CO.
P.O. Box 311
Palmyra, MI 49268
(517) 263-4756

STONEMOUNTAIN & DAUGHTER FABRICS
2518 Shattuck Ave.
Berkeley, CA 94704
(510) 845-6106
**www.stonemountainfabric
.com**

TANDY LEATHER
(877) 532-8437
www.tandyleather.com

THAI SILKS
1959 B Leghorn St.
Mountain View, CA 94043
(800) 722-SILK, (650) 965-7455
www.thaisilks.com

VOGUE FABRICS
718-732 Main St.
Evanston, IL 60202
(847) 864-9600
www.myvoguefabrics.com

Index